CLOSET DEVOTIONS

D1344440

Edited by
Michèle Aina Barale,
Jonathan Goldberg,
Michael Moon, and
Eve Kosofsky Sedgwick

CLOSET DEVOTIONS

RICHARD RAMBUSS

Duke University Press   Durham and London   1998

© 1998 Duke University Press
All rights reserved
Printed in the United States of America on acid-free paper ∞
Designed by Amy Ruth Buchanan
Typeset in Sabon by Tseng Information Systems, Inc.
Library of Congress Cataloging-in-Publication Data appear
on the last printed page of this book.

Virtue hath some perverseness.

—*John Donne, "To the Countess*
of Bedford"

Contents

ILLUSTRATIONS

ACKNOWLEDGMENTS

What was to become this book began with a generously open invitation from Jonathan Goldberg to contribute something to a volume of essays he was editing on sexuality and Renaissance literature and culture; for providing the initial impetus, for his indispensable reading of the book's final draft, and for so much more, to him go my most affectionate thanks.

I am also grateful to those who provided such stimulating forums for me to try out and refine my thinking on this subject before committing it to print. Thanks to Colleen Lamos and Helena Michie for hosting me at Rice University; to David Lee Miller for asking me to deliver one of the Hudson Strode lectures at the University of Alabama; to Mary Bly for the invitation to speak at "The Sacred Body in Law and Literature" symposium at Yale; to Jean Howard and Nicholas Radel for thinking to include me in the Shakespeare Association of America seminar they organized on feminism and queer theory; to the organizers of "Queer October" for having me back to Johns Hopkins; to the graduate students in medieval and Renaissance studies at Duke University who asked me to address the "Varieties of Desire" conference; to Jeffrey Masten for inviting me to present my work at the Center for Literary and Cultural Studies at Harvard; and to Valerie Traub, Stephen Campbell, and Pat Simons for bringing me to the University of Michigan as a participant in their "Rhetorics and Rituals of (Un)Veiling" conference.

It is with pleasure and devotion that I acknowledge my happy reliance upon a group of colleagues and friends, exchanges with whom have been so important to me over the past few years. For their assistance, encouragement, and engagement with my work I want to thank David Baker, Leonard Barkan, Cathy Caruth, Paul Elledge, Will Fisher, Geoffrey Harpham, Jeffrey Masten, Michael Moon, Supriya Nair, Patricia Parker, Gail Paster, Stephen Orgel, Joseph Roach, Michael Schoenfeldt, Debora Shuger, Alan Sinfield, Peter Stallybrass, Maaja Stewart, Ramie Targoff, Teresa Toulouse, Valerie Traub, and Joseph Wittreich. Larry Simmons and Josie Dixon presented me with Christ icons they knew I would like, and I have reproduced those images here. Thanks also to Richard Morrison,

Ken Wissoker, Paula Dragosh, and Amy Ruth Buchanan at Duke University Press for the care and enthusiasm with which they have overseen the making of this book.

I am especially indebted to John Guillory, who, over coffee one summer afternoon in Dupont Circle, helped me to see what this book was really about. Janice Carlisle read through several versions of the manuscript and improved it each time; she instantiates for me the meaning of colleague and of friend.

*   *   *

My research was generously supported by a fellowship from the Folger Shakespeare Library, as well as by grants from Tulane University and Emory University.

Portions of chapter 1 of this book first appeared in different forms as "Pleasure and Devotion: The Body of Jesus in Seventeenth-Century Religious Lyric," in *Queering the Renaissance,* ed. Jonathan Goldberg (Durham: Duke University Press, 1994); "Christ's Ganymede," *Yale Journal of Law and the Humanities* 7 (1995): 77–96; and "Homodevotion," in *Cruising the Performative: Interventions into the Representation of Ethnicity, Nationality, and Sexuality,* ed. Sue-Ellen Case, Philip Brett, and Susan Leigh Foster (Bloomington: Indiana University Press, 1995).

NOTE ON TEXTS

I have used the following editions: *John Donne,* The Oxford Authors, ed. John Carey (Oxford: Oxford University Press, 1990); *The Sermons of John Donne,* ed. George R. Potter and Evelyn M. Simpson, 10 vols. (Berkeley: University of California Press, 1953–62); *George Herbert and Henry Vaughan,* The Oxford Authors, ed. Louis L. Martz (Oxford: Oxford University Press, 1986); *The Complete Poetry of Richard Crashaw,* The Stuart Editions, ed. George Walton Williams (New York: New York University Press, 1972); *Thomas Traherne: Selected Poems and Prose,* ed. Alan Bradford (London: Penguin, 1991); and *John Milton,* The Oxford Authors, ed. Stephen Orgel and Jonathan Goldberg (Oxford: Oxford University Press, 1991). All citations of the Bible are according to the 1611 Authorized Version. In a few instances I have modernized some aspects of the seventeenth-century texts I cite.

Introduction

SACRED EROTICISMS

*The underlying affinity between sanctity and transgression has
never ceased to be felt. Even in the eyes of believers, the libertine
is nearer to the saint than the man without desire.*
— *Georges Bataille,* Erotism: Death and Sensuality

This is a book about devotion: devotion, specifically, as a form
of desire. Much, though not all, of this study turns on a re-
reading of English devotional literature, both verse and prose,
from the early to the mid–seventeenth century, a span that
traditionally has been esteemed as marking the apex of religious writing
in the language. My concern with this literature does not derive simply
from its cultural prestige, however. I am also drawn to it as a literature of *heightened affect,* produced as such, especially among those poets
grouped together under the name of "the metaphysicals," as a daringly
experimental expressive project. That is, I am interested in the manner by
which religious (and other ecstatic) texts represent and stimulate affect,
particularly in its most amplified registers. One means by which this process transpires in devotional writing involves its reliance upon structuring
analogies to erotic expression and experience. "If [Christ] come not yet
into thee, stirre up thy spirituall concupiscence," prompts Francis Rous in
a devotional manual titled *The Mysticall Marriage, or Experimentall Discoveries of the heavenly Marriage between a Soule and her Savior* (1631).
"Therewith," Rous continues, "let thy soul lust mightily for him."[1]

Who can engage the literature of Christian devotion and not be struck
by how often it speaks of religious affect in terms of—even as—sex? Of
course, to address God amorously as "My Lord, my Love," as George
Herbert does ("The Search," line 2), or to look forward to the coming nup-
tials of Christ and his Church, or to blazon the physical beauty of Jesus in
the throes of what is evocatively termed his Passion: all this was then and,
to a certain extent, remains now a devotional commonplace. But what
does *that* mean? Too often interpretation desists at the point of such a de-
termination, as if the status of being conventional would make a discursive

construct or a sentiment any less thick with significance. I will be arguing that, on the contrary, the very conventionality of such expressions marks them as all the more meaningfully impacted. Hence the project of *Closet Devotions* is to read through—indeed, to read into—the conventions and conceits of what I call, after Bataille, *sacred eroticism*.[2] My aim in doing so is to press beyond the impasse represented by the designation "simply conventional" and thereby to unsettle some of the usual pieties that continue to govern discussions of the interface between religion and eroticism, as well as between the soul and the body, the spiritual and the material.

Having invoked the question of the body's place in the sphere of religious devotion, I want to situate this book in relation to the seminal work that has been done on this topic over the past decade and a half. Through the endeavors of distinguished cultural historians such as Leo Steinberg, Caroline Walker Bynum, Peter Brown, and others, the body has begun to be restored to its place at the very core of pre- and early modern religious expression.[3] *Closet Devotions* looks to extend the scholarship that has been undertaken in these earlier periods to the seventeenth century and beyond. In doing so, I will be examining representations of the devout body, along with the body of Jesus and its various spectacularized figurations *in extremis,* in the canonical poetry of the period (particularly the verse of John Donne, George Herbert, Richard Crashaw, Henry Vaughan, and Thomas Traherne); in prose texts such as sermons, devotional manuals, prayer books, spiritual diaries, personal testimonies, and prophecy; and finally in some of the substantial religious materials produced over the course of the seventeenth century by women writers (including Aemilia Lanyer, Anne Wentworth, Elizabeth Singer, and Sarah Davy, among others). These texts afford us a plethora of affectively charged sites for tracing the complex overlappings and relays between religious devotion and erotic desire, as well as between the interiorized operations of the spirit and the material conditions of the body. Articulating a devotion that is profoundly attuned to the Christian doctrine of the Incarnation, of God becoming flesh—becoming a man—these religious works exhibit surprisingly little inclination to efface the corporeal. Rather, they proffer a spirituality that paradoxically bespeaks embodiment, doing so in ways that often enhance or extend the expressive possibilities of bodies and desires.

Following the work of Bynum and Steinberg, I will thus be arguing that Christianity's relation to the body cannot adequately be accounted for only in terms of an ascetic repudiation of the flesh—a task that, as

Bynum's studies of medieval female penitential practices illustrate, can itself be nothing short of corporeally spectacular. Like Bynum, then, I am interested in how religion has made use of the body and the passions in signifying, even amplifying, devotion. I am also interested, however, in how the erotic conversely—perversely?—uses the religious to enhance its own affects. Moreover, in view of the writings of Georges Bataille and Michel Foucault, as well as recent studies in the history of sexuality, I want to probe some of the terms under which the body and the bodily have been thus far recovered to devotion's expressive repertoires. As I will lay out in more substantive detail in what follows, I am especially troubled by the ways in which the pioneering and still prevailing scholarship on devotion has too readily circumscribed both the libidinal and the transgressive potentialities of the sacred body, whether it be the body of Jesus or a saint or an individual Christian devotee. In Leo Steinberg's bold study, *The Sexuality of Christ in Renaissance Art and in Modern Oblivion,* an astonishing assemblage of images that compromise modern decorum in their nearly exhibitionist presentation of a sexed and naked Christ, this circumscription takes the form of a hermeneutically delimiting theologism. For Steinberg carefully hedges with reference to *dogma only* the field of available meanings of and responses to representations of Jesus' arrestingly exposed body—as though, for instance, Michelangelo's nude, impressively muscled *Risen Christ* (fig. 1) would then (or now) stimulate reflection, as Steinberg implies, only upon the doctrine of the Resurrection.[4] In Bynum's work on female mystics and saints, these interpretively straitening impulses disclose themselves in her propensity to see the devotional body as operating chiefly in the most orthodox formats. One thus finds Bynum reading nearly every somatic expression of female piety, no matter how apparently outlandish or perverse it is to modern (or, for that matter, premodern) sensibilities, through a normalizing semiotics of marriage, impregnation, lactation, or food preparation: a set of terms that keeps the female body, even in its most ecstatic states, quite properly domesticated. "Women's symbols [of spiritual life]," Bynum thereby concludes in *Holy Feast and Holy Fast,* "did not reverse social fact, they enhanced it" (279). Bynum further notes that in spiritual expression women, in contrast to men, tend "to elaborate as symbols aspects of life closer to ordinary experience," which she then parenthetically delineates for us as "eating, suffering, lactating" (293).

Following Bataille's ecstatic theorems on the complementarity of the sacred and illicit,[5] my interests abide more with excess, transgression, and

Figure 1. Jesus as an icon of male beauty.
Michelangelo, *Risen Christ*, c. 1514–20. S. Maria sopra Minerva,
Rome, Italy. Courtesy of Alinari/Art Resource, New York.

the heterodoxies of gender and eroticism that can be embraced and inhabited through the mechanisms of devotion. The religious poetry of the metaphysicals, with its colliding decorums of spirituality and carnality, sanctity and profanity, provides a compelling site, we shall see, for this kind of foray through devotion's intensities and expressive perversities. But these effects can also be glimpsed here by returning for a moment to the enticement from Francis Rous's *Mysticall Marriage* with which we began: "If [Christ] come not yet into thee, stirre up thy spirituall concupiscence, and therewith let thy soul lust mightily for him." Note that what Rous proffers is not simply an invitation to love Christ; rather, it is a provocation to concupiscence—a "spirituall concupiscence," but concupiscence nonetheless. Rous's text aims to incite something more galvanic than any anodyne sentiment of devotional fealty. To do so, he invokes a form of sexual appetite—lust—that is no other than a sin, the very transgressivity of this carnal desire serving as the expressive mechanism by which religious affect is to be stimulated and enhanced. Nothing heats the passions, it has been said, like the taboo. ·

In considering sacred eroticism *as* eroticism, as a form of sexual expression, I do not mean to imply that some essential form of the erotic exists prior to its specific and changing cultural or historical instantiations. Nor that the sexual necessarily underwrites every desire or every semiotics of the body. That said, we nonetheless need to ask how it is that the sexual seems to appear so prominently in the devotional writing of this period. Was it, moreover, recognized as such—as sexual—then? What did it mean for these seventeenth-century Christians to envision and to speak of themselves as being ravished by God or lusting after Christ? Obviously it is not satisfactory to pass off such voicings of desire and passion as merely metaphorical, especially if that designation performs the function of enervating these expressions, of dulling their affective or transgressive charge. Another question—one no less legitimate to my thinking—is also what *we,* centuries later, may want to make of, how *we* may experience, this historical inheritance of sexualized devotion, with its erotic Christ— "a naked man, utterly desirable," as the title character in the 1995 film *Priest* (directed by Antonia Bird) finds himself, to his own dismay, viewing Jesus. At once a historicist and an unrepentant presentist, I look here to theorize devotional desire and to map the expressive forms it has both taken and *may take* in relation to bodies, affects, and eroticisms, the homoerotic no less than the heteroerotic. *Closet Devotions* does so principally from the vantage of the "prayer closet" of private religious devotion, a perhaps unusual site for such a query, but a culturally central and abiding one nonetheless.

As we see from *Priest,* as well as the tellingly overwrought public controversy attendant upon Disney's release of the film, the excitations and agitations of sacred eroticism are by no means relics belonging to a past, more baroque culture of religious enthusiasm now placidly dissipated. Hence throughout this study I have been mindful to pose early modern religious artifacts in relation to more recent representations and usages of devotional desire, ranging from Tony Kushner's critically lauded and commercially successful *Angels in America* plays to queer agitprop; from photographer Andres Serrano's *Piss Christ* (a metaphysical conceit of the sort that one feels could almost have been propounded by Donne in one of his characteristic feats of audacious juxtaposition, or concocted by Crashaw in accordance with his liquefacient poetics) to contemporary pornography, understood in this context specifically as a discourse of the hyper-visualized body and its operations. By means of such reframings across history and across cultural status—the early modern with the contemporary, the high with the low, the devout with the parodic—my aim here is not only to try to think outside some of the protocols governing current historicizing work on devotion and desire ("in those days they couldn't have meant *that*"—"that" typically being the sexual and, most often, the sexually transgressive). More important, by imbricating a reading of the canonical religious literature of the Renaissance with a variously fetched ensemble of contemporary cultural texts, I look to stage a historical salvo in Christianity's own terms—in Christianity's own canonic perversities—against its mobilization on behalf of a censoriously normalizing social and cultural vision, whether that ministration comes in the rigidly uncompromising guise of traditional orthodoxies and fundamentalisms or through the mainstreaming religiosocial tactics of the New Christian Right. Christianity, of course, exists as no singular theology, philosophical conception, or social structure. Yet, however it is constructed, Christianity's own myths, institutions, and cultural expressions offer too many transit points to the ecstatic, the excessive, the transgressive, the erotic to be allowed to serve tenably in such a censorious capacity, to be cast as a force field for the proscription of desire and its ever-wanton vagaries.

Religion and Christianity in particular rate among our culture's most venerated institutions. No doubt, then, there are those who will find the central concern of this book—the interrelations between devotion and eroticism in its several forms and registers—to be itself perverse. As what follows will show, however, those looking to deny any affiliation between these modes of desire are the ones outside the scope of tradition.

* * *

I listen to the message's transport, not the message.
— *Roland Barthes*, Sade/Fourier/Loyola

The first and longest chapter of this study, "Christ's Ganymede," treats the aspect of devotion and desire that has come to be the most phobically resisted and repudiated: the possibility that devotion to Christ might be invested as a site of erotic expressions, interests, and energies that are homoerotic.[6] To render a fuller treatment of Christian devotion and homoeroticism than this important topic has yet received, I afford a special place of prominence here to male devotional desire amorously attuned to a male Christ.[7] My other reason for highlighting male religious authors is that the seventeenth-century literary canon remains predominantly— though no longer exclusively—male, and I want to make my arguments concerning the constitutive excesses and transgressions of the sacred principally at a site where they might bear the greatest cultural capital.

The book's second chapter, "Devotion and Desire," looks to provide an account of sacred eroticism(s) that neither reduces religious desire into more or less sublimated sexual longing nor anesthetizes devotion's libidinal pulse. In doing so, this chapter replays many of the concerns of the preceding one, but both more expansively and more theoretically: more theoretically, inasmuch as I endeavor to provide a more phenomenological account of the tropes and terms of sacred eroticism, one that shies away from bounding their expressive force under the restraints of the "merely" metaphorical; more expansively, in that this part of the book opens more fully onto devotion's ecstatic trafficking across a wide purview of affectively imbued social positions (lover, bride, bridegroom, friend, ephebe, household intimate, servant, mother, father, child, pupil, and so forth) in its highly transitive, even volatile configurations of the bonds between Christ and Christian. While not leaving behind chapter one's structuring concern with homoeroticized religious expression, I look in this portion of the book to give more play to devotion's polytropic erotics—an erotics, we shall see, that is seldom constrained to a strictly dichotomous schematization of heterosexuality/homosexuality.

The final chapter of the book, "The Prayer Closet," delivers a material location for the devotional affects treated in the first two chapters. Here the relations between religious practice and the self's sense of itself—devotion's subjectivity effects, as it were—can be more fully elaborated. How are religious devotion and the various expressive forms it takes to be mapped onto the procedures of subjectivity, of how the self regards and acts upon itself? When does devotional desire work to undermine, rather than consolidate, the structures of selfhood? How does a developing, chiefly (but not exclusively) Protestant culture of private, personal devotion—"closet devotion" as it comes to be called in the period—function in terms of what Foucault has named technologies of the self, by which he means those techniques that "permit individuals to affect, by their own means, a certain number of operations on their own bodies, their own souls, their own thoughts, their own conduct, and this in a manner so as to transform themselves, modify themselves, and to attain a certain state of perfection, happiness, purity, supernatural power": in short, the work of the self upon the self?[8] In keeping with my emphasis throughout this study on Christianity's relation to the body, I frame these subjectifying concerns in materialist, and not simply spiritual or psychological, terms. More particularly, I am interested in how seventeenth-century devotional literature establishes the prayer closet both as a metafigurally incorporated condition of inwardness within the individual Christian and, at the same time, as a materialized place—a special room—within the Christian household, one whose architecture and even furnishing we find thoroughly detailed in the devotional manuals of the time.

Along with its function as an interiorizing apparatus, the prayer closet is increasingly designated in this literature as the private space in which the body—its gestures, motions, and voice—can be more fully brought to bear upon the performance of devotion. Correlative to the enhanced role accorded to the body in closet devotion, the prayer closet is also posited as a kind of vortex for the intensification of religious affect. "Godliness," Thomas Brooks thus contends in *The Privy Key of Heaven, or Twenty Arguments for Closet-Prayer* (1665), "never rises to a higher pitch than when men keep closest to their closets."[9] Materialized as such, as a special room in the house, the prayer closet is not only a privileged devotional place, but also a place of privilege, of economic and social prerogative. Accordingly, the literature of closet devotion—an emergent seventeenth-century religious subgenre, I suggest—is rather exclusively addressed to those who have both the means and the leisure for what another seventeenth-century divine calls "Closet-work." I stress this point here, at the outset of this study, as a check on any notion that religious devotion, even when it reaches its most ecstatic parameters, can utterly transume the contours of the social. Nonetheless, as much as religious devotion—even the sacred itself—is a social practice, its relation to the normal order of things is seldom strictly circumscribed to the orthodox. Rather, like desire and its vicissitudes, devotion can also take its pangs and its pleasures elsewhere. This book looks to that elsewhere.

I

CHRIST'S GANYMEDE

The King of the gods once loved a Trojan boy named Ganymede.
—Ovid, Metamorphoses

Both highly lauded within its own West Hollywood industry and seized during a St. Valentine's Day police raid on a Chicago adult theater, the gay porn videotape *More of a Man* opens, as these things go, with its leading man Vito on his knees.[1] Before him is a naked male form. Vito, still kneeling, hoarsely to the same: "You name it, I'll do it." The setting for this alluring scene of solicitation happens to be an empty chapel, and the unclothed male form Vito so addresses is an effigy of Jesus on the cross, dangling from the rosary beads bound up in his clasped hands—the video thereby offering Christ's as the first of the uncovered male bodies to be exhibited across its erotic field of vision. Commencing a sexual narrative in church, against a backdrop of votive candles and church bells, is in this case more than simply a gay male recasting of the devotional chic of Madonna's "Like a Prayer" music video, the "sacrilegious" sensation of the year before.[2] Nor, more important, is this staging, however scandalous it might appear to some, proffered as a profanation. Indeed, *More of a Man*'s allotment of a representation of Christ in his "Passion" its own place within gay pornography's carnival of desired and desiring male bodies is a provocation arguably more than a little overdetermined by Christianity's own contradictory, closeted libidinalities.

For here is an institution whose culturally venerable assessment of same-sex desire is (perhaps now more than ever) predominantly censorious, yet one which has also sought to stimulate devotion by the display made of a male body iconicized *in extremis*—a nearly naked man offered up to our gazes ("Ecce homo") for worship, desire, and various kinds of identification. What, then, is to be said of the place of Christ in the affective schemes of Christian devotion? In *Epistemology of the Closet* Eve Kosofsky Sedgwick remarks that while "Christianity may be near-ubiquitous in modern European culture as a figure of phobic prohibition, . . . it makes a strange figure for that indeed." "Catholicism in particular," she continues,

is famous for giving countless gay and proto-gay children the shock of the possibility of adults who don't marry, of men in dresses, of passionate the-atre, of introspective investment, of lives filled with what could, ideally without diminution, be called the work of the fetish. . . . And presiding over all are the images of Jesus. These have, indeed, a unique position in modern culture as images of the unclothed or unclothable male body, often in extremis and/or ecstasy, prescriptively meant to be gazed at and adored. The scandal of such a figure within a homophobic economy of the male gaze doesn't seem to abate: efforts to disembody this body, for instance by attenuating, Europeanizing, or feminizing it, only entangle it the more com-promisingly among various modern figurations of the homosexual.[3]

More of a Man offers graphic—hard-core pornographic—testimonial to this usually scrupulously closeted "entanglement," climactically emblema-tized by the video's final shot: a bedside freeze-frame of Vito's rosary be-side a spent condom. Narrativized as the coming-out story of this deeply conflicted, aggressively virile, Italian, Catholic construction worker, the video undertakes a reconciliation of Vito's devotion to Christ, his corre-spondingly fervent (though he feels illicit) sexual desire for the male body, and his emphatically maintained identity as a "man's man." Thus Vito's opening solicitation ("You name it, I'll do it") is embedded in an anx-ious supplication that Christ rid him of what he terms "all these crazy thoughts . . . okay, okay, these impure thoughts." But from this point on, coming as though it were the divine answer to his prayer (if hardly the one he expects), Vito is guided through a series of escalating homosexual en-counters. In the tape's next scene he thus heads from the "prayer closet" of the empty chapel to another kind of closet, one that's a more familiar set piece of gay porn: the water closet, or the public restroom. There he reciprocally penetrates and is penetrated by another man, sexual acts that are athletically performed through an orifice in the water closet door, the slang term for which is, incidentally, a "glory hole"—a naming that itself accords the scene something of a sacred nimbus. To this encounter, like all those that follow, Vito carries with him the rosary beads of the open-ing scene: a token, I take it, of Christ's sanctioning accompaniment. The conclusion of the tape finds Vito now "out" enough to ride shirtless atop a float in a gay pride parade. Then he heads right inside the float itself.

Accompanying him is Duffy, a comparably butch L.A. Dodgers fan, but also, as it happens, a dedicated AIDS activist. Vito and Duffy's coupling inside the gay pride float not only brings off their tape-long flirtation as the climactic sexual (and romantic) "number" of the pornographic narrative; this scene also consummates, as Mandy Merck suggests in her provocative discussion of *More of a Man,* a redemptive conjoining of religion, sex, and political activism.[4] Salvation is thus wrought for the symbolically, as well as ethnically, named Vito, but not at all in the terms of his original prayer, terms that would have maintained a phobic opposition between his religious devotion and his homosexuality, as well as between his virility and his desire for men. Redemption, the answer to prayer, instead arrives in the form of a coming out of the closet into pleasure *and* devotion.

Apropos of Sedgwick's intimations, as well as the homodevotional allurements of *More of a Man,* this chapter traces some of the circuits of male desire, vectored to and through Christ's body, that continue to magnetize the Christian prayer closet with a homoerotic penumbra. In doing so, however, I want now to turn back from the contemporary televisual medium of video pornography to another, in this case early modern, technology for processing (and producing) identity, desire, and affect. The representational mode I have in mind here is the seventeenth-century devotional lyric poem, an expressive achievement, I noted in the introduction, widely regarded as a high point of religious writing in English. Here we find voicings of devotion to Jesus that (in the reverse of Sedgwick's formulation) seldom look "to disembody this body." Here, particularly in the verse of those male poets loosely grouped together as "the metaphysicals," we find figurations of devotion, desire, and redemption that are indeed hardly less corporeally spectacularized than those that comprise the conversion-minded porn with which I began. And here, in the prayer closet of private devotion, we find John Donne, George Herbert, Richard Crashaw, and Thomas Traherne, among other religious writers of the period, more or less self-consciously reassigning in same-sex configurations (male God, male devotee) the erotic postures and blandishing conceits of the Renaissance love lyric. All this in the endeavor, as more than one of these authors frames it, of "courting" a profoundly desirable Christ, a beautiful Lord and Savior:

> Thou art my loveliness, my life, my light,
>> Beauty alone to me:
> Thy bloody death and undeserved, makes thee
>> Pure red and white.

In this stanza from Herbert's poem "Dullness" (lines 9–12), Christ's Passion is aestheticized and made amorous in terms of the conventional white-and-red color scheme of the erotic blazon. Jesus' wounded body likewise blooms white and red in one of Crashaw's several epigrams on the wounding of the Circumcision as a highly chromatic prefiguration of the Crucifixion: "Ah cruel knife! which first commanded such fair lilies / to change into such cruel roses" ("In circumcisionem," lines 1–2). From the religious application of such amorous conceits issues a mode of devotional expression that turns on a deeply affective, often unblushingly erotic, desire for Jesus and his body—"This beauteous form," as one of Donne's Holy Sonnets envisions it ("What if this present were the world's last night?"), "This sweeter BODY," as a Crashaw hymn adoringly echoes ("Office of the Holy Cross," "Compline").[5] "For beauty hee hath no match among men," the English divine Samuel Rutherford likewise asseverates in *Christ Dying and Drawing Sinners to Himself* (1647). "Christ hath a most goodly face," continues Rutherford: an estimation of physical beauty and desirability that is reflected in any number of Renaissance portraits of Jesus, such as the markedly handsome *Christ Carrying the Cross* (Circle of Giovanni Bellini) (fig. 2).[6]

Christ's physical attributes are also the subject of Leo Steinberg's *The Sexuality of Christ*. Steinberg's bold exposé of the denuded and phallically endowed images of Christ that abound in Renaissance visual art graphically illustrates the extent to which Christianity is an *incarnational* religion, one that can turn ostentatious in its desire to render the Savior as fully human and, what is more, as expressly, as functionally male. The poets with whom I am concerned here similarly show themselves to be deeply attuned—sometimes rapturously, sometimes bathetically—to what it means that the Word became flesh, that Jesus (in Pope Leo the Great's canonic formulation) was "born true God in the entire and perfect nature of true man, complete in his own properties, *complete in ours*"; that he was (as the Council of Chalcedon declares) "of one substance with the Father as regards his Godhead, . . . of one substance with us as regards his manhood; *like us in all respects,* apart from sin."[7] Or again, as an anonymous 1614 English sermon on "The Mysterie of Christs Nativitie" insists: "Undoubtedly he was a true man, and had a true, naturall, and not a celestiall and phantasticall body."[8]

Seventeenth-century religious verse is densely nuanced psychologically, yet arguably many of its most profound subjectivity effects are incited, in accordance with the incarnational theology I have here been calling to the

Figure 2. "Christ hath a most goodly face."
Circle of Giovanni Bellini, *Christ Carrying the Cross*, c. 1505–1510.
Courtesy of the Isabella Stewart Gardner Museum, Boston.

fore, by this poetry's reflection upon Christ's body in its extreme vulnerability *as a body,* as a truly human form, not a "phantasticall" one. Hence, the excruciating psychic and physical contortions of Donne's "Good Friday, 1613. Riding Westward." Here the poet pathically envisages the image of Christ crucified as "That spectacle of too much weight for me" (line 16), and he literally turns his back upon the Passion to ride away in the opposite direction. Despite Donne's renunciatory efforts, however, the poem remains an unnerving confrontation with just such a shattering sight:

> Could I behold those hands which span the poles,
> And tune all spheres at once, pierced with those holes?
> Could I behold that endless height which is
> Zenith to us, and to'our antipodes,
> Humbled below us? or that blood which is
> The seat of all our souls, if not of his,
> Made dirt of dust, or that flesh which was worn
> By God, for his apparel, ragged, and torn?
>
> (lines 21-28)

Consider also the eerie internalized monologue Herbert assigns to the physically brutalized Christ in "The Sacrifice," as his sacred body undergoes, step by step, the ritual desecration of crucifixion, all of which leaves the Savior wondering, in the poem's echoing, nearly hysterical refrain, "Was ever grief like mine?":

> Shame tears my soul, my body many a wound:
> Sharp nails pierce this, but sharper that confound;
> Reproaches, which are free, while I am bound.
> > Was ever grief like mine?
>
> (lines 217-20)

Coincident with their devotion to Christ's spectacularly exposed and traumatically violated physical body, these poets rarely show much inclination utterly to transume their own. Rather, as Donne (citing the church father Tertullian) puts it so encompassingly in a 1623 Easter sermon, "All that the soul does, it does in, and with, and by the body." [9] Donne's writing, like so much seventeenth-century devotional expression, espouses a devotion that is cathected onto the corporeal: a spirituality that, paradoxically, keeps returning us to the physical body and its operations, even—or all the more so—in any pietistic endeavor to discipline or rein them in. Caroline Walker Bynum makes a similar case in *Holy Feast and Holy Fast* concerning the hyperbolic penitential practices of late medieval female saints and mystics. The prodigious fasts and unnerving eating habits of these extraordinary women, their deliberate courting of physical illness, even their sallies into self-mutilation—all this, Bynum argues compellingly, is less a simple abnegation of the body than an ecstatic, devotional manipulation of the conditions of corporeality. Such feats should thus be seen, she writes, "more as elaborate changes rung upon *possibilities* provided by fleshiness than as flights from physicality" (6), as "the *experiencing* of body more than the *controlling* of it" (245). For these devotees, even denigrated flesh can be made to instantiate the faith of the soul it encases, the body being redemptively reappropriated as an implement of heightened devotional expressivity rather than repudiated as always no more than a gross weight or hindrance to it. To be sure, the forms of piety we find in the religious cultures of early modern England tend to be quite different from the medieval Catholic extravaganzas that light up Bynum's account. Nonetheless, I will be arguing throughout this book that numerous seventeenth-century Protestant devotional authors—those within the Church of England as well as those without—continue to employ the body and its metaphors as means to stimulate and to enhance devotional expression.[10] Like Donne, these poets and divines activate the corporeal as an expressive mechanism of devotion, one that is coenesthetic of "all that the soul does."

Following Bynum, then, I suggest that these religious texts offer an early modern discourse of the body and its passions no less than they provide a discourse of the soul. Yet I want also to reconsider and to interrogate some of the terms under which the bodily has been thus far recovered into view in prevailing accounts (including those of Bynum and Steinberg) of pre- and early modern Christianity. For, despite the talk here of foregrounding and extending corporeal meanings and operations within the sphere of devotion, this scholarship displays a recurring impulse to rein in or curtail the more manifold libidinalities of the very "fleshiness" (to use Bynum's term) it has itself insisted upon. Moreover, this policing of the flesh tends, we shall see, to be enforced most stridently (if often only implicitly) over questions of religion and the erotic, particularly the homoerotic.

The metaphysicals, with their characteristic mise-en-scène of the spiritual bordering the carnal, the sacred abutting the profane, supply what are perhaps the most provocative grounds for interrogating the orthodoxies of current scholarship on devotion, desire, and the body; indeed, the volatile heterodoxies of these poets make such reconsideration a requisite. Achieving their effects with a rhetoric of the extreme and often deliberately courting the perverse, Donne, Herbert, Crashaw, and their fellows have accrued from their own time down into ours more charges of excess, indecorousness, and queerness than one finds imputed to any other early modern literary practice. In fact, the ascription of gross impropriety and a hyperbolism bordering on unnaturalness are among the formative features of Samuel Johnson's construction (following Dryden) of a metaphysical "school" of poetry:

> Their thoughts are often new but seldom natural; they are not obvious, but neither are they just; and the reader, far from wondering that he missed them, wonders more frequently by what perverseness of industry they were ever found. . . . The most heterogeneous ideas are yoked by violence together; nature and art are ransacked for illustrations, comparisons and allusions; their learning instructs and their subtlety surprises, but the reader commonly thinks his improvement dearly bought, and though he sometimes admires, is seldom pleased. . . . Their wish was only to say what they hoped had been never said before. . . . What they wanted however of the sublime they endeavored to supply by hyperbole.

"Their amplification," he concludes with displeasure, "had no limits." [11]

Following Johnson (though leaving behind his censure), I am interested in what could be termed the experimental habitus of the metaphysicals: their desire, as he puts it, "to say what they hoped had been never said before." I am also interested in metaphysical transgressivity and the prevalence in these poets of exclamations of devotional affect so intensified that they encroach upon the taboo. This inclination to press the terms of the sacred to their limit—to an interface with the profane—is powerfully exemplified in Donne's Holy Sonnet "Batter my heart, three-personed God," one of the most anthologized religious poems from the period and one that will be a touchstone text for my discussion as well. In this astonishing sonnet, Donne's extreme agitations for spiritual satisfaction from his God take shape as a divine abduction and rape fantasy—one that is framed, as I will consider later, in metaphoric terms that cut back and forth across gender positions and forms of eroticism. At this point in the discussion, I want simply to suggest that the hyperbole, the downright violence of religious desire in a text like Donne's "Batter my heart," if not wholly recoverable, may perhaps best be appreciated by us now, not in terms of the canons of Bynum's social orthodoxies or Steinberg's theologism, but rather in something more like what I have been here offering as my own perverse metaphysical conceit in the juxtaposition of metaphysical religious devotion and contemporary pornography. However disparate in cultural status and representational history these forms may be, both are strikingly exhibitionist in their drive to bring into view the body and its most extreme performances and paroxysms, whether of pleasure or devotion—and often both at once. To put it another way: like pornography, metaphysical poetry is great in its excesses.

In keeping then with the metaphysicals' propensity for the hyperbolic and the transgressive, I will consider how discourses of the sacred can serve to authorize the ecstatic, the excessive, and the illicit. More particularly, I am interested in devotional modes and expressions that expand—and at times even violate—cultural orthodoxies, especially but not only those having to do with the body, gender, eroticism, and homoeroticism. A number of such prospects, as we have already begun to examine, become activated around the figure of Jesus and his body's privileged status within a Christian libidinal scheme that both abjects and stimulates same-sex possibilities. Moreover, we will find Christ's body—which is the body of God, but also the body made to bear all the corporeal functions, infirmities, and sins of humankind—sited at the breach between sacrosanct cultural boundaries. Christ's body, in other words, is one that *by its very nature* keeps exceeding, keeps transgressing the bounds of the licit, doing so in ways that touch upon the profane, the defiled—even, I am going to suggest, the sodomitical in its diffuse early modern shape as the cultural category of ultimate stigmatization.

ECCE HOMO:
CHRIST AND THE ORIFICIAL BODY

Ye sonnes of Salem, see Gods glorious Sonne,
Enrob'd with Wounds, and Blood, all goarie-gay!
—*John Davies,* The Holy Roode

. . . to hang *upon* him *that* hangs *upon the* Crosse,
there bath *in his* teares, *there* suck *at his*
wounndes . . .
—*Donne,* Death's Duel

It is precisely as the bearer of conflicted cultural encodings that Christ's violated body is so intently held in view in seventeenth-century devotional poetry. "See, see, ah see," John Davies repeatedly solicits in his lengthy, sensationalized Crucifixion poem *The Holy Roode* (1609).[12] Subtitled a "Speaking-picture," this thirty-page lyric presents Christ's Passion as a hypertrophy of the visual:

> But, O my Soule! to stirre, in thee devotion,
> Upon this ground of Griefe thine Eie still fixe:
> See here the King of Heav'ns Earthly promotion,
> Crown'd with sharp Thornes, and made a Crucifixe.
> . . . .
> Such Sight a squemish stomacke overturnes
> . . . .
> O see my Soule, ah cast thy carefull Eie
> Upon this Miracle-surmounting Wonder!
> The Body of thy God is wrencht awry,
> And . . .
>   Is . . . made crookèd that was ever streight.
> . . . .
> See how the sweat fals from his bloodlesse Browes
> . . . .
> Now, Eie of Sp'rite behold this spectacle . . .
> . . . .
> And see if you can any place espie
> About that Body, free from Wounds, or Bloes . . .
> . . . .
> Looke on this Crosse . . .
> (12–19)

And so forth, stanza upon stanza. Like Donne's "Good Friday, 1613" and Herbert's "The Sacrifice," Davies's *Holy Roode* directs us to fix our gaze in particular upon the profanation of Jesus' body:

> Behold his Body, that nere Filth could touch,
>   Is now defil'd with Blood, and festred Sores,
>   Both which (thou seest) that Body all begores!
> (18)

Begored and putrescent, Christ's body is here marked as defiled inasmuch as it is an opened and porous body, a site (to adapt the terms of anthropologist Mary Douglas) where corporeal (and, metonymically, societal) boundaries have been breached, where what belongs inside the body has spilled out onto its surface, thus polluting it.[13] In John Hayward's book of devotions called *The Sanctuarie of a troubled soule* (1604), "golden streames" issue from Christ's body and mix with this overflow of blood, tears, and gore, thereby spectacularizing the Crucifixion as the scene of utter hydraulic release (fig. 3).[14] The seventeenth-century New England poet Edward Taylor elaborates a similar devotional conceit:

> God's onely Son doth hug Humanity,
> Into his very person. By which Union
> His Humane Veans its golden gutters ly.
> And rather than my Soule should dy by thirst,
> These Golden Pipes, to give me drink, did burst.[15]

One doesn't need to travel very far, conceit-wise, to get from Taylor's "golden gutters," Hayward's "golden streames," and the liquescent Crucifixion woodcut to the consanguineous religious iconography of the contemporary photographer Andres Serrano, particularly his immensely controversial *Piss Christ* (fig. 4), an image whose complex of meanings lies in Serrano's own evocatively metaphysical juxtaposition of the sacred and the profane, of Christ and the stuff of the "golden gutters." Jesse Helms and the other Christian fundamentalists who denounced *Piss Christ* as blasphemous were right, I think, to recognize this photograph as a "shocking act."[16] Indeed, nothing would be further from my aim here than to drain off this image's shock value—or any of the value of shock value. Yet the insouciance, the perversion, of Serrano's representation of Christ must also be contextualized in terms of Christianity's own (orthodox) perversities. *Piss Christ* fully implicates Christ—just as the doctrine of the Incarnation necessarily does—within the human, within the processes of the body. "Inter faeces et urinam nascimur," Augustine unflinchingly asserted: we are born between shit and piss. And if this is humankind's reality, it must also be so for the Son of Man. As Serrano's shocking, and shockingly beautiful, photograph of a crucifix adrift in a refulgent red-gold color field of (defiling? purifying?) bodily fluid so powerfully recalls for us, the effect of the utter immersion of God within the conditions of corporeality turns out to be at once disconcertingly abasing as well as transformatively etherealizing—both for Christ and for the human body and its products. No less than Serrano's *Piss Christ*, the Renaissance devotional texts we have been considering understand this divinely mandated double-valencing, whereby the body of Jesus is rendered at once resplendent and "a meere Offence!" as Davies's poem likewise proclaims (18).

The sheer profanity of the Crucifixion is also registered in Herbert's

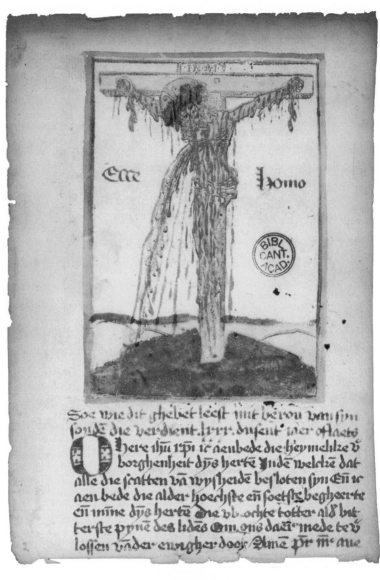

Figure 3. Christ ejaculating blood.
Woodcut, *Ecce Homo,* unknown origin, c. 1450. By permission
of the Syndics of Cambridge University Library.

Figure 4. Serrano's metaphysical conceit. Andres Serrano, *Piss Christ*, 1987. Courtesy of Paula Cooper Gallery, New York.

poem "The Cross," which ambivalently deems Christ's Passion a "strange and uncouth thing" (line 1). This uncouthness is more graphically depicted in *De Cruce . . . Ad sacram profanamque* (1606), a Latin treatise by the Dutch philosopher Justus Lipsius on the iconography of the cross, as well as the history and uses of crucifixion as a form of capital punishment. Like Donne's own poem called "The Cross" (which advances a kind of Protestant defense of the cross as a devotional emblem), Lipsius's folio-length *discursus* and its accompanying engravings honor and further spectacularize the cross by finding its form everywhere inscribed throughout the domains of the natural, the historical, and the mythic (fig. 5).[17] The image of the cross, as the title of Lipsius's study indicates, signifies no less within the purview of the profane, however, than it does in the sacred. Just how profane, how uncouth, is imaged in an arresting plate that depicts a cruciform image of execution by impalement (fig. 6). Here the unfortunate offender's leg is raised and bent akimbo to show explicitly that the tremendous spike whose point issues from his opened mouth entered his body through his rectum. In its collocation of cruciforms, Lipsius's *De*

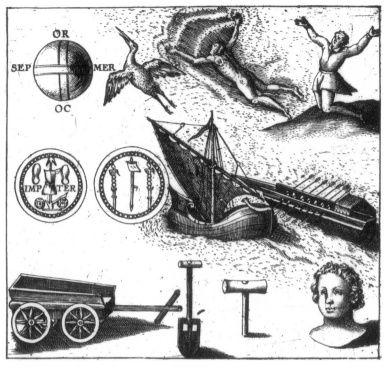

Figure 5. Nature's cruciforms.
Engraving from Justus Lipsius, *De Cruce,* 1606. Courtesy of
the Folger Shakespeare Library, Washington, D.C.

Cruce thus renders the central device of Christianity and the implement of Christ's Passion as the ultimate form of bodily denigration and offense, crucifixion here pictorially evoking a double sodomitical violation of the body—a penetration that is at once *per oram* and *per anum.*

At the same time *and in much the same terms,* the cross and the perforated, profaned male body it presents remain available to the devout as a powerful erotic icon. "What is this strange and uncouth thing? / To make me sigh, and seek, and faint, and die," Herbert continues in "The Cross," responding to Christ's Passion in terms of the lexicon and the gestural system of the conventional Petrarchan lover (lines 1–2). As in "Dullness," the poem I cited earlier, in which Herbert addresses Jesus as "my loveliness," devotion operates here within the scope of a Christian tra-

Figure 6. Crucifixion as sodomy. Engraving from Justus Lipsius, *De Cruce*, 1606. Courtesy of the Folger Shakespeare Library, Washington, D.C.

dition that finds Jesus' exposed and macerated body to be paradoxically both a sight of horror, shame, and defilement *and* a vision of astonishing, even erotic beauty—a devotional convention that is, I would maintain, no less perverse for being a convention. Davies's *Holy Roode* likewise offers Christ in his Passion as "The Paragon of Beautie"; "Can any Thing that hath but feeling sense / Be so obdurate," the poem asks, "As not to melt away, in Passion hot, / To see these Passions?" (10-11).[18] In the context of early modern devotional figurations such as these, Serrano's *Piss Christ*—a monumentally scaled, Cibachrome image that is nothing if not gorgeous— appears ever less the mere affront to Christianity many have taken it to be. Indeed, Serrano, who credits Renaissance art as a principal compositional source of inspiration for his painterly images, himself contends that "the best place for *Piss Christ* is in a church."[19]

*　*　*

Judging from sheer lyric output, however, no English poet was more enraptured by the image of God enfleshed, uncovered, and rendered corporeally vulnerable than was Richard Crashaw. In both English and Latin, Crashaw wrote and rewrote numerous epigrams, lyrics, hymns, and liturgical church offices that rhapsodically hold in view Christ's body and its often astonishing somatic effects and possibilities. What is more, along with the dozens of poems he plies on the Crucifixion, Crashaw was no less lyrically prolix when it came to such other markedly corporeal events and displays in the life of Christ as the complicated technicalities of his virgin conception, development in utero ("The mighty Son whom neither you [Nature] nor she [can] contain wholly / (believe it) is cramped by the fragile tissues / . . . / The quick organs swell with divine movement / (no more holy air moves the heavenly poles)" ["Deus sub utero virginis," lines 3–4, 7–8), and easy parturition; his circumcision in the Temple ("these first fruits of my growing death" ["Our Lord in his Circumcision to his Father," line 1]); the elaborate physical tortures he underwent on the road to Calvary; the preparation of his body for burial; and, finally, the post-Resurrection presentation of his still visible and manipulable wounds. The fulcrum of interest in these poems, indeed the trigger for their devotional profusions, is not merely the exhibition made of Christ's body, but the spectacularization of it as a body that is penetrable and penetrated: "But o thy side! thy deepe dig'd side," Crashaw thus rhapsodizes in "On the bleeding wounds of our crucified Lord" (line 13), a subject he returns to again and again throughout his several volumes of verse. What is more, Crashaw composes a number of sacred epigrams lyricizing the various implements—the priest's circumcising blade, Doubting Thomas's probing fingers, the whips, the thorns, nails, and lance used at Calvary—that had been employed at one time or another to open or to enter Jesus' body: "And now th'art set wide ope, The Speare's sad Art, / Lo! hath unlockt thee at the very Heart" ("I am the Doore," lines 1–2).[20] Even the Roman proctor's dismissal of Christ to his fate at the hands of the Jews is refigured by Crashaw, through his collocation of crimes against the body, as a form of bodily penetration: "Is murther no sin? or a sin so cheape, / That thou need'st heape / A Rape upon't?" he thus wonders in an epigram "To *Pontius* washing his blood-stained hands" (lines 1–3).[21]

Among those instruments that can penetrate and enter Christ's body is the poet's own tool, the pen. "Are NAILES blunt pens of superficiall smart?" Crashaw asks in his "Office of the Holy Crosse" ("Sixth Houre"). In "Adoro Te. The Hymn of St. Thomas in Adoration of the Blessed Sacrament," Christ is told that "Though hidd as GOD, wounds writt thee man" (line 22). In his extended version of the Marian hymn "Sancta Maria Dolorum," Crashaw accords the Passion a more highly wrought textuality, presenting it as the scene of reduplicating inscriptions involving both Jesus and the Blessed Virgin Mary, as "son and mother / Discourse alternate wounds to one another" (stanza 3). Here Christ's "Nailes write swords in her, which soon her heart / Payes back, with more then their own smart"—a "costly intercourse / Of deaths, and worse, / Divided loves." These reciprocating penetrations pen what Crashaw terms "This book of loves" (stanza 6), an amorous text into which he looks to be corporeally inscribed himself. In these terms, Crashaw's "Sancta Maria Dolorum" unfolds as a triangulated scene of mystic writing/wooing/wounding, with the poet hoping that by placing himself "in loves way" his "brest may catch the kisse of some kind dart, / Though as at second hand, from either heart" (stanza 7). The Hymn's conclusion shows him courting the Blessed Virgin, circuiting through her his desire for Christ, with whom the poet wants textually to "mix wounds" and thus share in the Passion:

> Rich Queen, lend some releife;
> At least an almes of greif
> To'a heart who by sad right of sin
> Could prove the whole summe (too sure) due to him.
> By all those stings
> Of love, sweet bitter things,
> Which these torn hands transcrib'd on thy true heart
> O teach mine too the art
> To study him so, till we mix
> Wounds; and become one crucifix.
> (stanza 10)

This "art" of penetrative transcription is evident in yet another epigram titled "On the still surviving markes of our Saviours wounds." There the text that "Naile, or Thorne, or Speare have writ in Thee" remains "Still legible" because the poet's pen, his means of access to Christ's body, "did spell / Every red letter / A wound of thine" (lines 2–8) in its very activity of writing the poem.

It appears, then, that for Crashaw's verse to represent—or, as he puts it, render "legible"—the body of Jesus is to remark its wounds, its points of penetration, its openings:

> Now you lie open. A heavy spear has thrown back the bolt of your heart.
>   And the nails as keys unlock you on all sides.
>
> ("Joh. 10. Ego sum ostium.")

In this epigram, Christ's violated body is once again figured as an opened cabinet or chamber. The architectural metaphor receives further elaboration in "On our crucified Lord Naked, and bloody," a poem that presents what is undoubtedly one of the period's strangest devotional conceits. In it Crashaw directs us to envision Christ's body as a "purple wardrobe," a kind of royal clothes closet, one that has been thrown open for the removal of a viscid robe of blood. This garment, Crashaw declares, is a lamentable covering for a body he says he would prefer to envision as remaining wholly naked:

> Th' have left thee naked Lord, O that they had;
> This Garment too I would they had deny'd.
> Thee with thy selfe they have too richly clad,
> Opening the purple wardrobe of thy side.
>   O never could bee found Garments too good
>   For thee to weare, but these, of thine own blood.

As George Walton Williams has cataloged, Crashaw recurrently tropes on bodies and various body parts as cabinets and closets, as secret spaces to be penetrated and infused with devotion.[22] In the "Hymn to the Name of Jesus," he thus first corporealizes, gives a body to, that name—"the wealthy Brest / Of This unbounded NAME"—and then he implores the now incarnate divine nomination to "Unlock" in itself "thy Cabinet of DAY" (lines 11–12, 127). Similarly, Crashaw adorns the verse "Letter to the Countess of Denbigh" with an emblem depicting the heart as a locked chamber (fig. 7). In the intensely erotic poem that follows, Christ is entreated to take aim at "The self-shutt cabinet of an unsearcht soul," "And 'mongst thy shafts of soveraign light / Choose out that sure decisive dart / Which has the Key of this close heart" (lines 36, 32–34).[23] Interestingly, in this instance Christ is figured, not as a penetrated body, but as the pene-

NON VI.

'Tis not the work of force but will
To find the way into man's will.
'Tis loue alone can hearts vnlock.
Who knowes the WORD*, he needs not knock.*

TO THE

Nobleſt & beſt of laces, the
Counteſſe of Denbigh.

Perſwading her to Reſolution in Religion,
& to render her ſelfe without further
delay into the Communion of
the Catholick Church.

WHat heau'n-intreated HEART is This?
Stands trembling at the gate of bliſſe;
Holds faſt the doo ,yet dares not véture
Fairly to open it , and enter.

Figure 7. The cabinet or closet of the devout heart.
Engraving from Richard Crashaw, *Carmen Deo Nostro*, 1652.
Courtesy of the Folger Shakespeare Library, Washington, D.C.

trating one. We are told, furthermore, that the "Dart of love" he has let
fly into the countess's "self-shutt cabinet" is a kind of liquid bolt: "hast
to drink the wholesome dart. / That healing shaft, which heavn till now /
Hath in love's quiver hid for you" (lines 46–49). A similar invitation is extended in another of Crashaw's vivid Circumcision epigrams: "Tast this,"
the spurting Baby Jesus enjoins in "Our Lord in his Circumcision to his
Father" (line 3)—"this" being the "seed of the purple font" of his just in-
cised male member ("In circumcisionem," line 6). Consider also a stanza
Crashaw adds to his Englishing of the *Dies Irae,* in which we are again
directed to the lower zones of Christ's body and its salvific workings: "O
let thine own soft bowells pay / Thy self; And so discharge that day"

(stanza 12). Crashaw's ecstatic supplication here melds the economics of atonement theology with—what?—scatology? Moreover, the poet erotically overcodes these "discharges" with the language of love, sighs, and amorous rescue: "If sin can sigh, love can forgive. / O say the word my Soul shall live."[24]

Robert Martin Adams wryly noted years ago in an essay on taste and bad taste in metaphysical poetry that Crashaw "has a sometimes disturbing way of dealing with orifices, which he likes to dwell upon."[25] As we have seen, Crashaw is especially given to dwelling upon the orifices opened in the body of Jesus, revealing him to be, as he is ecstatically heralded in Herbert's poem "The Thanksgiving," "King of wounds!" (line 3). But beyond this, what I find not so much disturbing as arresting in Crashaw's treatment of Christ's body is his propensity to represent it as almost nothing but orifices. Here (in English translation) is one of Crashaw's most unrestrainedly effusive wound poems:

"In vulnera pendentis Domini"
["On the wounds of the Lord hanging (on the cross)"]

Whether I call your wounds *eyes* or *mouths*—
surely everywhere are mouths—alas!—everywhere are eyes.

Behold the mouths! o blooming with lips too red!
Behold the eyes! ah wet with cruel tears!

Magdala, you who were accustomed to bring tears and kisses to the
sacred foot, take yours in turn from the sacred foot.

The foot has its own *mouths,* to give your kisses back:
This clearly is the *eye* by which it returns your tears.

With profuse sentimentality, Crashaw pictures the wounds of Christ as so many eyes to shed and collect tears, as so many mouths to kiss and be kissed.[26] What excites adoration here is the notion that Christ's body is exposed to be all openings and valves; no surface on it is completely sealed. Everywhere open, utterly accessible, this body presents no unbreachable borders of permeability and impermeability.[27]

Consider in these terms a stanza from Crashaw's own English rewriting of this same epigram:

O these wakefull wounds of thine!
Are they Mouthes? or are they eyes?

Be they Mouthes, or be they eyne,
    Each bleeding part some one supplies.
("On the wounds of our crucified Lord," lines 1-4)

All these sanguinary apertures in Jesus' body remain ever open, ever "wakefull": Christ's body, that is, won't ever be sealed up, won't ever be rendered impervious to us. Rather, Christ's "love sees us with these eyes," with these wounds ("Joann. 20:20. In vulnerum vertigia" ["On the marks of wounds"], line 3). While Crashaw's presciently surrealist figurations of Christ's wounds as dilated eyes and kissing mouths have struck some readers as devotional grotesqueries, these conceits were clearly erotically charged ones for the poet. Still another of Crashaw's Latin epigrams on Christ's wounds thus informs us that they were inflicted by "Amor" and that the instruments this amorous "miles," or soldier, used—"the bows, the quiver and the light darts"—are weapons drawn from the arsenal of Cupid ("Luc. 24. In cicatrices Domini adhuc superstites" ["On the wounds of the Master still present"], lines 1-2).

In texturing Christ's body with these proliferative, amorously emotive openings, Crashaw likewise presents it as a field of countless secretionary valves, all of which appear to have come unstopped at once:

"In vulnera Dei pendentis"
["On the wounds of God hanging (on the cross)"]

O streams of blood from head, side, hands, and feet!
O what rivers rise from the purple fountain!

His foot is not strong enough to walk for our safety (as once it was)
but it swims; ah—it swims in its own streams.

His hand is held fast; *but it gives, though held fast:* his good right hand
gives holy dews, and it is dissolved into its own gift.

O side, o torrent! for what Nile goes forth in greater
flood where it is carried headlong by the rushing waters?

His head drips and drips with thousands and thousands of drops
at once: do you see how the cruel shame reddens his cheeks?

The thorns cruelly watered by this rain flourish
and hope forthwith to change into new roses.

Each hair is a slender channel for a tiny rill,
a little stream, from this *red sea,* as it were.

> O too much *alive* [are] the *waters* in those precious streams!
> Never was he more truly the *fountain of life.*

In this poem, the penetrated male body turns erotically liquescent, a mechanism for a kind of ejaculatory excess, as it is again in Crashaw's "Vexilla Regis, the Hymn of the Holy Crosse": "Lo, how the streames of life, from that full nest / Of loves . . . / Flow in an amorous floud / Of WATER wedding BLOOD" (stanza 2). Correspondingly, Crashaw's devotional epigrams are themselves often little more than an accretion of reiterating ejaculations: "O streams of blood"; "O what rivers"; "ah—it swims"; "O side, o torrent!"

PISS CRASHAW

I don't really feel that I destroy icons. I feel that I create new ones.
—*Andres Serrano*

Serrano's *Piss Christ* belongs to a larger project involving the photographer's interest both in the formal, aesthetic qualities of various bodily fluids (his palette includes milk, blood, and semen, along with urine), as well as in the highly, and often contradictorily, charged cultural significances of these vital substances. Similarly, Crashaw's own strikingly chromatic poetic tableaux are notable for their extraordinary, even immoderate, figures of liquefaction, as well as for the remarkable transitivity of the liquids that stream and pool therein.[28] In "The Weeper," to take a much reviled, but nonetheless consistently anthologized example, the superflux of Mary Magdalene's penitential tears transmogrifies and swells into "milky rivers." This milky flow then somehow shoots heavenward, supplying the "cream" upon which "Every morn from hence / A brisk Cherub something sippes" (stanzas 4, 5). In "On the Still Surviving marks of our Saviours Wounds," Christ's blood, we have already noted, turns into ink for the poet's pen. More spectacularly still, in "In vulnera Dei pendentis," the Crucifixion lyric cited above, Jesus' body, awash "in its own streams," verges on being entirely liquefied, "dissolved into its own gift"—as is the case in Serrano's *Crucifixion,* another of his immersion photographs, this one using blood as its liquid color field (fig. 8).

In Crashaw's poem, the tide of "rushing waters" is a confluence of

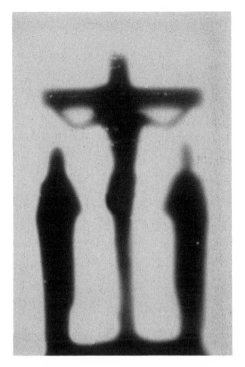

Figure 8. Blood bath.
Andres Serrano, *Crucifixion*,
1987. Courtesy of Paula
Cooper Gallery, New York.

blood and tears and possibly Eucharistic wine as well—"holy dews" revered here as "the fountain of life." These hybrid fluids likewise flow through his long poem *Sospetto d'Herode* ("The Suspicion of Herod"), where they are even more forthrightly eroticized. Elaborating the traditional conceit of Christ as honey, Crashaw ushers us inside another kind of devotional enclosure, one he terms the "Hive of Loves":

> Nor needs my Muse a blush, or these bright Flowers
> Other then what their owne blest beauties bring.
> They were the smiling sons of those sweet Bowers,
> That drinke the deaw of Life, whose deathlesse spring,
> Nor *Sirian* flame, nor *Borean* frost deflowers:
> From whence Heav'n-labouring Bees with busie wing,
>   Suck hidden sweets, which well digested proves
>   Immortall Hony for the Hive of Loves.
>
> (stanza 3)

Inside this apparently all-male "Hive of Loves," Christ allures with "hidden sweets," another fructifying discharge of the "deaw of Life" to be ingested by those the poem terms his "smiling sons." The sucking depicted in these "sweet Bowers" compounds the alimentary and the erotic (specifically the homoerotic), but the poet feels no need to be coy ("Nor needs my Muse a blush"), no need to obscure what he frankly acknowledges to be a highly amorous, male devotional liaison. For, unlike the mortal "deflowering" wrought by the change of seasons, the kind of insemination—the "immortal Hony"—Christ offers in his "Hive of Loves" is perpetually fecundating, effecting no less than a "deathlesse spring" for these "smiling sons."

In sum, then, like so much seventeenth-century religious expression, Crashaw's devotional verse displays little propensity to leave the body behind, to recuse the flesh from the operations of redemption. Crashaw's poetry instead insists upon the corporeal, intent on exploring its many expressive possibilities. His often exorbitantly rendered epigrams on Jesus' body, its countless wounds, and the vital fluids discharged from them stimulate Christian devotion in terms of a palpable foray through the permutations and permeabilities of bodies—Christ's excitingly vulnerable male body in particular. Crashaw's lyrics are devotional rhapsodies rung on what is outside that body that can be used to open and enter it (whips, nails, thorns, spikes, spears, knives, his own pen), as well as what can be made to stream out from it, once penetrated, in an unending flow (blood, tears, water, wine, ink, honey, cream, an inseminating "deaw of Life"). In thus envisioning Christ in his Passion as a highly fertile somatic field, one generative of numberless kissing mouths and tearful eyes, of countless orifices and dilated valves, of a literally promiscuous, hypersemantic mix of bodily fluids, Crashaw aligns religious devotion and its affects with the body and its most visceral operations. Indeed, to reinvoke an association I posited earlier, it could be said that Crashaw probes the openings in Christ's body, as well as their ecstatic flow and eruption of secretions, with an explicitness, a studied fascination, that evokes no discourse so much as contemporary pornography's fetishistic explorations of the erotic body and its paroxysms.[29] Like porn's spectacularized will-to-knowledge of the body—its orifices and valves—Crashaw's verse is devotionally interested in the form of Jesus *in extremis,* as an iconic male body rendered visible and open to desire. The fluid permeabilities of Christ's body, localized around the wound, the opening in the body—the site upon which so many of Crashaw's lyrics dote—thus provide the means for identification with him, for ecstatically "mixing wounds," for making the Passion commutable from the Son of Man to man.[30]

HOMODEVOTION

Let me be manly. Let me commit myself to my merciful Creator.
—*James Boswell*, London Journal

Real men love Jesus.
—*Evangelical Christian car bumper sticker*

In the course of an illuminating analysis of spirituality and eroticism in the poetry of George Herbert, Michael Schoenfeldt attends to a number of texts, related to those we have been considering by Crashaw (one of Herbert's devoted poetic disciples), that envision the penetration of Christ's body. "Passio Discerpta" ("The Events of the Passion") 4, "In latus perfossum," for instance, "depicts the 'remorseless steel . . . open[ing] up a path' in Christ, a path the speaker hopes his heart will follow." Similarly, Herbert's poem on the skeptical apostle Thomas, "Lucus 30 (In Thomam Didymum)" begins, Schoenfeldt comments, "with a striking image of a mortal penetrating the divine body—'The servant puts his fingers in you'—and sees Jesus' allowance of such penetration as a manifestation of his love."[31] Yet despite the fact that what Herbert has so graphically figured here is a scene of penetration involving a male mortal and a male divine body, Schoenfeldt's account of these poems no sooner brings into view Jesus' penetrable body than his consideration of it becomes repointed toward "the possibility of a feminized Christ" (249).

This impulse to recast Christ's gender as female recurs in Schoenfeldt's discussion of "The Bag," which he terms "Herbert's uncharacteristically grotesque portrait of the wounded Christ" (is this to say more like Crashaw's usual doings?), one that is said to express "the mystery of Christ's descent into vulnerable flesh as an adoption of tacitly feminine traits." This poem's central conceit is that the cavity lanced open in Jesus' side at Calvary is a corporeal pouch, a "bag," for carrying prayers, poems, letters—"anything to send or write"—up to heaven and "Unto my Father's hands and sight" (lines 31, 33). Christ, Schoenfeldt writes, thus invites his torturers to follow the spear in penetrating his body so they may "put [their messages] very neare my heart," and enticingly reminds them that "the doore shall still be open." . . . The poem's details—the action of "undressing," the placement in an "inne," the emphasis upon pregnability, the seductive promise that "the doore / Shall still be open"—all connote a sexual scenario which never fully surfaces, but which suffuses the process by which the almighty God of power becomes a vulnerable and compassionate deity. *The wound of "The Bag" functions as a kind of vaginal orifice, feminizing a traditionally masculine Christ.* Christ's willingness to assume a vulnerable body and be entered by all opens him up to the contamination of a fallen, and surprisingly feminine, sexuality. (249; emphasis added)

While this reading effectively draws out the ways in which Herbert represents Christ's *kenosis* in provocatively eroticized terms, we should question, I think, why "a traditionally masculine Christ" is to be reimagined here as "female." Certainly in this particular poem Herbert never stops referring to Christ as "he," never really blurs gender, never presents the Savior's vulnerable body as other than male. Indeed, the world of this poem appears to be another all-male one, populated by the Son of Man, his Father, the spear-wielding Roman soldier, and the spectators Christ addresses as "brethren" (line 30).[32] The "sexual scenario" evoked in "The Bag" is thus another markedly same-sex one. Where is, we might further ask, "the emphasis on pregnability" Schoenfeldt ascertains in "The Bag"? For Christ's body to be pierced "upon his side" (line 29) does not necessarily imply that he is also "impregnated." Not all acts (or thematics) of erotic penetration would have as their telos impregnation and reproduction. And finally, if one is meant to think of Christ's "bag" as evocatively genitalic, as Schoenfeldt rightly, I would say, encourages us to do, why should it have to be as "a kind of vaginal orifice"? Would it be going too far to see that pouch doubling as something like a kind of scrotum? "Unto my Father's hands and sight," Christ exclaims here in the midst of his Passion, "Believe me, it shall safely come" (lines 32–34).[33]

The notion of "Jesus as mother" seems to me to be more convincingly pursued when Schoenfeldt turns to Herbert's Latin lyric "Lucus 34 (To John, leaning on the Lord's breast)," in which he locates a figuration of "an overtly female Christ, nourishing with milk and blood his mortal disciples" (250). "Ah now, glutton, let me suck too!" Herbert immodestly importunes:

You won't really hoard the whole
Breast for yourself! Do you thieve
Away from everyone that common well?
He also shed his blood for me,
And thus, having rightful
Access to the breast, I claim the milk
Mingled with the blood . . .
(lines 1–7)

Crashaw also addresses a Latin epigram to John, the Beloved Disciple:

Enjoy yourself: hide your head in his majestic bosom, for then it
would never wish to be placed on a bed of everlasting roses.
("Sancto Joanni, dilecto discipulo," lines 1–2)

While his epigram is hardly less sensual than Herbert's, Crashaw bypasses an opportunity to frame in maternal terms the intimate encounter between Christ and the "dilecto discipulo" tenderly reposing at his breast. Nor does Crashaw demand, as Herbert does, his own turn at the bosom of Christ. "Enjoy yourself," he repeatedly encourages John, "and while he carries you in his holy bosom thus / o it will be enough for me to have been able to ride on his *back*." No sibling rivalry over "mother Jesus" here. Instead, Crashaw proposes another, equally striking corporeal metaphor for intimacy with Christ, one that has him mounting Christ's back, joining with him *a tergo*: "O sat erit tergo me potuisse vehi." Like those "smiling sons" sucking "hidden sweets" from Christ's "Hive of Loves" in *Sospetto d'Herode*, Crashaw again posits a devotional erotics that is homoerotic.

I want to stress here that I am by no means suggesting that these poets are incapable of representing bodies and desires in ways that traverse or trouble the categories of gender. On the contrary, gender and eroticism remain extraordinarily labile signifying fields in devotional expression and performance. Consider, for instance, Crashaw's epigram "Luke 11. Blessed be the paps which Thou has sucked":

Suppose he had been Tabled at thy Teates,
    Thy hunger feels not what he eates:
Hee'l have his Teat e're long (a bloody one)
    The Mother then must suck the Son.

What this unsettling epigram offers is, I think, less an emblem of religious androgyny than one of a more radical gender *undecidability*, the somatic operations envisioned by Crashaw being neither determinately male nor determinately female. Here Jesus is first imagined in terms of a son nursing at a mother's breast, and then he is accorded his own to suckle her; he bears a wound—one somehow concave and convex at once—that also functions as a protrusion; he is endowed with a "Teat" that is both mammary and phallic.[34]

Crashaw's "Blessed be the paps" is a particularly striking, but by no means unprecedented, instance of the malleability of gender within the figural space of devotional expression.[35] Accordingly, my aim here is not to underplay such traversals of gender and gendered positions, but rather to insist that we avoid peremptorily re-encoding every representation of the penetrable male body as feminized *because* penetrated. Are male bodies without their own orifices? In Crashaw's verse, as we have now seen at length, Christ's male body is replete with them and for that reason fascinating, deeply desirable, devotionally stimulating. What is more, Crashaw regularly presents Jesus' body as both penetrated and penetrating in the same figuration. In one of his several epigrams that turn on the conceit of Christ as Cupid, we are told that "In it [Christ's wounded side] there sate but one sole dart; / A peircing one. his peirced heart / . . . / The weapon, that he wore, he was" ("In cicatrices Domini Jesu," lines 9–12). Crashaw's Latin version of the same epigram represents Christ's cupidinous body as "both his dart and he himself the quiver for his darts" ("suumque / Et jaculum, & jaculis ipse pharetra suis") ("Luc. 24," lines 3–4). Herbert's "Artillery" likewise presents God and the poet who "woo[s]" him with "tears and prayers night and day" as "shooters both" (lines 19, 25).[36]

Accounts that fashion a paradoxically "female" or a "bisexed" Jesus often do so at the cost of too quickly effacing the primary maleness of his body and its operations, as well as, perhaps more important, the possibilities a male Christ affords for a homoeroticized devotional expression. The androgynous maneuverings now favored in critical and historical treatments of early modern religiosity thus never get at how devotion's *supra*natural imaginings can exceed and transgress the orthodoxies of the body, sex, and gender in ways that pass beyond the straightforward reversal of male into female. "This feminization of Christ"; "the vision of a bisexual or female Christ"; "Christ's suffering flesh was 'woman'"; "a relationship to the body of Jesus which is at once erotic and maternal"; "To enter into Christ is to return to the womb": formulations such as these have the effect (whether intentional or not) of rendering the poetry's erotically valenced scenarios of male penetration of a male body as more familiarly heteroerotic.[37] Here the male body penetrates, while the penetrated body turns "female," even if it is male.

GENDER ECSTASY

The inadequacy of this schema can be adduced by means of another example drawn from Crashaw's corpus—this one involving a female devout body. As we have been considering, Crashaw makes religious desire palpable in terms of a pervasive thematics of corporeal permeability and interpenetration. An orifice or perforation in the body becomes the portal for devotional access to Jesus: one thus enters him or is entered by him, and Christ and Christian together are deluged in the salvific streams that flow from the penetrated body. It bears reiterating here that in devotional writing—and perhaps most spectacularly so in Crashaw—gender seldom poses the limit to what the body can be imagined to enact or have enacted upon or through it. The positions of ravisher and ravished, penetrator and penetrated, can variously and successively be taken on by male, female, and undecidably gendered devotional bodies as they are rendered ecstatically expressive, devotionally stimulated.

In these terms, then, I want to take up Crashaw's extraordinary sequence of poems on Teresa of Avila, whose mystic experiences he choreographs as a series of shiftingly gendered, variously eroticized devotional tableaux. The headnote to "A Hymn . . . to Sainte Teresa," the first poem in the sequence, introduces this saint as "a WOMAN for the Angellical heighth of speculation, for Masculine courage of performance, more than a woman": terms that immediately realign gender identifications from the realm of essence to the space of a performative hypergender. In the poem that follows, a kind of "in the realm of the senses" hagiography, we learn that the child Teresa, having "Scarse . . . learn't to lisp the name / Of Martyr," grows consumed with the desire to become one: "SHE's for the Moores, and MARTYRDOM" (lines 15-16, 64). Heaven, however, has other plans, reserving her for "A death more mysticall and high"—and more erotic as well:

> THOU art love's victime; and must dy
> A death more mysticall and high.
> Into love's armes thou shalt let fall
> A still-surviving funerall.

> His is the DART must make the DEATH
> Whose stroke shall tast thy hallow'd breath.
>
> (lines 75–80)

Having been thus ravished by Christ's "DART," Teresa's mystic body is then laid open to what turns into a kind of angelic orgy, as

> The fair'st and first-born sons of fire
> Blest SERAPHIM, shall leave their quire
> And turn love's souldiers, upon THEE
> To exercise their archerie.
>
> (lines 93–96)

Teresa's multiply penetrated body becomes multiply orgasmic ("These thy DEATHS, so numerous" [line 110]), resulting in spiritual insemination and the fostering of converts—the poet himself in their number—these "Sons of thy vowes / The virgin-births with which thy soveraign spouse / Made fruitfull thy fair soul" (lines 167–69).

Yet what is so remarkable about Crashaw's rendering of Teresa's ecstasy is not the orgasmic overtones with which he, like Bernini's famous baroque sculpture, suffuses it. It is rather Crashaw's imagination of that ecstasy as the ecstasy of a *male* body (his own?) being possessed by a male lover, Jesus:

> O how oft shalt thou complain
> Of a sweet and subtle PAIN.
> Of intolerable JOYES;
> Of a DEATH, in which who dyes
> Loves *his* death, and dyes again.
> And would for ever so be slain.
> And lives, and dyes; and knowes not why
> To live, But that *he* thus may never leave to DY.
> How kindly will thy gentle HEART
> Kisse the sweet-killing DART!
> And close in *his* embraces keep
> Those delicious Wounds, that weep
> Balsom to heal themselves with . . .
>
> (lines 97–109; emphasis added)

The thematics of erotic penetration run over into the poem's next narrative section on Teresa's apotheosis. This time, however, the ecstasy-inducing "dart" is wielded not by Christ but by his Mother Mary, Crashaw now offering us a scene of female/female mystic congress:

> What joyes shall seize thy soul, when she
> Bending her blessed eyes on thee
> (Those second Smiles of Heav'n) shall dart
> Her mild rayes through thy melting heart!
> (lines 133–36)

In "The Flaming Heart," the sequence's third poem, contemplation of an artist's pictorial representation of Teresa's famous transverberation serves for further ecstatic play across gender. Here Crashaw accords the saint a more agential role than the passive posture she presented in the "Hymn," though, as we saw, her passivity there was valenced sometimes as female, sometimes as male, and sometimes both at once. Now Teresa "mockes with female FROST love's manly flame" (line 24), while the male seraph who serves as Christ's proxy on the scene is in turn overtly feminized: "Read HIM for her, and her for him" (line 11), we are instructed at the beginning of the poem, though this directive hardly "heterosexualizes" what follows. Crashaw then insists that the misguided painter rethink his rendering of this mystical encounter, particularly in terms of the gendered positions he has assigned to each party:

> Doe then as equall right requires,
> Since HIS the blushes be, and her's the fires,
> Resume and rectify thy rude design,
> Undresse thy Seraphim into MINE.
> Redeem this injury of thy art;
> Give HIM the vail, give her the dart.
> (lines 37–42)

The chastised artist would have understood this as the correct erotic alignment from the beginning, Crashaw insists, "Had thy cold Pencil kist her PEN" (line 20). For it is a phallicized Teresa who now wields "love's manly flame," and with it "the DART for it is she / (Fair youth) [who] shootes both thy shaft and THEE" (lines 47–48). The poet himself looks to be taken in turn by this erotically dominant nun: "By all thy brim-fill'd Bowles of feirce desire / By thy last Morning's draught of liquid fire; / . . . / Leave nothing of my SELF in me" (lines 99–100, 106). Eventually the angel is restored his shaft, but Teresa retains "the equall poise of love's both parts," having been made "Bigge alike with wounds and darts" (lines 75–76).

Accorded a mystic body both impregnable and phallic, Teresa's ec-static experiences overrun any template that organizes gender or eroticism in terms of a binary structure. Yet this is not the same, I would argue, as claiming that the format of gender is wholly abdicated in her trans-ports, in these expressions of devotion at white heat. Indeed, Teresa— "a WOMAN for the Angellical heighth of [her] speculation, for Masculine courage of performance, more than a woman"—seems not to transcend but rather to occupy all imaginable gender space. Nor do I think that the poems' exhilarated circulation through these engenderings is wholly con-tainable within the soft contours of the merely androgynous. This saint, as Crashaw represents her, could instead be taken as an early modern ex-ample of those whom Eve Sedgwick has described in another context as "just plain more *gender-y* than others—whether the gender they manifest be masculine, feminine, both, or 'and then some.' " [38] Similarly, gender is not transcended in Teresa's ecstasies; rather, it is palpably taken up and on, gender's concomitant forms, postures, and attributes serving as a tensile field for the expression of Crashaw's trenchantly corporealized mysticism. And even though his manipulations exceed the kinds of dichotomous models of gender and sexuality upon which notions of androgyny and ef-feminacy are arguably most often forged, I am no more inclined to dub this "gender trouble" than I am to call it androgyny. What is embraced is instead a kind of gender ecstasy.

HISTORICISM AND EROTICISM

For advanced students only, one is tempted to say, are Prof. Steinberg's
discussions of the hand of Christ—as child and as adult on his own groin. And
only for rather specialized tastes perhaps is the question of his erection.
—Michael Levey, "Behold the Man," a review of Steinberg's The Sexuality of
Christ *in* The Washington Post Book World [39]

Gender is not the only transitive category here. As we have already seen, devotional texts can be no less fluid across forms of eroticism in the kinds of congress they envision between Christ and Christian. Before further elaborating this claim in terms of a reading of Donne's Holy Sonnets, however, I want first to address another aspect of why recent scholarship has remained so little concerned with the *vagaries* of devotional desire, particularly its homoerotic flexions. This reason is genealogical, having to do with the widespread adoption by Renaissance critics of interpretive models honed in scholarship on the body's role and meaning in *medieval* religiosity. As I indicated in the introduction, the historian Caroline Bynum holds an especially influential position on this account. Her work has powerfully demonstrated the extent to which "the extravagant penitential practices of the thirteenth to the fifteenth century, the cultivation of pain and patience, the literalism of *imitatio crucis* are . . . not primarily an attempt to escape from body. . . . Rather, late medieval asceticism was an effort to plumb and to realize all the possibilities of the flesh" (*Holy Feast,* 294). These medieval practitioners of asceticism and ecstasy "were not rebelling against or torturing their flesh out of guilt over its capabilities," she continues, "so much as using the possibilities of its full sensual and affective range to soar ever closer to God" (295). Bynum is a luminous guide to Christianity's historical legacies of an often startlingly vivid corporeality. What makes a critical consideration of her work particularly germane for my concerns here is the emergence of Bynum's medieval scholarship as a recurring gloss on seventeenth-century religious writing as well.[40] Furthermore, in "The Body of Christ in the Later Middle Ages: A Reply to Leo Steinberg," a largely critical, essay-length review of Steinberg's *The Sexuality of Christ,* Bynum herself extends her interpretive models and investments in the direction of Renaissance cultural materials.[41]

Unlike many of the literary critics now adapting the protocols of her work to Renaissance texts, however, Bynum is herself reluctant to admit the erotic as a significant component of the extreme physicality she finds catalyzing so much religious expression in the Middle Ages. Accordingly, she notes quite critically that "the recent outpouring of work on the history of the body, especially the female body, has largely equated body with sexuality." Against this tendency, she urges us to "wipe away such assumptions before we come to medieval source material. Medieval images of the body have less to do with sexuality than with fertility and decay" (*Fragmentation and Redemption,* 182). Bynum thus contests what she takes to be Steinberg's anachronistic imputation of sexual significance to the vast number of pictorial representations his book gathers in which the focal point of the image is the display, and sometimes even the manipulation, of Christ's penis. It is only the suspicion of the modern viewer, Bynum argues to the contrary, that smuggles sexuality into these images, or into any artifact of the profoundly somatized religious cultures of the Middle Ages and the Renaissance. "Twentieth-century readers and viewers tend to eroticize the body and to define themselves by the nature of their sexuality. But did medieval viewers? For several reasons, I think we should be cautious about assuming that they did" (*Fragmentation and Redemption,* 85). "Nor," she adds, "did medieval people understand as erotic or sexual a number of bodily sensations which we interpret that way" (86).

Bynum's caveats against seeing the body "that way" are surprising given that her work is otherwise invested, as I have noted, in the task of recovering into view the spectacular efforts of devotees, saints, and mystics—"religious virtuosi," she aptly names them (*Fragmentation and Redemption,* 34)—"to plumb and to realize *all the possibilities* of the flesh," to activate "its *full* sensual and affective range" (*Holy Feast,* 294–95; emphasis added). But before further scrutinizing the latitude of sensual possibilities Bynum's work allows, I want first to address her polemical use of Steinberg's book in staging the case against eroticizing premodern bodily expression and exhibition. For Bynum's critique strikes me as a rather misdirected volley.[42] Despite its provocative title, Steinberg's *The Sexuality of Christ in Renaissance Art and in Modern Oblivion* is actually far less concerned with any notion of Christ's "sexuality" than it is with the denotation of his gender and genitality.[43] Moreover, Steinberg, as I remarked in the introduction, carefully circumscribes with a series of absolutely orthodox doctrinal explanations any possibility that these images of Christ's naked body and his occasionally erect penis could have anything at all to do with sexuality or erotic desire—be it Christ's, the artist's who rendered it such, or even the viewer's. According to Steinberg, the depiction of Jesus' uncovered body, and the rendering of his virile member as an object of *ostentatio,* is always *only* an emblem of the Son of God's Incarnation, of his complete descent into human form and all its weaknesses: "The sexual member exhibited by the Christ Child, so far from asserting aggressive virility, concedes instead God's assumption of human weakness. It is an affirmation not of superior prowess but of condescension to kinship, a sign of the Creator's self-abasement to his creature's condition" (47). Thus scrupulously left unexplored by Steinberg is any more carnal notion of the Incarnation, any possibility that such an *ostentatio genitalium* might, not instead but *also,* signify erotically, as the *ostentatio vulnerum* (the display of Christ's wounds) so ardently does in the devotional love poetry of Richard Crashaw, the poet, incidentally, whom Steinberg most often cites in his book. Indeed, what is most remarkable about *The Sexuality of Christ*— apart from its astonishing illustrations—is just how little concerned it is (Bynum's critique notwithstanding) with questions of eroticism and affective response, questions that still remain, even here in this controversial and courageous study, consigned to the closet of what Steinberg himself dubs "modern oblivion."

The anxious topic of erotic responsiveness to representations of Christ in his Passion is addressed, however, in Richard C. Trexler's essay, "Gendering Jesus Crucified." In replying to Steinberg and Bynum, Trexler argues "that not completely unlike other gods, Jesus, whether in his image or in the vision made of him in imitation, might physically seduce his devotees and even those who ridiculed him."[44] Trexler also reminds us that the intention of the artists who supply such representations cannot be absolutely determinative of how those images will be received by viewers: "We can be sure that the meaning of Jesuses on the Cross lies less in the intentions of the image-makers than in the sense of self with which male, and female, devotees and ridiculers felt themselves attached to the figure" (119). Indeed, this short, provocative essay is full of fascinating evidence that points to a premodern recognition of and, in many cases, anxiety over the possibility that representations of a nude Christ could induce erotic effects. Trexler, for instance, refers us to Gilio da Fabriano's influential dialogue *On the Errors of Painters* (1568), a text in which the case for clothing all holy images, including those of Jesus, is clinched with the citation of Pliny's story of Pheidias's *Venus,* a statue so beautiful that it incited certain "lussuriosissimi giovini" to masturbate in front of it and then ejaculate onto the sculpture (116). Bynum, in her "Reply to Leo Steinberg," determines that there is "reason to think that medieval people saw Christ's penis not primarily as a sexual organ but as the object of circumcision and therefore as . . . wounded, bleeding flesh" (86). However, the worry expressed here by Gilio is not only that male viewers would see Christ's exposed penis as a sexual organ, but that their own might be incited in response to it.

In recognizing the potential eroticism of an encounter with the Christ image, Trexler notes that "few scholars have raised the problem of the male gazing sensually at the male form" (116). Yet this important question is subsumed in Trexler's own preliminary account of the same-sex (devotional) male gaze by his inclination (and we have seen this before) to regard the male form of Jesus not as masculine but as feminine. For instance, Trexler directs us with evident enthusiasm to the *Isenheim Altarpiece,* where "Jesus' awful wounds have healed in the very earth." "If saying that this body has been regendered is problematic," he continues, "I shall use the word rejuvenated. Now it is soft and creamy, and Jesus' hair, no longer its earlier Mediterranean black, has turned a remarkably northern, or, may I say, feminine, blond. *Che bella!*" From here, he declares: "I believe that we should look at the impact that the effeminized—or dependent—masculinity of the humiliated Jesus Crucified had, and still has, on Christians' actions" (118). Although such directions may not take us very far into the problematic of "the male gazing sensually at the male form," much more troubling is Trexler's citation and apparent endorsement of Wendy Doniger's argument in *Women, Androgynes, and Other Mythical Beasts* that religious devotion always entails heterosexual object choice, even if recasting the gender of either the divinity or the devotee is required to straighten that relation.[45] This may be true of all the Hindu mystical texts Doniger treats, though it seems doubtful to me.[46] In any event, such compulsory heterosexuality is certainly not the rule in Christian devotional relation to Christ.

Although less rhapsodic than Trexler ("Che bella!"), Bynum on occasion does concede some kind of erotic quality to the devotional experiences of the female saints and mystics she studies.[47] This may seem ironic, given her critique of Steinberg; yet when it comes to the sexual, what Bynum allows on the one hand she is quick to reprove with the other. Exemplary of this practice is her exegesis of Catherine of Siena's stunning vision of marrying Christ, not with the ring of gold and jewels as we find depicted in any number of paintings, but instead with the fleshy band of his circumcised foreskin: "Oh Jesus, gentlest love," Catherine thus intones in one of her letters, "as a sign that you had espoused us you gave us the ring of your most holy and tender flesh at the time of your holy circumcision on the eighth day. . . . [J]ust enough flesh was taken from him to make a circlet of a ring. . . . Notice that the fire of divine charity gave us a ring not of gold but of his own purest flesh."[48] Bynum comments, "When Catherine of Siena spoke of the foreskin of Christ as a wedding ring, she associated that piece of bleeding flesh with the eucharistic host and saw herself appropriating the pain of Christ. It is we who suspect sexual yearnings in a medieval virgin who found sex the least of the world's temptations" (*Fragmentation and Redemption*, 86). Perhaps so, but I feel tempted to wonder whether, if indeed Catherine found "sex the least of the *world's* temptations," it was not more a matter of her other-worldly "sexual orientation" (so to speak) and its erotic object choice in Christ than it was a function of the kind of nearly absolute abrogation of the sexual propounded in Bynum's account.

Bynum's method for treating matters such as Catherine's vision of sealing her marriage to Christ with such an extraordinary piece of jewelry unfolds with a nearly heuristic force. Typically, we are first enticed with an expression of desire for union with Christ—say, for example, the twelfth-century monk Rupert of Deutz, who (as Bynum narrates the scene) "climbed on the altar, embraced the crucifix, and felt Christ's tongue in his mouth" (*Fragmentation and Redemption*, 86): an image of divine French kissing that would, no doubt, strike many of us as powerfully erotic—provocatively homoerotic. But then Bynum issues the requisite chastisement for succumbing to the temptation to take such expressions "that way." Similarly in *Holy Feast and Holy Fast*, Bynum returns to Catherine of Siena, this time citing Catherine's ecstatic exhortations to other women about "putting on the nuptial garment" of Jesus and "climbing up Christ's body from foot to side to mouth" (178). But, Bynum then cautions, we are not to regard such an expression as "erotic" or "nuptial" in the least. Why? Because, first of all, Catherine equates this kind of union with suffering and pain. That, Bynum determines, is "extremely unerotic." Second, and perhaps more interesting, this saint's devotion is not to be eroticized because Catherine sees Christ, we are told here, as "either a female body that nurses or a piece of flesh that one puts on oneself or sinks into":

> Catherine understood union with Christ not as an erotic fusing with a male figure but as a taking in and a taking on—a becoming—of Christ's flesh itself.
>
> In fact, Catherine clearly associated Christ's physicality with the female body, underlining thereby both her capacity for assimilation to Christ and her capacity, like his, for service. . . . And she repeatedly called Christ's wound a breast. (178)

Not unlike Crashaw in his Passion poems, Catherine desires a union with the exposed and opened body of Jesus, a form of ecstatic congress she imagines and enjoys in the most graphically physical of terms. But whereas Crashaw's rapturous poetic figurations typically (though not always) retain the primary maleness of Christ's body, Catherine, as Bynum points out, at times reconceives that body across genders as a female form. In "sinking into" the body of Christ and sharing his Passion (both his suffering and his bliss), Catherine thus sees herself intimately engaging with another female body. Like Crashaw, Catherine envisages eroticized devotional intercourse as a same-sex act: in melding her body with Christ's, this visionary female saint sees herself sharing the "nuptial garment" with another desired female body.[49] But for Bynum this is just the reason why we are not to think of as sexual Catherine's feverish yearnings to embrace, kiss, mount, take in, put on the body of Christ. Their corporeal union could not be erotic, the unspoken supposition of Bynum's argument dictates, because then we would have to recognize it as homoerotic.

Bynum states that her aim is to expand our sense of the semiological significations allotted to bodies, bodily parts, and bodily processes, instructing us that "medieval symbols were far more complex—polysemic as anthropologists say—than modern people are aware" (*Fragmentation and Redemption,* 116). Yet we have seen that she herself can be quick to delimit the erotic—and especially the homoerotic—potentialities of her own devotional polysemy of the medieval body. Near the conclusion of *Holy Feast and Holy Fast,* Bynum determines that "our modern assumptions obscure the fact that food *is* food and body *is* body" (300). Significantly, this naked essentialism shows up in Bynum's argument immediately before the possibility arises of *sexualized* corporeal meaning, of what she cursorily dismisses as a twentieth-century, post-Freudian interpretive legacy "that the body means sexuality" (300–301). Here, in other words, one form of essentialism—food is food; body is body—simply replaces another—body is sex—with the alimentary being the essentialism of choice.[50]

My sense is that we need to consider carefully what kinds of bodies have been heretofore recovered to the historical repertory of devotion's practices and expressions. Bynum, in fact, broaches her agenda for the reembodiment of religious culture at the conclusion of one essay in *Fragmentation and Redemption:* "If we want to express the significance of Jesus in both male and female images, if we want to turn from seeing body as sexual to seeing body as generative . . ." (117). But let us stop here. Why should this argument be structured in terms of an opposition? Indeed, why should we turn away from regarding the body as always at least potentially sexualized, as a truly polysemous site where various meanings—including an array of erotic ones—coincide, compete, and collude with each other in making the body *meaningful?* And even granting the opposition Bynum advances between the body as generative and the body as sexual, why should we want to prioritize the former? Why affirm generation as always preferential to eroticism? Evidently, that is what Bynum would direct us to do, not only in our study of medieval religiosity but also in our own historical moment, given the oddly nostalgic lament that concludes *Holy Feast and Holy Fast* over "the impoverishment of twentieth-century images" (302). It is striking, and I think telling as well, that here the modern reflex for reading the body erotically is implicitly linked to a notion of the impoverishment of contemporary culture.[51] One form of cultural impoverishment that Bynum's own work on the devotional body and its desires fails to consider, and regrettably may even have contributed to, is the obfuscating turn away from devotional envisionings of the body's homoerotic possibilities, possibilities as richly present in the medieval religious materials she studies as they are in the seventeenth-century devotional verse to which we now return.

"THAT I MIGHT RISE"

Like Bynum's work on Christian devotion and the body, Bataille's account of religion as a cultural system is underwritten by incriminations of semiological impoverishment. In contrast to Bynum, however, Bataille's concern lies precisely with the *de*-eroticization of the meanings of the sacred, as well as with the foreclosure of the ways in which the sacred engages with the profane and the transgressive. Writing from within an ecstatic philosophical space conceptually far removed from the interpretive chastenings Bynum levels in the name of historicism, Bataille postulates a cross-cultural, cross-temporal erotics of religion in which "the sacred and the forbidden are one, [where] the sacred can be reached through the violence of a broken taboo" (126). Yet Christianity, as Bataille sees it, has from its inception looked to sever this reciprocally constitutive coupling of the holy and the taboo, doing so much to its own impoverishment.[52] "Misunderstanding the sanctity of transgression," he charges, "is one of the foundations of Christianity" (90). Although Bataille marks Christianity as the exception to his axiom that transgression is complementary, even requisite to the production of sacrality, it strikes me that in just such terms he has delineated the devotional contours of Donne's most famous Holy Sonnet:

> Batter my heart, three-personed God; for, you
> As yet but knock, breathe, shine, and seek to mend;
> That I may rise, and stand, o'erthrow me, and bend
> Your force, to break, blow, burn, and make me new.
> I, like an usurped town, to another due,
> Labour to admit you, but oh, to no end,
> Reason your viceroy in me, me should defend,
> But is captived, and proves weak or untrue . . .
> (lines 1–8)

Like nearly all of Donne's devotional verse, this sonnet begins at once anxiously and impudently, with the poet forthrightly declaring the inadequacy of all the divine measures thus far undertaken on his behalf: "for, you / As yet but knock, breathe, shine, and seek to mend." In place of these more orthodox ministrations, Donne goes on to advance his own program for redemption, one that climaxes with his desire to be, like a Christian Ganymede, carried off by God and ravished:

> Yet dearly'I love you, and would be loved fain,
> But am betrothed unto your enemy,
> Divorce me, untie, or break that knot again,
> Take me to you, imprison me, for I
> Except you enthral me, never shall be free,
> Nor ever chaste, except you ravish me.
> (lines 9–14)

Remarkably, it isn't enough for Donne to be enthralled, to be ravished—raped—by Christ alone, as Crashaw's christocentric poetics would probably have framed the desire. Pursuing his own fantasia of eroticized devotional excess, Donne instead enlists the entire Christian Godhead in the endeavor: "Batter my heart, *three-personed God*"—a trinitarian gang bang.

Surveying some of the history of criticism concerned with this remarkable sonnet, one finds that it is scholars from an earlier generation, those writing in the 1950s and 1960s, who candidly address and repeatedly fret over the moral and erotic implications of Donne's final metaphorical turn, noting that it seems to "open a field for scatological interpretation," that it evokes a "notion of God as 'corrupting' man." [53] But it is really no such thing, we are here eventually reassured. What may look to be a case of a male poet begging to be figuratively sodomized by his male God is not so after all; for, these readings insist, the eroticized violations Donne so fervently prays for would be metaphorically enacted on his soul—his *anima*—and, we are further instructed, "with Donne (as with Shakespeare, Spenser, and others) the soul is always feminine." [54]

Feminizing the soul is often the practice in Renaissance devotional materials; but it isn't always so—as it isn't in another of Donne's devotional sonnets, "Oh my black soul!" in which the poet's similarly unregenerate soul is nominated as "he" and "himself." [55] For the moment, however, I am less concerned with contesting the sexual politics that underwrite the scholarship of a previous generation of critics than I am in remarking their willingness to address head-on, if only ultimately to vanquish, the homoeroticism of Donne's poem. Such willingness stands in marked contrast to contemporary critical readings of "Batter my heart," a body of commentary that has rather more effortlessly heterosexualized Donne's ultimate figure for the release he so desires. William Kerrigan, for example, usefully contextualizes "Batter my heart" in terms of what he sees as a particularly Donnean theology of accommodation, a system that entails the poet working out fully, even eagerly, "the most anthropomorphic consequences of anthropomorphism—in short, to imagine with some detail the sexuality of God."[56] Yet Kerrigan himself is inclined to work out those consequences and to detail that sexuality only insofar as they can be made to accommodate a heterosexualized coupling between God and man. Here is his paraphrase of the poem: "If the good man weds God, then the sinful man weds God's 'enimie,' and if God would claim this recalcitrant soul, then he must grant divorce and possess *her* by force" (351–52). Striking here is the shift in gender, as Kerrigan's account modulates from talk of the "good man" to God's efforts to recapture the sinner and "possess *her* by force." From this point on, Kerrigan endows Donne's sonnet with a female voice, reconstructing its "battered heart" as "the ravished vagina" (335). Kerrigan's essay dates back to the mid-1970s, but feminine regendering continues to be standard critical practice, as instanced by Stanley Fish's more recent essay, "Masculine Force: Donne and Verbal Power." Although his reading is kinkier than Kerrigan's inasmuch as it allows for the erotic possibilities of other orifices, Fish likewise finds "that Donne now assumes the posture of a woman and . . . spreads his legs (or cheeks)"; "the woman," he concludes, "is now asking for it."[57] Or as Wilbur Sanders put it more lyrically and more insidiously some years earlier, "The poem ends on a conscious note of sweet female passivity."[58]

Sex-change is likewise the preferred operation in feminist and gender-oriented criticism concerned with Donne's religious verse. Debora Shuger thus considers Donne in the course of her account of the vicissitudes of *female* sacred eroticism, finding his structuring of devotional subjectivity to be "erotic, abandoned, and female" (*The Renaissance Bible*, 190). In a more explicitly feminist discussion, Ann Baynes Coiro notes that Donne "usually talks to his God as one aggressive guy to another," only to shy away from her own aptly phrased recognition when the scene between these "guys" becomes sexualized: "The most complete self-abnegation he can imagine is, in 'Batter my heart,' to place himself before God as a woman, a woman begging to be raped."[59] The direction Coiro sketches for a reading of Donne's sonnet is especially interesting in that it is presented in a Modern Language Association volume on *Approaches to Teaching the Metaphysical Poets*. Coiro's aim—an important one—is to recover these poets, whose misogyny has been assailed over the past several decades, as tools in the service of making the classroom a space where all sorts of constructions and deployments of gender can be interrogated: "We need to talk with our students," she urges, "about the gender of any persona, about how we as readers form the persona's gender, about how the gender forms the poem, and about the implied but silent other who is also shaped by the gender of the speaker and by us" (84). Yet missing in this useful pedagogical concatenation is any analytical trajectory along which questions of sexuality can explicitly be raised—crucial questions, I maintain, for tracing the affective bearings of a male devotional desire directed to a male deity. Thus, while the lines of inquiry Coiro opens here would allow us and our students to map a number of gender-marked axes through Donne and the other metaphysicals, the elision of other kinds of erotics— those existing outside or alongside the heteroerotic—has the unwitting effect, as gender subsumes sex, of producing its own "silent other," its own act of effacement. Let me be more specific. Coiro finds that Donne must be abjectly placing himself before God as, or like, a woman because he voices a desire to be ravished. But undergirding this kind of default re-gendering is the uninterrogated presumption that such a desire may take only a single form, namely a heterosexually modelled one. In other words, if the ravisher (God) is male, then the would-be ravished (Donne) must be seen as "female."

While I question her equation in this instance of the desire to be ravished with womanliness, Coiro's account does pointedly register that Donne's sonnet "intended to shock" (85). Conversely, Achsah Guibbory reads "Batter my heart" in terms that not only heterosexualize Donne's coupling of salvation and sexual violation, but thoroughly domesticate the poem as well. In her chapter on Donne for the *Cambridge Companion to English Poetry: Donne to Marvell*, Guibbory describes the sonnet's amorous scenario this way: the speaker, she writes, is "like a woman who loves one man (God) but is betrothed to another (Satan), and wants to be rescued, even by force." Thus, "Christ is the bridegroom," while the poet adopts the "conventionally 'feminine,' passive role of bride." [60] Yet the connubial narrative Guibbory reads into "Batter my heart," while orthodox enough in form, is unwarranted by the sonnet itself, this critic taming Donne's poem of the very outrageousness that is surely its point. For although Donne sees himself as currently betrothed to the devil, he never asks God to intervene and make a proper "bride" out of him. The sonnet, in other words, fails to end with the expected and complementary call for a re-betrothal to Christ as a more appropriate spouse for the Christian. Indeed, there is little that is proper about Donne's sonnet and its multiply metaphorized scheme of redemption, one that is predicated upon a series of violent and violative actions: the Godhead is to take a battering ram to a hard heart; to besiege and steal away a town that is "due" to another; to provoke a divorce. And, after all this, it isn't remarriage that the poet says he then desires, but rather something that is, I think, meant to be felt as far more transgressive. For Donne says he wants to be ravished, and hence what is offered as the sonnet's devotional climax is his insistent solicitation that God would rape and enthrall this desirous devotee.

Donne's Holy Sonnet "As due by many titles I resign / Myself to thee, O God," dramatizes this eroticized battle for the soul in metaphorical terms that are much the same as those we find in "Batter my heart." In this poem, however, Satan is cast in the role of Donne's ravisher, thereby usurping God's amorous prerogatives:

> Why doth the devil then usurp in me?
> Why doth he steal, nay ravish that's thy right?
> Except thou rise and for thine own work fight,
> Oh I shall soon despair, when I do see
> That thou lov'st mankind well, yet wilt not choose me,
> And Satan hates me, yet is loth to lose me.
> (lines 9–14)

Though ravished, the poet retains his masculine subject position in this sonnet: "I am thy son," Donne reminds God (line 5). Similarly, nowhere in "Batter my heart" does Donne apostrophize himself or his soul as "she"; nor does he accord himself the position of a "woman," much less a bride, over the course of the poem's envisioned path to redemption. Instead, despite enduring cultural proscriptions that have tended generally, though not monolithically, to feminize any body subject to penetration,[61] Donne's desire in view of divine ravishment remains bawdily assertive, even priapic: "That I may rise, and stand, o'erthrow me" (line 3). Thus, to return to Fish's formulation, while the poet may be spreading his legs and his cheeks—"I . . . / Labour to admit you, but oh, to no end" (lines 5–6)—being so taken here does not entail effeminization or castration. Indeed, it is as though Donne wants the Godhead to ravish him, "to break that knot again," *in order that* he will be rendered potent, erect. Moreover, if there is any taking on of a feminized subject position in "Batter my heart," it is one Donne looks to abjure in seeking severance from the devil: "Divorce me, . . . / Take me to you" (lines 11–12). Satan is the one who has made a "woman" of him, a rectifiable situation if only God would himself "rise" (as Donne likewise urges him to do in "As due by many titles") and finally take him as his own, ravish him, make more of a man of him.

The erotics of salvation in "Batter my heart" are thus specified to be homoerotic ones. Such is also the case in a sexy religious poem simply called "Love," written by Donne's later contemporary Thomas Traherne, who likewise indulges a divine rape/rapture fantasy:

> Did my ambition ever dream
> Of such a Lord, of such a love! Did I
>   Expect so sweet a stream
> As this at any time! Could any eye
>   Believe it? Why, all power
>   Is used here.
> Joys down from Heaven on my head to shower,
> And Jove beyond the fiction doth appear
>   Once more in golden rain to come
>   To Danae's pleasing fruitful womb.
> (stanza 3)

From the pleasure of imagining himself drenched and impregnated with Christ's "sweet . . . stream," like both the mythological Greek maiden Danae and the biblical "bride of God" (line 9), Traherne shifts his metaphors across genders, across eroticisms in the poem's final stanza. There he offers himself to Jesus as "His Ganymede! His life! His joy!" (line 31). Now, the poet exults, whether "He comes down to me, or takes me up / . . . I might be His boy" (lines 32–33). As Christ's Ganymede, Traherne rapturously takes as his own the name and status of the handsome shepherd whom Zeus, in the form of a giant eagle, had carried off to heaven to serve as his cupbearer and male beloved (fig. 9).[62] But Ganymede is also the name that is slang in the period, as one seventeenth-century dictionary puts it, for "any Boy, loved for carnal abuse, or hired to be used contrary to Nature to commit the detestable sin of *Sodomy*."[63] Instancing another dovetailing of the profane and the sacred, the figure of Ganymede had moreover been widely adopted in the Renaissance as an emblem of the soul's ecstatic ascent to God and its triumph over the temptations of the world, an allegorical meaning Herbert may be evoking in his exhorta-

Figure 9. "That I might be His boy."
Michelangelo, *Ganymede*, c. 1532. Courtesy of the Fogg Art Museum,
Harvard University Art Museums. Gifts for Special Uses Fund.

tion that the country parson must keep his soul as "fervent, active, young, and lusty as an eagle" (201). As Leonard Barkan notes, Claude Mignault's commentary on Alciati's emblems remarkably aligns Jupiter's desire for the youthful Ganymede and Christ's invitation "Suffer little children to come unto me." [64] In the mythography of Alexander Ross's *Mystagogus Poeticus* (1647), Jesus himself is presented as "the true Ganimedes, . . . the fairest among the sons of men." [65] However Ganymede is allegorized, be it as Christ or Christian, Traherne's amorous lyric indicates that the devotional appropriation of this mythical figure hardly entailed a corresponding evacuation of all his original (homo-)erotic significances.[66]

Throughout this discussion I have been insisting upon the homoerotic currents of devotional desire against the grain of a significant amount of current scholarship that, in its own dehistoricizing ways, has pronounced devotion "pure" of sexual expressiveness or has found the erotic present here only by heterosexualizing it. But my point is not to homosexualize Donne or Traherne, to "out" them from their prayer closets. Such a gesture would be conceivable only at the cost of dislocating these early modern writers to a modern conception of sexuality yet to be consolidated at this time. As a significant amount of recent work on the history of sexuality has articulated, a notion of sexuality as one's essential identity was not operative when these poets wrote. That particular subjectifying construction had to await the late-nineteenth- and even early-twentieth-century crystallization of a binarized model of *sexual selfhoods,* homo and hetero.[67] Many (though probably not all) of us tend to express and experience sexuality in terms not simply of what we do, but of *who* we are, inhabiting our sexuality, in other words, as a full-blown subjective orientation, as a maker and marker of a core identity. Pre- and early modern conceptions of sex, however, were organized more in view of first a theological and then a juridical index of erotic actions that one might perform, some licit, many not, but acts that were widely thought to be theoretically predicable of anyone. In that respect, to speak of someone in this period as a homosexual — or even as a heterosexual — courts anachronism. David Halperin puts this point cogently: "Where there is no such conception of sexuality, there can be no conception of either homo- or heterosexuality — no notion that human beings are individuated at the level of their sexuality, that they differ from one another in their sexuality or belong to different types of being by virtue of their sexuality" (26).

Hence Christians were indiscriminately apprised from early modern pulpits to be vigilant against the allurements of buggery and sodomy —

a sin, cautions Puritan divine John Rainolds, to which "men's natural corruption and viciousness is prone."[68] Sodomy: the natural form of unnaturalness—for all men. Noting that "every natural man and woman is born *full of all sin* . . . as full as ever his skin can hold," the New England Puritan Thomas Shepard thus exposes the human heart as "a foul sink of all atheism, sodomy, blasphemy, murder, whoredom, adultery, witchcraft, buggery." "It is true," he continues,

> thou feelest not all these things stirring in thee at one time . . . but they are in thee like a nest of snakes in an old hedge. Although they break not out into thy life, they lie lurking in thy heart; they are there as a filthy puddle in a barrel, which runs not out, because thou happily wantest the temptation of occasion to broach and tap thine heart.[69]

Samuel Danforth, another seventeenth-century American preacher, similarly warns that the "holiest man hath as vile and filthy a nature, as the Sodomites."[70]

Although it bespeaks redemption, not castigation, Traherne's poem "Love" is likewise not legible according to modern notions of sexuality that are premised on the classificatory scheme of two different, even dichotomous, kinds of sexualities, with every person being the subject of one or the other. Instead, Traherne's devotional ecstasies traverse complementary, not opposed, erotic identifications with both a ravished maiden and a too beautiful boy swept up to serve at bed and board in heaven. The amorous desires expressed by Traherne cannot thus be summarized as either hetero- or homosexual: "I am His image, and His friend. / His son, bride, glory, temple, end," "Love" concludes (lines 39–40). The poet is thus Christ's counterpart, his friend, his son, his boy; he is his bride, his boy-bride, his end—Christ's Ganymede.

In thus opening the prayer closet, I am not looking to rescript early modern religious and literary representations in accordance with modern concerns and modern categories of sexual interest and identification. Nor am I simply concerned to make these artifacts answer my own desire— though I would also be reluctant to deem every such gesture an altogether illegitimate mode of textual consumption. My chief point is instead to contest an unwarranted imposition on devotional expression of a flattening, overly normalizing metaphorics of unvariegated heterosexuality, a social and historical construction that, at least as it is now imagined and experienced—that is, as a category of determinative self-identification—no more existed in the seventeenth century than did its deviant twin (another later "invention") homosexuality. At the same time, the lack of a modern, ontologizing apparatus of sexuality—what Foucault calls "the regime of sexuality"—should not be seen to preclude our engagement with erotic meanings in these texts. Indeed, the very absence here of a polarizing system of sexual types tends to open these works in the direction of a greater plasticity of erotic possibilities, possibilities not entirely containable by our own (often only supposititiously coherent) sexual dichotomies.[71] Concomitantly, I want to insist that any account of the erotics of Christian devotion, whether premodern or modern, needs to consider as well its homoerotics. Stimulated by a spectacularized, denuded, and penetrable male form—the ravished, ravishing body of Jesus—the amorous expression of the prayer closet requires as much.

SACRED SODOMY

Blesst Lord, my King, where is thy golden Sword?
Oh! Sheath it in the bowells of my Sin.
—*Edward Taylor*, Preparatory Meditations 2.16

Whatever is the subject of a prohibition is basically sacred.
—*Bataille*, Erotism

In his recent autobiographical essay "Tongues Untied: Memoirs of a Pentecostal Boyhood," Michael Warner brilliantly and movingly overlays his own conversion narrative of a boyhood of fervent evangelical Christianity with another of his emergent gay identity, doing so in terms that make plausible, even inevitable, disclosures like the following: "Jesus was my first boyfriend. He loved me, personally, and told me I was his own."[72] From here, Warner goes on to discuss, with reference to Bataille as well as to Marcuse, how religion "makes available a language of ecstasy, a horizon of significance within which transgressions against the normal order of the world and the boundaries of self *can be seen as good things*" (15). We have seen this sort of ecstatically authorized transgression in Traherne and Donne, with their use of metaphors of illicit sex—rape, debauchery, sodomy—to body forth divine operations that are world-altering. Nor, it's worth adding, is this salvific transgressivity played out exclusively within the terrains of the homoerotic, as we see from Donne's no less perverse handling of the revered biblical trope (culled from the Song of Songs) of

Christ's marriage to his Church. In another of the Holy Sonnets, "Show me dear Christ, thy spouse, so bright and clear," Donne advances the astonishing analogy that the true Church is most true, most faithful, not when she remains a chaste wife to Christ, but rather when her divine husband plays pander and she, like a whore, opens herself to all comers:

> Betray kind husband thy spouse to our sights,
> And let mine amorous soul court thy mild dove,
> Who is most true, and pleasing to thee, then
> When she'is embraced and open to most men.
> (lines 11–14)

Salvation in Donne's sonnet is in the mode of a divinely sanctioned debauchery. Herbert works a related trope in his poem "Church-music," which analogizes the "wounding" pleasures of sacred music to what sounds like a recuperative resort to a brothel:

> Sweetest of sweets, I thank you: when displeasure
>   Did through my body wound my mind,
> You took me thence, and in your house of pleasure
>   A dainty lodging me assigned.
> (lines 1–4)[73]

While both these poems cast devotional desire in heteroerotic terms, neither one routes it through the scripturally sanctioned metaphorics of marriage between Christ and Church or God and soul. Donne and Herbert instead prefer to court a more transgressive sacred eroticism.

To return once more to "Batter my heart," Donne's no less transgressive desire for a limit-experience with his God is here vehiculated, I've argued, through a same-sex rape fantasy—a rape fantasy that also performs as a seduction, as an overweening attempt to woo a trio of divine lovers who hitherto have been either disinclined or uninformed on how best to serve their servant's desires. To put it in these terms is also to recognize that the power dynamics in play in "Batter my heart" are far more polyvalent than the various "abjection readings" of the sonnet, feminist and non-feminist alike, have thus far allowed. For although he solicits ravishment, indeed demands to be enthralled to divine love, Donne never relinquishes his pushy imperatives. Instead, he willfully, aggressively calls for his own undoing: "Batter my heart"; "o'erthrow me," "bend your force"; "Take me to you, imprison me"; "break that knot again."

It is here that I would locate, not only the simultaneously exalted and abjected devotional body, but also the conditions of devotional subjectivity itself—this place where the subject is attenuated between the hyperbole of his or her own agency and longing at one pole and a matching desire for the self's utter abasement, even dissolution at the other.[74] From this vantage, what Donne wants from God looks a lot like what Leo Bersani says one should get from sex, and from passive anal sex in particular. Tracking what he sees as a more radical, though nervously muted, pulse in psychoanalytic erotic theory, Bersani argues in his controversial essay "Is the Rectum a Grave?" that the value of sex resides not in some intersubjectively grounded sense of self to be derived from the experience, but in its potential for effecting precisely the opposite.[75] Bersani points to Freud's *Three Essays on the Theory of Sex* and the "somewhat reluctant speculation" hatched there that sex, especially in its more ecstatic parameters, is tied to sensations or affective experiences that pass outside or beyond those attendant upon psychic organization, processes that can disrupt the perceived coherence of the self. Hence, Bersani asserts, what sex can do—and do valuably—is to effect a temporary undoing of the self, a shattering of the subject. "The sexual," he determines, "emerges as the *jouissance* of exploded limits" (217)—although here Bersani might just as well be evoking the conversion/perversion experience envisioned by Donne as advancing a notion of sex as a tautology for a pushy masochism. Indeed, the term *pervert*, in a meaning now gone out of date, was once as likely to name the religious convert or heretic as it was to stigmatize the sexual outlaw.[76]

With Donne, the convert/pervert at hand, the question would then have to be, Are the Holy Sonnets redeeming sodomy, or are they sodomizing redemption? Given his proclivity for excess, it may seem inevitable that Donne in particular would pursue the sacred to the utmost limit posed by sodomy—a category of sexual and (perhaps even more important) social dissidence that, in its recurring early modern encouplement with the capital crimes of sedition, sorcery, and heresy, was seen to instantiate utter profanity, a gross social disorderliness that, unchecked, could undermine society and nature on an almost cosmological scale and potentially bring down the apocalyptic fate of this iniquity's namesake city.[77] But even aside from Donne's own perverse inclinations, the sacred path toward sodomy may already be overdetermined insofar as Christ's own body could be seen as assimilable under early modern conceptions of the sodomitical, a category of transgression that prominently included, but was by no means limited to, same-sex sexual activity. No less then than now, sodomy was a shiftingly defined and inconsistently applied rubric, one that potentially named just about any sex act (pederasty, but also heterosexual anal and oral intercourse, bestiality, incest, masturbation, prostitution, even, at least in one case, sex between Christian and Jew) that might be construed as undermining married, procreative sex and its serviceability to a system of social alliance.[78]

Although this line of my discussion becomes more speculative—some no doubt would even say wishful, an appraisal that I would not take entirely as a rebuff—I want to pursue this sodomitical Christ by returning to Steinberg and pressing the case he makes for "the sexuality of Christ." Recall his implication that the single point of those many Renaissance images that compromise decorum by denuding Christ's body and displaying his penis is the provision of explicit evidence that God had become man indeed:

> If the godhead incarnates itself to suffer a human fate, it takes on the condition of being both deathbound and sexed. The mortality it assumes is correlative with sexuality, since it is by procreation that the race, though consigned to death individually, endures collectively to fulfill the redemptive plan. Therefore, to profess that God once embodied himself in a human nature is to confess that the eternal, there and then, became mortal and sexual. This understood, the evidence of Christ's sexual member serves as the pledge of God's humanation. (15)

This is the doctrine of the Incarnation, the core premise of the Christian redemptive scheme: Jesus can save us, not because he is God, but because he is necessarily also demonstrably a man, one of us. Remarkably, as Steinberg argues, the place where this tenet can be most graphically read in Renaissance iconography is Christ's groin: this the bodily site where the mystery of the Incarnation is most manifestly endowed—the penis at the center of the confession of faith (fig. 10). "And is not this reason enough," Steinberg demurely proposes, "to render Christ's genitalia, even like the stigmata, an object of *ostentatio?*" (19).

Steinberg further contextualizes the Renaissance convention of this *ostentatio genitalium* in view of a Christian tradition that regards sex in its procreative capacity as doing battle with sin and its attendant penalty of human mortality: although themselves sullied by sin, "unconquered, the nuptial weapons fight with death, they restore nature and perpetuate the race," as Bernardus Silvestris's *De mundi universitate,* an influential

Figure 10. Carnal Incarnation.
Perugino, *Madonna and Child,* after 1500. Samuel H. Kress Collection,
© 1997 Board of Trustees, National Gallery of Art, Washington, D.C.

medieval allegory, celebrates.[79] Likewise emblematic of power and human vitality, "the organ of the God-man," Steinberg declares, "does better"—though, I would add, it also does *other*. For Christ's male member vanquishes death by grace and specifically not by procreation: "It obviates the necessity for procreation," Steinberg contends, "since, in the victory over sin, death, the result of sin, is abolished" (47). Nor can this conquest be cast as one in which the significance of the sexual is simply abrogated by means of Christ's lifelong, imperturbable chastity. Indeed, for that virginity to count as anything like a meaningful achievement, Jesus must be physiologically capable and potent. Martin Scorsese's controversial, though actually quite devout, 1988 film version of Nikos Kazantzakis's *The Last Temptation of Christ* makes this very point by means of a hallucinatory reverie Christ experiences while hanging on the cross.[80] Within the delirious dreamspace of his Passion, Jesus imagines himself marrying Mary Magdalene, making love to her, and becoming a father; the "last temptation" thus appears here as a fantasy of domesticity and sexual normativity, a normativity represented in this sacred context as what is necessarily rejected in the scheme of redemption.

To return to Renaissance iconography, Christ's sexual capabilities are figured, Steinberg contends (in one of the most controversial aspects of his argument), by a number of images showing the Savior with what looks to be an erection. However we construe these representations, the point remains that Christ must be endowed with what Steinberg terms "sexuality," a sexuality that is redemptive, a sexuality that could even be said to be the fulfillment of sexuality. Yet Christ's is also a sexuality conspicuously not in the service of procreation, his naked, multiply penetrated male body iconicized for us as a spectacle of nonreproductive, but fully operational eroticism. Thus, to play out to its end Steinberg's argument and the line of incarnational theology it calls to the fore, with Christ we have another kind of sexual expression, "another sexuality"—one that is manifestly not procreative, one that exceeds, even displaces sex pointed toward generation. And, as we have seen, in that direction, the direction of the sexual that is nonreproductive, lies the sodomitical.

Not that one is likely to find Christ explicitly positioned over there; not even Donne goes so far as to *name* Christ, or himself in his desired relation to Christ, a sodomite. Such a way of designating this relation, however forthrightly it is homoeroticized, would be implausible here inasmuch as the name *sodomy* anathematized what was most heinously *contra naturam*, and what could be more natural than a man loving his God?

Naming Christ or Christian the sodomite may thus be untenable, almost illogical, but this is not to say that it passes in the period as absolutely unimaginable, unspeakable: "St John the Evangelist was bedfellow to Christ and leaned alwaies in his bosome, . . . he used him as the sinners of Sodoma." So another scandalous poet of the time, Christopher Marlowe, is reputed to have maintained, if the memorandum of his heresies sent to Elizabeth I after Marlowe's death by informant Richard Baines is to be credited.[81] However we assign this inflammatory speech act—whether to a freethinking Marlowe, or to a libelous Baines, or as the unconscious of the culture uttering what on occasion needs to be said in order to be kept as censored—it is worth considering what it means that a declaration of a sodomitical Christ is circulated in the service of constructing a plausible, if excessive, case of heresy, of what one could (but must not) be seduced into believing. We might also wonder what, apart from its baldness, separates "Marlowe's" blasphemy from Donne's and Traherne's uncensored devotional fantasies of themselves becoming Christ's Ganymede.

The difference, I suggest, is vast and at the same time nominal. Certainly context marks one division. The sodomitical declarations attributed to Marlowe are part of a case made to predicate the sodomitical of Marlowe himself, a case whose logic, as such matters were wont to go, is unflinchingly circular: Marlowe, in other words, would see Christ's relationship with his beloved disciple as sodomitical because Marlowe is himself a sodomite, and we know Marlowe is a sodomite because he says things like Christ sodomized his beloved disciple. Furthermore, as the work of a number of historians of sexuality has uncovered, early modern sodomy typically emerges into view as such, as sodomy, only in the most stigmatizing contexts, when its perpetrator can also be branded a heretic (Marlowe was additionally charged with being an atheist), or a traitor, or some other sort of outrageous violator of the social order.[82] Given sodomy's supposed world-negating power, it is unlikely, Jonathan Goldberg argues, "that those sexual acts called sodomy, when performed, would be recognized as sodomy, especially if, in other social contexts, they could be called something else, or nothing at all" (19). Thus when desire that might be deemed sodomitical was assimilable under another name, some more proper or productive social relationship—be it friendship, patronage, pedagogy, the routine sharing of a bed between master and servant, even, I add, a male Christian's eroticized devotion to his male God—such expressions might very well pass unremarked, unstigmatized. That was the early modern tendency, and it may still be our own. The sodomitical scandal of "Marlowe's" declaration that Jesus used Saint John "as the sinners of Sodome" is that it doesn't permit any other way to name the homoerotic affects of Christian devotion, that it doesn't allow for any other more proper cover for what is imagined, metaphorized, and desired within the prayer closet as closet.

* * *

Nor are such devotional provocations merely curious mementos from a foregone, more corporeally expressive religious culture. Rather, they provide a distant mirror to hold up to our own time, a moment (despite the menacing political ascendancy of the Religious Right and the repressive "culture wars" it has spearheaded) in which Christ and Christianity have once again been brought out of the prayer closet in the possibilities they can offer for a transgressive coordination of pleasure and devotion. We thus have, for example, *More of a Man,* the redemption-minded gay porn videotape with which I began, and its achievement of a spectacularized chiasma of devotional axes: religious, erotic, and political. A vector of homodevotion likewise crosses through Antonia Bird's film *Priest,* which, like Scorsese's *The Last Temptation of Christ,* met with a host of religious denunciations and public protests upon its theatrical release. In the film's emotional climax, a handsome, young (and, interestingly, rather conservative) priest confesses his homosexuality to another of his order. Significantly, the terms of the priest's confession fully implicate Christ and the crucifix he has hung on his bedroom wall in the desires he has agonizingly sought for so long to repress: "I sit in my room sweating. I turn to him for help. I see a naked man, utterly desirable. I turn to him for help, and he just makes it worse."

Utterly desirable or not, God is a manifest absence in Tony Kushner's epically scaled *Angels in America.* Nonetheless, this two-part play understands something of the affective (and not only ideological) space religion continues to claim in the American national imaginary. At the center of Kushner's self-titled "Gay Fantasia" is the character of Prior Walter, a gay man with AIDS, anointed to be the ending millennium's "Prophet. Seer. Revelator": a queer augur who tells us he "get[s] hard" every time he hears the voice of the angel beckoning him to take up his apocalyptic role, a prophet who literally "humps" the supernal mystic text with which he is presented and over which he eventually shares a shuddering orgasm with his (male? female?) heavenly visitor. This erotic epiphany may in the end come off as more overblown than sublime, but it remains worth citing in this context at some length:

ANGEL: Open me Prophet. I I I I am
          The Book.
          Read.

PRIOR: Wait. Wait.
          How come . . . How come I have this . . . um,
          erection? It's very hard to concentrate.

ANGEL: The stiffening of your penis is of no consequence.

PRIOR: Well maybe not to *you* but . . .

ANGEL: READ!
          You are Mere Flesh. I I I I am Utter Flesh,
          Density of Desire, the Gravity of Skin:
          What makes the Engine of Creation Run?
          Not Physics But Ecstatics Makes The Engine Run:

(The Angels's lines are continuous throughout this section. Prior's lines overlap. They both get very turned-on.)

PRIOR   *(Hit by a wave of intense sexual feeling)*: Hmmmmm . . .

ANGEL: The Pulse, the Pull, the Throb, the Ooze . . .

PRIOR: Wait, please, I . . . Excuse me for just a
          minute, just a minute OK I . . .

ANGEL: Priapsis, Dilation, Engorgement, Flow:
          The Universe Aflame with Angelic Ejaculate . . .

PRIOR   *(Losing control, he starts to hump the book)*:
          Oh shit . . .

ANGEL: The Heavens A-thrum to the Seraphic Rut,
          The Fiery Grapplings . . .

PRIOR: Oh God, I . . .

ANGEL: The Feathery Joinings of the Higher Orders,
          Infinite, Unceasing, The Blood-Pump of Creation!

PRIOR: OH! OH! I . . . OH! Oh! Oh, oh . . .

ANGEL: *(Simultaneously)*: HOLY Estrus! HOLY Orifice!
          Ecstatis in Excelsis! AMEN! [83]

Consider also the guerrilla art image (available at the historic 1993 national lesbian and gay rights march on Washington as a crack-and-peel sticker) of an appropriated Renaissance Madonna and Christ Child—but

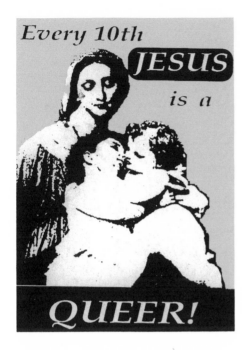

Figure 11. Queering Christianity. Crack-and-peel sticker from 1993 lesbian and gay rights march on Washington, D.C.

a Christ Child who turns toward and adoringly clutches a similarly beatific male cherub. Underneath this devotional ensemble is the slogan "Every 10th Jesus is a queer!" (fig. 11). Canonical Christian iconography has also been recast as the grounds for the expression of homoerotic desire in the work of American painter Marsden Hartley, whose "Christ Held by Half-Naked Men" presents a strikingly all-male pietà (fig. 12). Hartley places Christ's languid body in the arms of a shirtless, muscular fisherman, who is seated in front of an aggregation of similarly barrel-chested, hyper-virile men. The striking mismatch between the pronounced muscularity of these displayed male torsos and Jesus' tiny bearded head underscores the corporeality and the homoeroticism of Hartley's pietà against the attribution of any more strictly spiritualized or psychologized meaning to Christ's Passion.[84] More outrageous still is the pietà of Chilean-born artist Juan Davila, whose painting "Holy Family" directly copies Michelangelo's venerable sculpture. Here, however, instead of cradling Christ's denuded corpse, the Virgin Mary holds forth a giant, full-color cock and balls: a fetish image that is the logical, if pornographic, condensation of all those

Renaissance paintings and drawings cataloged by Leo Steinberg in which the visual—and devotional—focal point is no other than the display of the God-Man's phallus.[85]

At issue in these more contemporary homodevotional expressions, as in the canonical seventeenth-century religious lyric poetry of the metaphysicals, is, I would argue, not just a perverse desire to pervert the sacred—which, of course, can itself be a form of pleasure and one I would not want to underplay. Rather, it is more a sense of how perverse the sacred is to begin with, of how the sacred body *as such*—even the sacred body of Jesus, that body whose eroticism is not serviceable to marriage, procreation, domesticity—already glistens with the sheen of the transgressive, holding forth both devotional and erotic possibilities of contravention and excess.

CODA: MISS SCHREBER

Fancy a person who was a Senatspräsident allowing himself to be f....d.
—Daniel Schreber, Memoirs

Such transgressivity, however, is by no means exclusively or even particularly circumscribed to the homoerotic devotional cathexes I have looked to foreground. Although this account has been insisting upon the recognition of sites within the domain of Christian sacred eroticism that are not subsumable under a strictly heterosexual model of desire, I am not suggesting that the (perhaps more usual) metaphorical operations of casting either Christ or the male devotee in the feminine role is itself any less queer. Here we find a case in which the convention is no more conventional—no more heterosexually conventional—than the deviation from it. Donne, as Izaak Walton's "Life of Donne" (1640) relates, in excited anticipation of his death, donning his shroud and looking like a bride at the dress rehearsal for her wedding: is this any less perverse than Traherne's desire to be made Christ's Ganymede, his boy lover?[86] Or Donne's own same-sex rape fantasy in "Batter my heart"? Cast in any of these terms, Christian desire—the desire for Christ—remains other than straight and straitening, though differently so, I think, inasmuch as each of these metaphoric scenarios provides its own affront to any *tout court* enforcement of compulsory heterosexuality within the symbolic order. In one devotional conjunction we have Christ and Christian in ecstatic congress with each

Figure 12. Homodevotion.
Marsden Hartley, *Christ Held by Half-Naked Men,* 1940–41. Hirshhorn
Museum and Sculpture Garden, Smithsonian Institution, Washington, D.C.

other as males; in the other, they come together as male and performative female. Then again, in still other eroticized devotional scenarios, gender, at least as a defining status or position, hardly seems a determinative denotation whatsoever (Crashaw's "Blessed be the paps which Thou hast sucked" epigram, for instance).

The conventions and the meanings (both discursive and experiential) of sacred eroticism will be treated at greater length and more theoretically in the next chapter of this book. In concluding this part, I simply want to point out that the queerness of the male Christian devotee offering himself to Christ as his bride or his female beloved has rarely been addressed or appreciated. The perversity of this topos can be set in relief, however, through one of Freud's most famous case histories, his diagnostic reading of Daniel Schreber's *Memoirs of My Nervous Illness* as a "Case of Paranoia." Schreber, a high-ranking German judicial magistrate or Senatspräsident, believed that his body was being penetrated from on high by what he describes as heavenly "rays," a bizarre admixture of sunbeams, God's nerve fibers, and divine spermatozoa. By means of this continuing process of impregnation, Schreber finds himself undergoing a double conversion: one that takes him from his lifelong agnosticism to religious belief, but also from maleness to a nascent femininity, his body being re-outfitted from the inside out with female organs and traits. Before this conversion, Freud reports, "he had been inclined to sexual asceticism and had been a doubter in regard to God; while after it he was a believer in God and a devotee of voluptuousness." This was "not the sexual liberty of a man," Freud continues, "but the sexual feelings of a woman. He took up a feminine attitude towards God; he felt that he was God's wife."[87] As such, as God's wife, Schreber—or "Miss Schreber," as the divine voices he hears in his head like to tease and entice him (20)—envisions himself becoming the holy mother through whom the redemption of the whole world might be conceived and birthed in terms of "a new race of men" (17).

In the meantime, Senatspräsident Schreber, the converted devotee of voluptuousness—God's slut, as he also identifies himself here (23)—religiously gives himself over to sensuality. "Voluptuousness, so the voices assured him, had become 'God-fearing,' and he could only regret that he was not able to devote himself to its cultivation the whole day long" (31). Freud continues:

> If he presses lightly with his fingers upon any part of his body, he can feel these nerves, under the surface of the skin, as a tissue of a thread-like or

stringy texture; they are especially present in the region of the chest, where, in a woman, her breasts would be. (32)

Freud, in the course of his analysis, remarks upon this "surprising sexualization of the state of heavenly bliss" (30). What is really remarkable, however, is not so much the erotic content of Schreber's religious fantasies, but how little there is within them that we haven't already encountered in some form or another within the canon of seventeenth-century devotional poetry. The "assumption of a feminine attitude towards God" (34); the supersensuality of his spiritual expression and feeling; the notion of a religious salvation wrought upon and through an exquisitely sensate body; the thematics of corporeal penetration; the eruptive conjunction of the holy and the taboo within the penumbra of the sacred: this, for the analyst, is the "surprising" content of Schreber's ecstatic delusions. Despite the fact that he believes these experiences to devolve from his own, unique anointing, the stuff of Schreber's religious fantasia is recognizable as a striking recapitulation of the orthodox postures and tropes of Christian devotion in their most hyperbolized presentation. Schreber's *Memoirs* are, to be sure, an essay in devotional exorbitance as well as egotism and delusion. Yet the border separating Schreber's porno-devotional encounter with his God and conventional sacred eroticism at times appears, in the context of the materials we have been considering here, to be little more than the difference between engaging the tropes of sacred eroticism metaphorically or inhabiting, investing oneself in them, absolutely literally. And even that dividing line, we shall see, can be stretched into a membrane that is all too porous.

DEVOTION AND DESIRE

But after all, the Christian pastoral also sought to produce specific
effects on desire, by the mere fact of transforming it—fully and
deliberately—into discourse: effects of mastery and detachment, to be
sure, but also an effect of spiritual reconversion, of turning back to God,
a physical effect of blissful suffering from feeling in one's body the
pangs of temptation and the love that resists it.
—Michel Foucault, The History of Sexuality

There is a Cupid more divine I finde
Than that same wanton wandring boy that's blinde.

. . . .

There is a Venus too, but not like this;
One whom the Trinitie will court and kisse.
—John Saltmarsh, Poems Upon some of the
holy raptures of David

 "Amorous languishments," "luminous trances," "Delicious
DEATHS," "dear and divine annihilations," "Bottomles treasures / Of pure inebriating pleasures," "divine embraces,"
"soul-peircing glances" that set "the house on fire / And melts
it down in sweet desire": these are among the "thousand unknown rites /
Of joyes and rarefy'd delights" accruing to the one who would "have her
GOD become her LOVER." So entices Crashaw's ode on "Prayer" (lines
69–83, 120–24). What is remarkable about this poem isn't so much the
unabashedly sexy allure it accords devotional life, but rather how little its
erotics owe in the end to that canonical wellspring of *marital* imagery for
metaphorizing sacred love, the Song of Songs. Instead of Scripture, this
Christ is more apt to take his amatory cues from Cavalier erotic lyric,
specifically Thomas Carew's "A Rapture." Carew's exuberantly licentious
("No wedlock bonds unwreathe our twisted loves"), nearly blasphemous
("We only sinne when Loves rites are not done") celebration of the pleasures of the sensual body has been plausibly christened "the sexiest poem

of the [seventeenth] century,"[1] and Crashaw's sacred lyric immodestly echoes it throughout its own tireless orgasmics, throughout "the many Heav'ns at once" (line 123) it bestows upon the devout soul. Endowed with a libertine "power / To rifle and deflour" and urged to "Seize her sweet prey" (lines 114-15, 107), this lover of God is transported by Crashaw well beyond the anxious virgin longings, the drawn-out connubial preparations, the thereafter promises of heavenly bliss held forth in the allegory of the Canticles to a here and now experience of devotional rapture.[2]

For gestures such as these, Crashaw's fame (and notoriety) is as the English poet most apt to fly decorum in the pursuit of spiritual ecstasy through almost wanton sensory stimulation, a waywardness critics have tended to link to Crashaw's perversely Romanist inclinations, to a notion that his religious as well as aesthetic temperament was never sufficiently anglicized.[3] But if other English poets seldom match the pitch of Crashaw's fever-dream religion, the devotional materials of the period—whether Romanist, Anglican, or dissenting, whether ecclesiastical or popular—are nonetheless deeply textured, as we have been considering, in the affects of passion, pleasure, and erotic longing.[4] Sometimes the literature of devotion even evokes outright cupidity, as when John Saltmarsh admiringly, even enviously, describes Solomon in his *Meditation upon the "Song of Songs"* (1636) as "ravisht with a holy lust."[5] Francis Rous likewise invites us in his devotional handbook *The Mysticall Marriage* (1631) to "looke on [Christ] so, that thou maiest lust after him, for here it is a sinne, not to looke that thou maist lust, and not to lust having looked" (13). Similarly, Baptist convert Sarah Davy is described as "drinking . . . the Rivers of the pleasures of God, of being sick of Love to the blessed Jesus Christ, whom she had chosen her Savior, Bridegroom, Lord, and King; whose love, beauty, and glory ravished her heart."[6] To speak thus of the allure of devotional life, of enjoying God as one's lover, of Christ acting as Eros or Cupid, the arrow-armed male god of love: all this is commonplace here—a point that has been duly remarked in any number of accounts of seventeenth-century religious literature, accounts that typically have had little more to say about this permeative suffusion of erotic imagery and energy into the devotional expression of the period beyond remarking its utter conventionality.

By reading *through* that conventionality, I want to reopen the question of sacred eroticism and accord a more unsettled meaning to such Christian commonplaces. This unsettling will spread out fractally across several interpretive registers, including those of propriety and priority, the figurative and the literal, and the spiritual and the material. What can these crossings of the languages of desire and devotion be said to mean? Which term should bear the emphasis, the place of precedence, in the phrase *sacred eroticism:* the sacred or the erotic? Are the voicings of amorous devotional desire always only metaphorically meant? Under what pressures might such expressions overflow their circumscription as metaphor and begin to be taken—to be *experienced*—as something else? Furthermore, does this interchange between religion and sex still obtain in our own time? If so, what does the imbrication of these two forms of desire now signify? In taking up such questions, we will be able further to theorize the consideration of devotion, affect, and corporeality begun in the first chapter of this book. Whereas the vantage taken there, however, was principally from the perspective of the transgressive and even the perverse, I am here chiefly concerned with what passes as more conventional in the domain of Christian devotion. Moreover, while this inquiry will continue to avail itself of the riches of seventeenth-century lyric poetry, I also want to open up its purview more fully to other kinds of early modern devotional materials, including published sermons, prayer manuals, emblem books, spiritual autobiographies, and missionary accounts.

THE GOD OF LOVE

That our sensuality by vertue of Christ's Passion, be brought up into the substance. — Hugh Cressy, Revelations of Divine Love (1670)

"There is nothing more pleasant and comfortable, . . . more ravishing and soule-contenting to a true Christian, than the frequent and serious meditation of Christ," begins Alexander Grosse in the preface to a collection of his sermons titled *Sweet and Soule-Perswading Inducements Leading Unto Christ* (1632).[7] Samuel Rutherford's *Christ Dying and Drawing Sinners to Himselfe* (1647) likewise allures with the prospect that in Christ's "drawing there is love-sicknesse, and lovely paine in Christs ravishings." Here Jesus is depicted as a lover so passionate, so insistent in his wooings, as to be very nearly rapacious in his salvific efforts: "When Christ cannot obtaine and winne the content and good-liking of the sinner to his love," Rutherford writes, "he ravisheth, and with strong hand drawes the sinner to himselfe; when invitation doe not the business, and he knocks, and we will not open, then a more powerfull work must follow." Rutherford thus concludes that "Christ drives such as will not be led" (282). Both evoking and answering the violence of devotional desire in "Batter my heart," Rutherford tenders the kind of strong-armed Savior Donne's Holy Sonnets so arduously long for—a lover who won't be denied.

Ravishment and redemption are similarly conjoined in Traherne's "Love," a lyric whose fluid erotics and gender identifications I placed alongside Donne's sonnet in the previous chapter. "O nectar! O delicious stream! / O ravishing and only pleasure!" Traherne begins. The enduringly popular communion manual *A Weeks Preparation Towards a Worthy Receiving of the Lords Supper* (1679) carries its own notion of eroticized devotional imbibing to the more public sphere of the communion ritual. Here the sacrament serves in the work of "weaning the senses from sin to devotion," as one both consumes Christ and is in turn consumed by him:

> A little before his passion, he made himself my meat, and my drink, to enter within me, for which cause I am to hold his pains as mine own. . . . O that I could enter into his enflamed heart, and see the furnace of infinite fire, that burneth therein, and melt in those flames . . . issuing forth full of love.[8]

John Saltmarsh's equally incendiary treatise *Holy Discoveries and Flames* (1640) removes us from the Lord's Supper to the space of private devotion—"The Bride-chamber" he terms it—a site of reciprocal amorous stimulation between Christ and Christian: "here is nothing but revellings and divine espousals, . . . here is the sweet celebration of the spiritual marriage, . . . the interchange of sacred courtship . . .; here is no mourning, no lamenting, nothing but love-songs, and sweet epithalamiums, mutuall enjoyments & admirations of each other."[9] More sexually explicit still is Edward Taylor: "The Soule's the Wombe. Christ is the Spermodote / And Saving Grace the seed cast thereinto" (Meditation 2.80).[10]

Not that these Christians always represent themselves as being satiated with the degree of pleasure God has thus far accorded them. Again Donne comes to the fore as the desirous devotee who desires yet more, who remains to be satisfied. His Holy Sonnet "Since she whom I loved hath paid her last debt" commences with the declaration that the poet has surrendered his wife—"her soul early into heaven ravished" (line 3)—to God, who is here cast as both a rival paramour for Anne and a jealous would-be lover of Donne himself. Upon the loss of his wife, Donne informs God, "I have found thee, and thou my thirst hast fed." It remains unclear, however, whether by feeding this thirst God has satisfied desire or rather heightened it, for, as Donne goes on to complain, "A holy thirsty dropsy melts me yet" (lines 7–8).

Herbert's "Frailty" is another expression of unfulfilled devotional long-ing, a poem that in effect casts God as something of an erotic tease, one who has yet to make good on his promised allures: "Affront those joys, wherewith thou didst endow / And long since wed / My poor soul, ev'n sick of love" (lines 19–21).[11] "Love-sick" likewise names Henry Vaughan's characteristic devotional state, both in a poem of that title and in "Cock-crowing," where he beckons God: "who, but thee, knows / A love-sick soul's exalted flight?" (lines 33–34). "Do not despise a love-sick heart!" Vaughan again blandishes in "Begging" (II) (line 14). Some of the pleasures for which this poet longs are cataloged in his ode "To the Holy Bible." While more measured than the feverish flight of the senses launched out of Crashaw's prayer book, the "mild act of love" Vaughan here predicates of the Scriptures likewise incites a concatenation of sensual acts and affects: "quick'ning kindness, smiles and kisses, / Exalted pleasures, crowning blisses, / Fruition, union, glory, life" (lines 23, 29–31). Herbert's pastoral conduct manual *A Priest To the Temple* (1632) similarly represents the Bible as cache of "moving and ravishing texts" (198). Francis Quarles proffers the pleasures of the Scriptures with a more voluptuously developed con-ceit in his *Sions Sonets* (1625), blazoning an opened Bible as the uncovered body of a new bride. The two testaments, Old and New, thus become

> These curious Apples of thy snowy brests,
> Wherein a Paradise of pleasure rests;
> They breathe such life into the ravisht Eye
> That the inflam'd beholder, cannot die.
> How orient is thy beautie! How divine![12]

Although I have thus far derived all these examples of seventeenth-century sacred eroticism from male authors, there is also, of course, a significant body of religious writing in the period that gives voice to the devotional desires of women. And it is no more demure. Elizabeth Moore, eulogized in Edmund Calamy's *The Godly Mans Ark* (1657), regularly spoke of being "deeply in love" with Jesus, of finding him "altogether lovely, and most desirable to my soul," of "pant[ing] after Christ and Christ alone."[13] Addressed to those who "endeared are to piety," An Collins's *Divine Songs and Meditacions* (1653), while hedged with conven-tional disclaimers of poetic modesty, is similarly indulgent when it comes to the pleasures of being the Lord's beloved. Collins's verse beckons us to a heady devotional world of "bliss unspeakable" and "transcendent ravishing delights": "But tasting once how sweet he is, / And smelling his perfumes, / Long can she not his presence misse."[14] Like Quarles, Collins scripts her devotional desire in terms of luxuriant poetic figures derived from the Song of Songs. Yet Quarles posits his sacred eroticism at a more mediated allegorical remove. Recall that in his sonnet the beloved, the putative object of desire, is neither the soul nor God, but the Bible, which functions here as an explicitly feminized go-between, a female-gendered corpus across which the love between a male Christian and his male God can be routed. Collins, however, directly installs herself at the center of the Christian allegory of divine courtship and eventual connubial bliss, this poet advancing herself as a devotional agent of particular desirability: "Yet as a garden is my mind enclosed fast / . . . / Apt to produce a fruit most rare, / That is not common with every woman / That fruitfull are" (57).[15] These lines echo Song of Songs 4:12 ("A garden enclosed is my sister, my spouse; a spring shut up, a fountain sealed"), a text that is usually explicated with reference either to the Virgin Mary or to the corporate Church. But Collins makes this idealized ascription individually her own, the brio of her self-assertion complicating the biblical text's imagery of proper female humility and passivity.

The anonymous author of *Eliza's Babes: or the Virgins-Offering* (1652), while likewise putting herself forward as Christ's "blest Spouse," elaborates another devotional convention of the time in christianizing the tropes of secular love poetry:

> Shoot from above
> Thou God of Love,
> And with heav'ns dart
> Wound my blest heart.
> (lines 1–4)

This stanza is from a poem called "The Dart," and its god of love turns out to be Christ in the guise of Cupid.[16] This commonplace conflation of Christ and Cupid, the two male gods of love, suggests as much the continuity as the conflict between erotic and spiritual libidos:

> Descend sweet life,
> And end this strife:
> Earth would me stay,
> But I'le away.

I'le dye for love
Of thee above,
Then should I bee
Made one with thee.

And let be sed
Eliza's dead,
And of love dy'd,
That love defi'd.
(lines 5–16)

The problematic of how spiritual desire seems to reduplicate as well as to replace erotic longing—both forms of desire here go by the same name, the name *love*—is not always so neatly managed as it appears to be in "Eliza's" quaint closed couplets, however. Later in the century, Elizabeth Singer imbues her *Devout Exercises of the Heart* with "such Fires as seem to speak the Language of holy Passion."[17] Holy passion may be what Singer looks to ignite, but her devotions come off as so sexy that they are reissued with a prefatory admonishment from Isaac Watts on how Singer's "pathetick and tender Expressions . . . may be perversely profaned by an unholy Construction" (11). "Let all such Readers stand aloof," he warns, "nor touch these Sacred Leaves, lest they pollute them" (14). Yet Watts's proscription against "unholy Construction," of course, entices as much as it interdicts, enfolding into the realm of possible (if censured) meanings the very notion of a devotional pornography it seeks to disallow.

BRIDE OF CHRIST

Then let them know, that would enjoy
The firme fruition,
Of his Sweet presence, he will stay
With single hearts alone,
Who . . . their former mate,
Doe quite exterminate.
—*An Collins, "A Song expressing their*
Happiness who have communion with Christ"

What Watts terms *construction*—the question, that is, of how eroticized devotional expression is to be interpreted, indeed experienced—goes to the heart of Anne Wentworth's *A Vindication* (1677), an autobiographical pamphlet that engages the conventions of amorous religious devotion in ways that are still more problematic. The author, who believed herself to be a prophet, had been expelled from her nonconformist Baptist fellowship for leaving and publicly repudiating her husband. *A Vindication* is Wentworth's public retort to charges that such actions make her out to be "a Proud, Passionate, Revengeful, Discontented, and Mad Woman."[18] She maintains instead that she did what she did only as "I was commanded of God" (7), an authority whom she now obeys specifically as "my soul's beloved" (4)—her spouse, her new husband. "And if this be to be mad," Wentworth determines, "I confess my self to be beside my self to God; whose Love constrains me, and whose spirit has in this manner after an irresistible but sweetest manner captivated my proper understanding, will and affections" (8). Wentworth then declares, "My heavenly bridegroom is come" (9), and she doesn't appear to be talking metaphor.

Consider in this context Francis Rous's proposition in *The Mysticall Marriage:* "The soule," he directs us to contemplate, "hath but one husband at once" (18). Accordingly, the Christian's previous spouse (by which Rous means one's past unregenerate way of life) "must be slaine, and by death, put off," if "Christ Jesus, the new and true husband of the soule shall be put on in regeneration" (20). Rous's exhortation derives, of course, from an allegorized application of a biblical stricture of monogamy. In the same vein, the poet An Collins declares that Christ will betroth himself only to those whom "their former mate, / Doe quite exterminate" (31). Wentworth, while not going quite so far as to see her own former mate thus dispatched, does press the notion of the soul's monogamous marriage to Christ far enough beyond allegory to find in such commonplaces the warrant "to absent my self from my earthly Husband, in obedience to my Heavenly Bridegroom, who call'd and commanded me in a way too terrible, too powerful to be denied" (4). It thus becomes apparent over the course of Wentworth's account that what is at issue for her is not simply a matter of prioritizing the will of God above that of an earthly mate, nor of dedicating herself to Christ as though she were figuratively his bride. Instead, she represents herself as having exchanged husband for husband: "Then was the full communion between Christ and my Soul, the Love knot, the comely bands of Marriage" (12). "Then," she continues, "did he espouse me unto himself for ever."

That Wentworth has "wickedly left" her husband and "unduly published things to the prejudice and scandal" of him (2); that she now intends to provide for herself economically ("my own hands may administer to my necessity that I may not be burdensome to any" [5]); that she will continue to proclaim her prophetic vocation ("despise not Prophesie," we are here cautioned [18]): none of this, she insists, warrants the charges of pride and disobedience with which she has been incriminated. Rather, these very actions and intentions, Wentworth contends, should secure her public stature as just the opposite.[19] Reversing every accusation she faces, Wentworth stresses above all that she is merely acting in accordance with a principle of obedience, *wifely* obedience: "I shall not be an unfaithful wife for obeying the voice of my heavenly Husband, in answering his call, and submitting to his will," she declares in a companion tract.[20] Working yet another redirection of the charges made against her, Wentworth further justifies her course of action by insisting that "in the true reason of the case, I have not left my Husband, but he me," citing what she terms his habitual "cruel usage" of her, the many "miscarriages of my Husband" (*A Vindication*, 5, 7). Although Wentworth does indicate that she might conceivably take her "former" husband back if he were to alter his ways, such a reconciliation is here never really registered as much of a possibility. Being forced to return to him, Wentworth asserts, would "make a rape of my Soul," and the tract concludes with her reiteration that "my Maker is my Husband" (*A true Account*, 18, 17).

Interestingly, Wentworth associates her marital hardships with the matter of female authorship and, more specifically, with her extradomestic appointment as a national prophet: what she terms a "more than ordinary call and command of God to publish the things which concern the peace of my own Soul and of the whole Nation" (*A Vindication*, 6). This prophetic commission is what Wentworth's husband "in a most cruel manner hindered me from performing, seizing and running away with my Writings" (5). She further charges that he "has wounded and oppressed me for 18 years" (13). It has been suggested by a recent editor of Wentworth that we regard the time span by which she measures her oppression as merely emblematic, that Wentworth so frames her account because eighteen years marks the duration of time the woman in Luke 13, "a daughter of Abraham," suffered a bodily infirmity until she was healed by Christ's touch.[21] Yet it also needs to be said that while Wentworth represents—presumably even experiences—her life and spiritual career typologically (as evidenced by her habitual autobiographical appropriation of fragments of biblical texts and stories), her typologies seldom float unmoored from some concomitant grounding of material referentiality:

it would be very easie for me, from the great Law of self-preservation to jus-
tifie my present absence from my earthly Husband to all persons who have
learnt to judge of good and evil . . . and who have tenderness enough duly to
weigh various tempers of minds, and the different circumstances of bodies.
Forasmuch as the Natural constitution of my mind and Body, being both
considered, He has in his barbarous actions towards me, a many times over
done such things as not only in the Spirit of them will be one day judged a
murdering of, but had long since really proved so, if God had not wonder-
fully supported, and preserved me. (*A Vindication,* 4)

Once again, Wentworth makes it clear that she is not to be understood as
though she were speaking only figuratively here. In forsaking her "barbarous" earthly husband for a better, heavenly one, she sees herself escaping
a life of spiritual impairment—what she graphically terms a "murdering"
of her spirit. But in appealing specifically to those "who have tenderness
enough duly to weigh . . . the different circumstances of bodies," Wentworth is also disclosing that she seeks relief from a life of spousal abuse,
of physical domestic battery, a life that she says she fears one day will (in
her word) *really* end in her murder.

Here, as with her arrestingly literal realization of the topos of Christ-
as-spouse, we see that for Wentworth there is no impermeable divide between the soul and the body, the other-worldly and the this-worldly, even
the metaphorically meant and the actually perceived; instead, these fields
of meaning and experience are always pressing, impinging upon each
other. Nor should we be surprised to learn that this continues to be so in
Wentworth's dealings with her new, divine husband. Unsettlingly imitative
of her past spouse's battery of "fierce looks, bitter words, sharp tongue
and cruel usage" (*A Vindication,* 5), not to mention the threat of physical
violence he embodies, Christ himself ultimately proves to be no less the
domestic tyrant when his new bride would willfully follow her own mind:
"for eleven months together I withstood the Lord," Wentworth confesses,
"till from Heaven he threatened to kill me, and took away my sleep from
me: and then the terrors of the Lord forced me to obey the command"
(*A Vindication,* 7). Domestic violence evidently has its place even in the
marriage to God.

A FIGURATIVE GOD

"My God, my God, Thou art . . . a figurative, a metaphorical God," Donne exclaims in his *Devotions upon Emergent Occasions* (1624).[22] I have dwelt at some length upon Wentworth's *Vindication* and its materialist typologisms to exemplify, however, that the conceit of Jesus as lover or spouse cannot always be adequately accounted for *as a conceit and nothing more*. Within this well-worn devotional commonplace, Wentworth finds her sanction for publicly annulling one marriage and contracting another (somewhat) more satisfactory one in its place. Yet this is not to suggest that she should be seen as a naive literalist, blind to allegorical schemes of sacred signification. Instead, Wentworth appears to engage her faith and her calling at a point where the word of God is the word of God, where the experiential difference between what is typologically meant and what is literally meant is moot, where what matters is that it is meant. To illustrate what I am attempting to recover here, let me pose an admittedly—and literally—far-fetched analogy between the early modern Baptist Wentworth and some other, present-day nonconformists. I have in mind the snakehandlers of Appalachia and their own arrestingly literal enactment of a scriptural text, that of Mark 16:18: "They shall take up serpents; and if they drink any deadly thing, it shall not hurt them." So declared Christ as his parting benediction to his beleaguered disciples. These daredevil fundamentalists and the female prophet Wentworth are separated, of course, by a good deal more than just a historical gap of some three hundred years. Nonetheless, they could be seen to stand akin as instantiations of the ever-available potential of the most expressively powerful religious conceits—to feel, for instance, so beloved, so personally chosen by God as to be his bride; or to be so securely in God's care that it is as though one could, even *should,* pass around rattlesnakes—of the potential of such conceits to overflow their usual circumscription as being only figures of speech. For Wentworth, this overflow builds up under the dual pressures of a violently abusive husband and a prophetic mandate to preach and to publish. For the snakehandlers, the trigger appears to be a desire ritually to spectacularize the extreme difference between the highly performative enactment of their faith and the hollow motions of a miracle-less, mainstream Christianity. And once having exceeded a framework of "mere metaphor," religious conventions can further serve to authorize, as we find here, perspectives and behaviors that are themselves far from conventional.

What, then, if someone began to act as though she—or, for that matter, he—actually, not only figuratively, were Christ's lover? This appears to be just the status Anne Wentworth felt compelled to take to herself. But I want further to suggest that many of the examples of devotional eroticism I have been here adumbrating tend in their own ways to exceed and even contravene schemes of meaning that would sublate them as mere analogy and nothing else. These devotional guides and stimulants do not offer up their highly wrought amorous scenarios simply as analogies in the service of evincing, however dimly, some aspect of the otherwise ineffable mysteries of spiritual life. Rather, they bespeak a devotion that is—and not just is like—an erotic experience, an affective shock that seldom registers as "just" spiritual.

Let me flesh out this contention in terms of an example that recurs throughout the literature of Christian devotion: the amorous set piece, once again derived from the Canticles, of the lover reclining at the beloved's breast. "You shall lay soule and head down in the bosome, and between the brests of Jesus Christ; that bed must be soft and delicious, it is perfumed with uncreated glory," Samuel Rutherford entices in *Christ Dying and Drawing Sinners to Himselfe* (13). Anthony Horneck evokes an equally hedonistic prayer closet encounter in *The Passion of our blessed Lord and Saviour Jesus Christ* (1700?), though interestingly he reverses the usual assignment of erotic positions. For Horneck makes himself the (male?) erotic aggressor, as he pulls Christ's beautiful body up against his own, refusing to release him: "My Beloved is Fair, having Dove's Eyes, as in the chiefest among ten thousand! Oh that I had my Beloved, I would not let him go, but he should lye all Night betwixt my breasts!"[23] In her visionary diary, the Quaker Ann Bathurst records in similar terms how Christ had come to her the night before: "I held Him and would not let Him go, but that He would lie all night as a bundle of myrrh between my breasts, and He was willingly held."[24]

In a related context Pierre Bourdieu contends, much to the point I am arguing here, that "practical belief is not a 'state of mind,' still less a kind of arbitrary adherence to a set of institutional dogmas and doctrines ('beliefs'), but rather a state of the body."[25] Yet according to prevailing accounts of affective religiosity, Bathurst, Horneck, and Rutherford would probably be regarded as invoking the erotic electricity of such intimacies as simply evocative, and then only in the most approximate ways, of the "passion" with which Christ "courts" our souls or of the "fire" with which we should in turn "burn" for him. No doubt such limited analogizing of

the divine to the human, even the spiritual to the carnal, is a central characteristic of pre- and early modern religious expression, as well as of some
of the more affectively expressive Christian cultures of our own time. The
poetics of sacred typology have already been much discussed by others,
however, and it is not in that direction I wish to head here.[26] "Touch him
hard with thy faith," urges Rous in *The Mysticall Marriage;* "sucke him
strongly with thy love, that more vertue may come out of him" (305).
There is something too muscular about Rous's provocation, something in
how strongly it flaunts its own sensuality, for its horizon of meaning to be
set only at some metaphorical remove and not also felt as a hyperbolized
"state of the body."

Recall also that passage I cited earlier from the communion manual
A Weeks Preparation, in which the overwhelming experience of receiving
communion effects a "weaning of the senses from sin to devotion." Note
that this is not a weaning from the senses. Rather, what is envisioned
in these preparatory meditations is a process of corrective redirection
whereby the faculties are seduced away from sin and toward what is both
a worthier and a more sensually gratifying object of stimulation—incarnated, we have seen, in the figure of a Christ poised to consume the devout
with desire: "O that I could . . . melt in those flames . . . issuing forth full
of love" (80). "Bring all your senses, see, heare, feele, tast, and smell, what
transcendent sweetnesse of heaven is in this love," Rutherford similarly
enjoins in *Christ Dying and Drawing Sinners to Himselfe* (284). Even Foucault, in the passage from his introductory volume of *The History of Sexuality* cited as an epigraph to this chapter, is in danger, I think, of putting
the relation between pleasure, devotion, and their discourses in terms that
are too monolithically repudiative: Christianity, he writes, looks to produce "a physical effect of blissful suffering from feeling in one's body the
pangs of temptation and the love that resists it" (23). The problem with
such a formulation is that it imagines that the only pangs available therein
are those that come by way of denial and asceticism. This is not to deny
that pleasures can indeed be found along such a *via negativa,* that sensual ecstasy may also be wrought through disciplining a fervidly abject
devotional body or subjectivity. But what I would foreground here is the
existence of a powerful vein in seventeenth-century English religious writing that, in keeping with the redeemed libertinism of Crashaw's ode on
"Prayer" with which we began, forthrightly advances religious devotion
as a practice of pleasure.

Hence we find treatises like *A Practical Discourse Concerning Death*

(1689) by William Sherlock, Dean of St. Paul's, in which the case for Christianity (despite the book's dour title) comes dressed as an argument for hedonism. Sherlock's evangelism is premised on the notion that men — and there is indeed something gender-specific about the address of this text, beginning with its title page harkening to the lawyers of the Temple — that men are naturally, and quite properly, disposed to the pursuit of pleasure: "We cannot blame any Man who lets loose his affections upon that which is his happiness; for there neither can nor ought to be any bounds set to our desires or enjoyment of our true happiness."[27] Yet Sherlock also insists that not all pleasures are equally pleasurable. Surprisingly, his calculus appears to be less concerned with the moral rectitude of various enjoyments than it is with the sheer intensity of pleasure they are able to afford — something, Sherlock argues, that can be calibrated "in value proportionally to the length and certainty of its continuance" (8). Since "there are infinitely greater and better things, reserved for us in the next World" (27), the problem with those men who hanker after pursuits that could disqualify them from the more lasting, hence more pleasurable pleasures of heaven, is that they are, in the end, not libertine enough.

Not that Sherlock sees Christian men foregoing all enjoyments now in order to merit the greater ones of the hereafter: "Ask a devout Soul, what transports and ravishment of Spirit he feels, when he is upon his knees, when with St. Paul he is even snatched up into the third Heavens, filled with God, overflowing with praises and divine joys," Sherlock enthuses (41). But then he goes on to insist — and this distinguishes him from many of the other devotional writers I have been treating — that the pleasures with which he allures on God's behalf are strictly noncorporeal ones. Indeed, for Sherlock these devotional processes entail the abnegation of the body rather than its redemption. "The union to these earthly Bodies," he intones with exuberant disgust, "is the meanest and most despicable state of reasonable Souls" (44).

Sherlock likewise sets the soul in opposition to the body in the passage on the Pauline transports of devotion I cited a moment ago. "And does it not then become a man, who has a reasonable soul," Sherlock thus continues, "to seek after these rational, these manly, these divine Pleasures, these pleasures of the Mind and Spirit, which are proper and peculiar to a reasonable Creature?" (41). From here, he endeavors to structure a de-carnalized devotional pleasure — a form of religious affectivity that is neither corporeally oriented nor corporeally expressive — hatched in terms of a series of implicit, contiguous oppositions: soul/body; rational faith/religious enthusiasm; spiritual pleasure/sensual abandonment; and finally, of course, what is manly/what is feminine or effeminate. Yet while he disavows the body, Sherlock nonetheless continually expresses the spiritual in the idiom of the corporeal, thereby smudging the clarity of his own emphatic spiritual/sensual divide. Hence in the very endeavor of disavowing an effeminizing sensual religious devotion, Sherlock's own rhetoric becomes itself transported in an evocatively ganymedic reverie of ravishment, of the Christian man "snatched up" to heaven and there "filled" with his God.

EXTRAMARITAL DESIRE AND DEVOTION

'Tis the life of pleasures!
To see my self His friend!
—Traherne, "The Vision"

David had his Jonathan, Christ his John.
—Herbert, "The Church-Porch"

To this point, I have been principally concerned with the permutations of a conjugally oriented devotional eros. Sherlock's part-Pauline, part-ganymedic fantasy of ravishment recalls for us once again, however, that there are voicings of amorous religious desire that do not speak the language of marriage. This is not to dispute the centrality of the Song of Songs (along with an influential body of allegorizing medieval commentary on it) as the locus classicus for a kind of sacred eroticism patterned on the social model of the marriageable couple, of Christ as the divine spouse for a bride-like Church or individual Christian soul. But a consideration of the affects of devotion would be incomplete without attending to the various expressions of longing for union with or through God that take shape outside the domain of conjugality. What, then, are the other social formations, alongside those of marital courtship and wedlock, by which devotion becomes suffused with desire and eroticism?

One such possibility lies in the relation of friendship, the early modern conventions of which can be strikingly passionate in both their emotive and their physical registers.[28] Almost always conceived as a same-sex relation in which attraction is predicated upon some point of likeness, friendship afforded a patently normative social mode for framing the loving relations between a male Christian and the male God with whom he desires affiliation. The devotional usage of the bond of friendship is particularly notable in Herbert's poetry. While his verse abounds in sighing, crying, wooing, and other stock Petrarchanisms, the repertoire of connubial conceits deployed so frequently by other religious writers goes surprisingly underutilized in Herbert's nonetheless amorously inclined religious poetry. For when he is not being hailed as a father, king, or divine employer, Herbert's God—"my Joy, my Love, my Heart," as he is called in "The Call" (line 9)—appears at least as often in the guise of a beloved masculine friend as he does in the role of heavenly spouse.[29] The poems "Paradise," "The Pilgrimage," and "The Bag," for instance, each position God in the place of friend, as does the famous ending of "Jordan" (II):

> But while I bustled, I might hear a friend
> Whisper, *How wide is all this long pretence!*
> *There is in love a sweetness ready penned:*
> *Copy out only that, and save the expense.*
> (lines 15–18)

This poem commences, as others have also noted, with a string of sexually suggestive terms for the conceptual processes of fabricating devotional poetry: "My thoughts began to burnish, sprout, and swell" (line 4). The voice of Christ-the-friend concludes the poem and quiets the poet's bustling, not so much by effacing this opening note of eroticism, but rather by asserting that all the love, all the sweetness ever to be desired has already been made available to him without all this endeavor. In "Unkindness" Herbert again looks to relate himself to Christ in terms of friendship:

> Lord, make me coy and tender to offend:
> In friendship, first I think, if that agree,
>   Which I intend,
>   Unto my friend's intent and end.
> (lines 1–4)

The problem, as the poem's penitent refrain goes on to disclose, is that with respect to Christ, the poet hasn't upheld the social protocols of friendship: "I would not use a friend, as I use Thee" (line 5). Similarly in "The Sacrifice" Christ himself casts the trauma-inducing shock of his Crucifixion as in part a betrayal, a failure of friendship: "All my disciples fly; fear puts a bar / Betwixt my friends and me" ("The Sacrifice," lines 49–50).

Alexander Grosse's sermonic volume of *Sweet and Soule-Perswading In-*

ducements, although prefixed with an epigraph from one of Bernard's nup-
tially oriented sermons on the Canticles, also repeatedly invokes friendship
as a favored mode for figuring the social and emotive relations Christians
may enjoy with their God. Grosse thus introduces Christ as "the Friend
comforting [the Christian] in his heaviness" (sig. A2). Later he adds that
"the soule which truly receives Christ in the Gospell, is an everlasting
lover of Christ" (33). But then, instead of making the expected turn here in
the direction of the marital, Grosse elaborates the meanings of this lover
relation in terms of a biblical analogy that points to another homosocial
relationship, one that, like friendship, was often idealized in the period as
profoundly affective, even amorous. This is the bond that exists between
master and servant: "The soule," Grosse thus proclaims, "is an everlasting lover of Christ; as *Hyram* loved *David* ever, an everlasting servant
to Christ" (33).[30] Like the chain of erotically imbued identity positions
amassed in Traherne's poem "Love" ("I am His image, and His friend, /
His son, bride, glory, temple, end"), the couplings of God and his devotee envisioned by Grosse traverse a succession of affectively charged social
relations: "we professe our selves to be schollers in Christ's schoole," he
writes, "servants in Christ's family, members in Christ's body, subjects,
friends, and the Spouse of Christ" (57). As Roland Barthes notes of Igna-
tian meditational practice, the "*I* takes advantage of all the situations the
Gospel canvas provides in order to fulfill the symbolic motions of desire:
humiliation, jubilation, fear, effusion, etc. It has absolute plasticity: it can
transform itself, reduce itself according to the needs of comparison" (64).

This kind of traversal of intimacies also provides the framework for *The
Privy Key of Heaven* (1665), Thomas Brooks's treatise on private prayer.
"You are his friends," declares Brooks, citing John 15:15 as his scriptural
touchstone (194). Reminding us that friendship depends upon private intimacies, including the exchange of secrets ("To be reserved and close is
against the very law of friendship" [186]), Brooks makes this biblical
notion of our friendship with Christ the crux of his argument that private
devotional practices are as much a Christian duty as public attendance at
church:

> Consider that the near and dear relations that you stand in to the Lord call
> aloud for secret prayer. . . . Now, a true friend loves to visit his friend when
> he may find him alone, and enjoy privacy with him. A true friend loves to
> pour out his heart into the bosom of his friend when he hath him in a cor-
> ner, or in a field, or under a hedge. (194)

The dynamics of solitary prayer will be treated at length in chapter 3; what I want to foreground here is the degree to which Brooks's idealized devotional couplings slide back and forth between positing Christ and Christian as friends and presenting them as each other's amorous beloved: "You are the spouse of Christ," continues this passage on our "near and dear relations" with Jesus. "True lovers," Brooks then concludes, "are always best when they are most alone"; hence for him the prayer closet represents the site of the most profound sacred eroticism.

The elision of (male) friendship into the amorous is even more strikingly parlayed at the conclusion of *The Privy Key.* Citing relevant biblical prooftexts, Brooks reminds us again that

> Lovers love much to be alone, to be in a corner together, Cant. vii.10-12. Certainly the more any man loves the Lord Jesus, the more he will delight to be with Christ in a corner. There was a great deal of love between Jonathan and David—1 Sam. xviii.xix. and xx. compared—and according to their love, so was their private converse, their secret communion one with another; they were always best when in the field together, or when in a corner together, or when behind the door together, or when locked up together; and just so would it be with you, did you but love the Lord Jesus Christ with a more raised and a more inflamed love; you would be always best when you were most with Christ in a corner. (294)

In the course of recent governmental hearings in Israel concerning the question of equal rights for gays and lesbians in the armed forces, a liberal member of the Israeli parliament armed herself with the very same biblical verses cited here by Brooks to stage the claim that Jonathan and David were lovers. Predictably, if no less disappointingly, her assertion generated an onslaught of violently phobic repudiations and threats from the conservative clergy.[31] But for the seventeenth-century Puritan minister Brooks, the conflation of male friendship and erotic love is, as this passage illustrates, a patently natural conceptual move to make.

One reason this is so has to do with the kind of transitivity across social relations and identity positions we have found to be characteristic of the Christian devotional imaginary. Beyond this, however, Brooks's modelling of the love between lovers upon the pair of Jonathan and David—intimate male friends whose love for each other, the Bible tells us, surpassed their love of women—requires, I think, further contextualization in terms of then newly emergent notions of marriage as (among other things) a relation of intimate companionship, a relation of conjugal *friendship:* what, in short, social historians have termed the companionate marriage.[32] In his important work on collaboration and companionship, Jeffrey Masten points to a number of discursive overlappings between the idea of a companionate marriage and the early modern ideals of passionate male friendship, noting that in the seventeenth century these two relations are repeatedly framed in analogous terms.[33] Brooks's devotional effusions throw into relief just how dependent the structuring of the companionate marriage was upon homoeroticized male friendship—a social formation that is historically anterior to this new version of heterosexuality, providing it with many of its emotive contours. Affectively charged mutuality, affinity, companionship, equality, as well as the range of intimacies evoked by Brooks's phrase "private converse":[34] these values and expressions had been largely the provenance of the same-sex friendship relation, and they thus can be exemplified by Brooks in terms of the famous male couple Jonathan and David. Yet, in a way that is already suggestive of how the affective repertoire of the same-sex friendship is to be taken over and reinscribed heterosexually, Brooks endeavors in just such homoerotic terms to make both comprehensible and appealing the conjugal ideal according to which he would also figure the Christian's relation "in a corner," "under a hedge," in the prayer closet, to his consort Christ: lovers as friends, friends as lovers.

*   *   *

We have been considering how the conventions of passionate male friendship served as a basis for representing the intimacies to be enjoyed between man and God. This same framework can also provide for some deeply affective, sometimes even amorous, conceptions of fellowship among Christians, of a Christian society structured in terms of the passionate conjoining of devout men with each other in the intimacies of friendship, as well as in the bond of shared devotional pleasures. "The bliss of other men is my delight," Traherne thus declares in his poem "Goodness" (line 1). John Winthrop, governor of the Massachusetts Bay Colony, advances a more detailed, though similarly affective socioreligious program of community building through a loving brotherhood in devotion. His model Christian society would be structured so "that every man might have need of other, and hence they might be all knitt more nearly together in the Bond of brotherly affeccion," "in a most firm bond of love and friendshippe."[35] In his essay "New England Sodom," Michael Warner offers a cogent analysis of this Puritan body politic and erotic, showing how its affective ligatures, whether sexual or not, are nonetheless pointedly sexualized.

Warner also notes that Winthrop's utopic social vision of brotherly "love and friendshippe" is neither addressed to nor particularly concerned with devout women: "By 'brotherly' he means male" (339). This is not to say, however, that the religious homosocial was exclusively a male domain. We can garner how a seventeenth-century Christian woman might put to devotional use the structures and terms of passionate friendship from Sarah Davy's *Heaven Realized, or the holy pleasure of daily intimate communion with God* (1670), a book that is directed, its male editor informs us in his preface, "especially [to] young Gentlewomen" (sig. A4ᵛ). Interweaving prayer, devotional meditation, and Baptist conversion narrative, *Heaven Realized* is another amorously effusive religious text, adorned with expressions of desire appropriated from the Psalms, as well as the Song of Songs. Davy thus recounts how as a young girl she was captivated by a sermon on the text of Canticles 4:7–8: "Thou art all fair my love, there is no spot in thee." The notion of the "beauty of a soul in Christ," she reports, "filled me with desires and longings to be such a one" (7–8). In the time that passed before these hopes were answered, Davy's desire "to be such a one" apparently became attached to a corresponding longing to *know* "such a one." For the answer to her prayers and longings does not come in terms of a direct, personal revelation of Christ himself. Instead, after several years of isolation ("None could I find to declare my trouble [to]" [12]), the disclosure of God's love takes the form of a providential encounter with a remarkable friend-to-be:

> One day the Lord was pleased by a strange providence to cast me into the company of one that I never saw before, but of a sweet and free disposition, and whose discourse savour'd so much of the Gospel, that I could not but at that instant bless God for his goodness in that providence; it pleased the Lord to carry out our hearts much towards one another at that time, and a little while after the Lord was pleased to bring us together again for the space of three dayes, in which time it pleased God by our much converse together, to establish and confirm me more in the desires I had to join with the people of God in society and enjoy Communion with them according to the order of the gospel. (20–21)

Curiously, only at this point does Davy reveal that the exceptional, unnamed companion with whom she has enjoyed "much converse"—converse that leads to conversion—is another woman: "she was of a society of the Congregational way called Independents" (21). Through her, "through the help of my friend" (24), Davy comes to embrace "the order of the Gospel" (21) and at last to experience the "beauty of a soul in Christ."

In keeping with the conventions of the conversion narrative form, Davy's spiritual enlightenment is framed in the highly affective terms of "sweet experiences" and "sweet breathings" (25)—a "full enjoyment of him" (22). Yet there is also a way in which the object of sacred eroticism is for Davy as much her new female friend as it is Jesus himself. This is registered in how closely the expression of her feelings for her friend overlap and reduplicate her patently erotic expressions of devotion to Christ. For example, Davy finds her "soul much carried out in love to Christ" (8); correspondingly, she says of her friendship that "it pleased the Lord to carry out our hearts much towards one another" (21). What is more, just as her friend was the "instrument" (24) by whom Davy is led to Christ, Christ himself reciprocally serves as a sanctioning conduit for the passionate conjoining of the two women: "Then," Davy writes, "were our hearts firmly united, and I blessed the Lord from my soul for so glorious and visible an appearance of his love, for I had many sweet refreshments given me at that time" (21). Similarly, the Lord, like the friend, provides his new convert with "sweet comfort and refreshings" (23), with "sweet evidences of his tender love" (26). Indeed, only Christ can console Davy upon the absence of her friend: "When she was gone, I was sensible of the great mercy the Lord had been pleased to show me, but in an instance snatched it from me again. . . . But after a few reflections . . . my soul was again filled with hungerings and thirstings after God, for a more clear and full enjoyment of him" (21–22).[36]

Davy's interlacings of desire, amorous love, and friendship—sentiments that ramify at once in relation to her union with Christ and her bond with her female friend—are threaded together even more tightly when she declares that Christ has revealed to her as his preeminent commandment the injunction "that as I have loved you so you would love one another with a sincere pure unbounded love" (37). Not surprisingly, Davy situates this exhortation within the framework of the friendship bond. Christ, she teaches, is here directing us to

love one another as I have loved you, or to love thy friend as thou lovest thyself, most willing to do that which may be for thy friends good, although it be to some prejudice to thyself; this is love, and by this you shall know that you are my disciples: if you love one another. (37–38)

Love for God, as well as love from God, is thus married to the divine dicta of friendship. For Davy, sacred eroticism is a triangulated affect, routed through—but also routed to—a special female friend.

Christ likewise appears "between women" (to recast Eve Sedgwick's indispensable phrase) in the religious friendship and missionary partnership of Katharine Evans and Sarah Cheevers.[37] Together these Quaker visionaries several times left their homes, husbands, and children to travel throughout England, Ireland, and Scotland in the 1650s, preaching and distributing Quaker literature. In 1658 Cheevers and Evans undertook a more ambitious evangelical mission, heading toward Alexandria in imitation of the apostolic travels of Saint Paul. Along the way, they were detained and interrogated under the Inquisition in Malta. *A True Account of the Great Tryals and Cruel Sufferings undergone by those two faithful Servants of God* (1663), an autobiographical report of their imprisonment by Catholic authorities, records both the futile efforts of the inquisitors to shake the convictions of the women and the ecstatic visions and dreams that sustained them in their imprisonment. This jointly authored text is also a record of passionate female friendship founded on religious devotion and evangelical fervor. For among the many deprivations and indignities suffered by these women during their three-and-a-half-year confinement, their greatest misery arises when they are threatened with separation from each other. "Death it self," Evans writes, "had been better than to have parted in that place."[38] Even when their jailers look to remove a gravely feverish Evans to a room cooler than the confines of their prison cell, she staunchly maintains: "I said, I rather chuse to dye there with my Friend, than to part from her."

Evans and Cheevers speak of each other throughout *A True Account* interchangeably as "My Friend" (18), "my dear Sister in Christ Jesus" (25), and "my Mate" (20). Evans, moreover, appropriates the language of the marriage bond to ward off their jailers: "The Lord hath joyned us together," she declares, "and wo be to them that should part us" (27). Evidently, such terms had more binding force within the divinely sanctioned union of these women than they did in relation to their individual husbands, whom Cheevers and Evans (as their continual missionary endeavors indicate) were always leaving at home. When the women were indeed temporarily placed in separate cells, Evans looked to comfort her despondent "mate" with letters recounting the devotional ecstasies bestowed upon her by Christ: "I told her," Evans writes, "of the glorious Manifestations of God to my Soul, for her comfort, so that I was ravished with Love, and my

Beloved was the chiefest of ten thousands" (42). Once again, the same-sex bond of religious friendship—clearly the most important human relationship for Cheevers and Evans—is vectored to and through an eroticized Christ.

RELIGION AND SEX

> . . . *I'le ask*
> *One question, and I pray thou woulds't unmask;*
> *How is my Saviour such a lover turn'd?*
> *Is he grown wanton, amorous, that mourn'd?*
> *Is he recover'd of his wounds, and fit*
> *To court and woo a beauty?*
> —*John Saltmarsh*, Poems Upon some of the holy
> raptures of David

In his memoir of a Pentecostal boyhood, Michael Warner has written, "You can reduce religion to sex only if you don't especially believe in either one" ("Tongues Untied," 15).[39] I do believe in at least one of them, and thus do not mean to be here restaging the kind of reductive "discovery" that would unveil affective religiosity to have been more or less imperfectly sublimated sexuality all along. Yet I also do not want to censure out of hand any treatment of devotion's plethora of eroticisms as simply a retrojected imposition on early modern cultural materials. Indeed, what would be far more dehistoricizing is to impute an innocence or naïveté concerning the sexual suggestiveness of these devotional aids to their own early modern authors, editors, and users. One site where such a knowing awareness declares itself, I have already noted, is in the chastening interpretive advisements that accompany a number of the works themselves. Hence William Sherlock's emphatic declarations in *A Practical Discourse Concerning Death* that the pleasures comprising his practice of Christian hedonism are to be strictly divorced from those that gratify the sensual appetites of the body. Hence also Isaac Watts's editorial anxiety over a profane reception of Elizabeth Singer's "pathetick and tender Expressions" of longing for Christ, her altogether desirable lover—expressions that, Watts himself concedes, "powerfully engage all animal Nature in their Devotion" (11).

For another example—one that appears earlier in the century and hence at a further historical distance from the remonstrances against affective religiosity that are to become more pronounced by the century's end—we can return to Francis Quarles's *Sions Sonets*. Though offered to readers for "your pleasures," these epithalamic lyrics come ready-glossed so as not to be received as "loose and lascivious" (122). Thus an exclamation such as "O How I'm ravisht with eternall blisse!" is marked in the text by an asterisk—a typographical chaperon that glosses this ecstatic sentiment with the chaste explanation, "By heavenly contemplation" ("Bride's Sonet XI," stanza 1). In other cases, however, such built-in interpretive structures and strictures were apparently deemed insufficient to deter the sort Quarles in his dedicatory preface names the "wanton Reader" (122), the one who would use a devotional text to stimulate the wrong kinds of desire. Should that transpire, the fault, according to a revamped 1737 edition of the communion manual *A Weeks Preparation,* would lie as much with the text itself as it would with the cupidinous tendencies of the user. Thus in the foreword he contributes to what is now called *The New Week's Preparation,* the Duke of Newcastle upbraids the original *Weeks Preparation* as "a Book, which has already been found so injurious to Christianity, and has brought so great and many Scandals upon the reasonable Service of Almighty God."[40] Newcastle cites a string of eroticized devotional entice-ments from the old version's preparatory prayers and meditations as the culprits: "Art thou afraid of being too much enamoured with this Jesus? O my Love, my Joy, my Jesus . . . Thou wert within me. Thou only pleas-est me, and thee only I desire" (iii). Such "rapturous and wanton expres-sions," with their "unnatural Heats and extatic Fervors," are here scorned as "a Disgrace and Reproach to the dignity of a Rational Nature" (iv). Newcastle furthermore castigates the "Manner of Address" of the origi-nal version's prayers as "fitter for a dissolute Lover, than for an acceptable worshipper of the all-pure and all-knowing God" (v).

Backed by the imprimatur of the Church of England, Newcastle's rail-ings against "rapturous Rights of unhallowed love" and "spiritualiz'd Concupiscence" (iv) accord with the critique—and in some cases the wholesale repudiation—of amorously inflected devotion that grows even more emphatic in the eighteenth century. Of more interest to me, how-ever, is how that critique is advanced here in terms of an early modern notion of sexual sublimation as Newcastle (erroneously) ascribes the of-fending manual's original, overheated composition to the frustrated "car-nal and wanton Appetites and Wishes of unmarried Nuns and Friars" (4). Despite what Caroline Bynum and others have argued, we can thus see here that reading symptomatically is not in every case a historically in-sensitive imposition of Freudian constructs onto a pre-Freudian past. A notion of the sublimation of the erotic into the religious likewise haunts Watts's anxious defence of Singer's "Language of Rapture address'd to the Deity." In this case, however, the hysterical symptom is invoked by Watts only to be deemed inapplicable to the writer at hand:

> I know also that this soft and passionate Turn of religious Meditation has sometimes been imputed to Injuries and ill Treatment in the Marriage State, whereby the same Affections are wean'd from an undeserving Object, and pour'd out in amorous Language upon an Object supremely worthy and divine. (12)

"But neither has this Reproach any Pretence in this present case," Watts concludes—as though he were insisting that Elizabeth Singer is nothing akin to the likes of an Anne Wentworth.[41]

* * *

Clearly, then, there is an early modern awareness of how a discourse of amorous devotion to Christ could speak and be spoken of as a discourse of the erotic. That the sexual is not, as it has been recently maintained, something we moderns "read into" these texts is evidenced by these strain-ing early modern endeavors to read it *out*.[42] Moreover, the excitations that Newcastle, Quarles, Watts, and Sherlock censure are the same ones others look to court. And somewhere between these poles lies the counsel offered by the medieval mystic Saint John of the Cross in *The Dark Night of the Soul*. There he considers the case of those who, "when there comes to them some spiritual consolation or delight in prayer," find to their dis-may that "their humours are stirred up and their blood . . . excited."[43] Yet, he instructs, "when the spirit and the sense are pleased, *every part of a man* is moved by that pleasure to delight according to its proportion and character"—including, the saint notes unabashedly, "the lower part" (359; my emphasis). "And hence," he continues, "come these motions"—mo-tions, we are told, that "arise and assert themselves" (361, 359). John thus evokes (in terms explicit enough to cause the regular excision of these pas-sages from later editions and translations of *The Dark Night*) the scene of novices and young devotees at prayer with erections—thus stimulated not despite, *but because of* the intensity of their devotions. And, surprisingly (or not), his counsel for them is don't worry; just continue on praying.

Donne offers something of a Renaissance analogue in a 1617 sermon on the text of Proverbs 8:17, "I love them that love me":

> All affections which are common to all men, and those too, which in particular, particular men have been addicted unto, shall not only be justly employed upon God, but also securely employed, because we cannot exceed, nor go too far in imploying them upon him. (*Sermons*, 1:237)

His contention that upon God we can make good every desire—even every addictive excess of desire—is exemplified by the lustful but nonetheless devout Solomon, "whose disposition," Donne notes, "was amorous, and excessive in the love of women." Even "when he turn'd to God," Donne continues (and here he might as well be recounting the amorous approaches of his own devotional poetry), Solomon "departed not utterly from his old phrase and language, but having put a new, and a spiritual tincture, and form and habit in all his thoughts, and words, he conveyes all his loving approaches and applications to God." Donne thus treats sexual appetite and spiritual longing *in their most intensified registers* as homologous forms of desire, insisting that in God we can find "fit subject, and just occasion to exercise *the same affection* piously, and religiously, which had before so sinfully transported, and possest" us (1:236; my emphasis). Indeed, Donne further implies that the "voluptuous man" is the one best qualified for success in the devotional endeavor he later terms the "amorous seeking of Christ" (237, 250). Or as Bataille would put it centuries later: "Even in the eyes of believers, the libertine is nearer to the saint than the man without desire" (*Erotism*, 122).

In Donne's account, as well as in Bataille's, the religious and the sexual are accorded adjacent psychic or, perhaps better, affective sites. It's in the mix of religion and the erotic—particularly, as I argued earlier, the erotically transgressive—that devotion becomes stimulated, heightened. This is especially so in Donne and the metaphysicals, notorious for their often disquieting alignments of the spiritual and the corporeal, the sacred and the profane: a "school" of writers, to recall the censure of Samuel Johnson, whose amplification knew no limits. Consequently, an appreciation of this expressive amplitude is what tends to go missing in accounts that sublate the erotic galvanism of devotion to Christ into "mere" metaphor or that dampen the potential here for excess and transgression by making orthodoxy and doctrine the only applicable categories of meaning.

Perhaps one reason the erotic was so readily appropriable to early modern religious expression and experience is that there did not yet exist a distinct discourse for sexuality in the seventeenth century, that the sexual had not yet been accorded the status of a discursive or experiential domain unto itself. Yet even now the interface between religion and eroticism still obtains—though perhaps today it is more often the case that *religion* provides the proximate language for expressing heightened sexual affect than vice versa. "Oh God, I'm cumming" may be the only words with which many of us now pray, and who is to say that this isn't prayer, that this is only metaphorical? What is more, if the sexual went underconceptualized in these earlier periods, it arguably now has become overconceptualized, to the degree that the category of the perverse in sex per se may for us be nearly emptied out. Religion, on the other hand, remains from a post-Enlightenment point of view a warehouse of perversions. Looking to religion has thus become a means of amplifying eroticism, of reinfusing it with an alluring transgressivity.

It is in these terms that I would account for a manifestly profane text like a "Jack Off for Jesus" handbill, distributed in San Francisco several years ago to advertise a gay safe-sex party ("vestment check provided") in celebration of the Pope's departure from the city during his American tour. In contrast to this pontiff's pronounced disinclination to find much room at the table for lesbians and gays, the handbill's muscled, t-shirted Christ beckons "Cum unto me" from beside a trinity of ejaculating penises. Very knowingly, this image hyperbolizes the pervasive, if typically deeply closeted, homoeroticism that has, we've seen, in numerous instances structured devotion to Christ. Yet while the provocation of men having sex "for Jesus" functions as antihomophobic political satire, the handbill at the same time means, I think, to be enticingly erotic—all the more so in the *frisson* of its highly transgressive cathexis onto what stand among the culture's most venerable icons. Or consider an advertising tableau from what bills itself as the *Abusive Furniture Catalog,* which matter-of-factly determines that "no single piece of s&m equipment [has] stronger impact than the cross." In a blurb that congeals the rhetorics of menace, ecstasy, and quaintly old-fashioned salesmanship, we find that the "home dungeon" model the catalog offers for sale and shipment is "easily assembled or disassembled," "sturdy enough to hang your victim either by the arms or by the legs"; "a piece," the ad concludes, "with a frightening power available to you at a very reasonable cost." Only $99.95.[44]

"Blasphemy has always seemed to require taking things very seriously." So Donna Haraway recognizes at the outset of her highly iconoclastic, antihumanist, yet profoundly religiomythic "Cyborg Manifesto."[45] Ac-

Figure 13. Sacred eroticism: Divine Love and Anima as paired Cupids. Otto van Veen, *Amoris divini emblemata*, 1615. Courtesy of the Folger Shakespeare Library, Washington, D.C.

cordingly, I think it would be a misreading to regard these images, as well as the other profanations I have cited over the course of this study, as operating in terms of mere, hence banal, irreverences. "Blasphemy," Haraway continues, "is not apostasy"; it is rather a form of faithfulness, she explains, though a faithfulness that is the obverse of "reverent worship and identification."[46] Similarly, I see cultural texts such as the *Abusive Furniture Catalog*'s S/M cross, or the revisionary, homoeroticized pietàs of Marsden Hartley and Juan Davila (discussed in chapter 1) as recognizing—even being (as Haraway recaptures the term) *faithful to*—the visceral power of the religious. With their own newfangled (or, as it turns out, not so newfangled) metaphysical conceits, these texts and images propound the ever-tempting conjunctions of sexuality and religious devotion as expressive mechanisms for heightening affective response, for stimulating that which would pass beyond the more ordinary operations of eroticism.

Religion, as I have been arguing throughout this book, could likewise be sexy in the seventeenth century. Hence in considering the relations between devotion and eroticism, our aim should be neither to reduce religion into sex nor to desexualize devotion. At the same time, we need to be wary of any blanket spiritual allegorization of the more sensual and corporeal provocations of religious experience, a move that all too often results in the erotic penumbra of sacred eroticism being chastely vaporized. Nor, given how profoundly, how constitutively, imbricated religion and eroticism are in these texts, does it seem to me to be a wholly tenable operation, as some others have undertaken, to determine which one of these two powerfully expressive discourses of desire has the place of precedence as the origin of the other.[47] The term *devotion,* as we know, can signify either erotic attachment or religious worship and oftentimes, we have further seen, both at once. Hence, rather than seek to disentangle such affiliations of pleasure, devotion, and eroticism, we might therefore look, following Donne, to bring these overlapping networks of desire into an expressive rapprochement (fig. 13). Through an osmosis of eroticism fueling religious affect and religiosity heightening erotic desire, devotion to Christ becomes sexualized, becomes (to recall Bourdieu's formulation) a state of the body and its passions, no less than it is an exertion of the soul. The range of texts we have been concerned with here—early modern and postmodern, high and low—strikingly document that the erotic and the religious are not always thought of or experienced as two necessarily separate domains. Instead, we find relays along which the soul and the body, the figurative and the material, the other-worldly and the this-worldly, even the sacrosanct and the profane, have served, sometimes in contest with each other, sometimes in collusion, in the stimulation of devotion and ecstasy. This is to say that religion and sex have done, and still continue to do, each other's affective work.

3

THE PRAYER CLOSET

But thou, when thou prayest, enter into thy closet, and when thou hast
shut thy door, pray to thy Father which is in secret, and thy Father,
which seeth in secret, shall reward thee openly.—Matthew 6:6

The command in the Text sends us as well to the Closet as to the
Church.—Thomas Brooks, The Privy Key of Heaven

Organized gestures, which is to say ritualized and codified gestures, are
not simply performed in "physical" space, in the space of bodies. Bodies
themselves generate spaces, which are produced by and for their
gestures.—Henri Lefebvre, The Production of Space

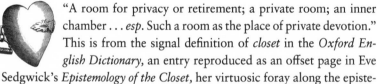 "A room for privacy or retirement; a private room; an inner chamber . . . *esp.* Such a room as the place of private devotion." This is from the signal definition of *closet* in the *Oxford English Dictionary,* an entry reproduced as an offset page in Eve Sedgwick's *Epistemology of the Closet,* her virtuosic foray along the epistemic and performative relays between occlusion, disclosure, and (sexual) identity (65). Yet the primacy of place accorded the *prayer* closet in the *O.E.D.*'s catalog of closet meanings should serve to remind us that the closet has been a material structure—a space—as well as a set of subjectifying structural relations, one moreover that was framed, particularly in its early modern forms, with a religious referent. Over the course of the seventeenth century, Christian devotion, especially in its most affectively amplified registers, comes to be an increasingly closeted expression. The devotional literature of this period, both prose and poetry, thus abounds in injunctions sending Christians to the closet, to the intensified experiences of the individual encountering God in this private, hence deemed more intimate, place. "Let us then often retire to our Closets, and give our Souls the Pleasures of Conversing thus with God," William Dawes urges in a devotional manual that lays out *The Duties of the Closet* (1693). "If therefore we desire to become Friends of God, if we would enjoy his

Conversation," insists Dawes, "it must be in our Closets."[1] So too Samuel Smith in *The Christians Guide* (1685): "Devotion requires solitude. We have our Master's word and decision in the case. *When thou goest to pray,* says he, *enter into thy closet.*"[2] "Godliness," adds Thomas Brooks in *The Privy Key of Heaven, or Twenty Arguments for Closet-Prayer* (1665), "never rises to a higher pitch than when men keep closest to their closets" (162). Detailed in these texts as a fully materialized place—as a room in the household—the prayer closet produces this "higher pitch" because in it, in private, devotion may transpire more manifestly through the nervures of the body even as it is stirred within the recesses of the soul. Coincident with this expressive conjunction of body and soul, the prayer closet, we shall see, also becomes the space to which effusions of sacred eroticism are increasingly relegated, closeted.

THE CARE OF THE SOUL

And shall we then grudge to bestow that Care upon our Soules,
which we so freely undertake upon our Bodies?
—*William Dawes,* The Duties of the Closet

Eroticism for those philosophers of the erotic I have been drawing upon here—Freud, Bataille, Donne—involves losing the self beyond the self: the experience Bataille calls dissolution (*Erotism,* 17–18). "The whole business of eroticism," he avers, "is to destroy the self-contained character of the participators as they are in their normal lives" (17). Conversely, it appears that the cultivation and consolidation of selfhood emerges as the principal project of a good deal of the literature of closet devotion, the most subject-centered genre of religious writing. "Whoso truly loves himself will love his Closet and his Prayers," declares Edward Wettenhall, another Anglican bishop, in his devotional handbook titled *Enter into thy Closet* (1663).[3] Here, as in other works of this genre, the material isolation of the prayer closet is advanced, not only as the premier forum in which to invoke the presence of God—private devotion, Daniel Featley claims in *Ancilla Pietatis* (1633), "hath a deeper channell"[4]—but also as a necessary condition for enhanced spiritual self-awareness. Another primer on private prayer, Elnathan Parr's *Abba Father* (1636), similarly instructs, "Privacie is to bee chosen, that beeing sequestred from company, we may more fully descend into our owne hearts."[5] Bishop Joseph Hall provides the same counsel in *The Art of Divine Meditation* (1633): "Solitariness of place is fittest for meditation." "Retire thyself from others," he urges, "if thou wouldst talk profitably with thyself."[6] With a continued emphasis on the spatiality of devotional practice, Hall specifies how "one finds his closet most convenient, where his eyes, being limited by the known walls, call in the mind after a sort from wandering abroad." One thus retreats to solitude, enters the closet, not only to approach God, but also to engage the self. As facilitated by the closet, an intensified encounter with oneself emerges in this literature as no less an integral aspect of devotion than prayer or scriptural study or even churchgoing. As the nonconformist Oliver Heywood puts it in his own *discursus* on *Closet-Prayer* (1668), "Soliloquy in the heart, helps to a colloquy with God."[7]

Accordingly, we find the period's many popular prayer books, devotional manuals, and guides to godliness distributing their pedagogy more or less equally between lessons on the proper framing of worship and supplication and detailed instruction on the technologies of self-acquaintance and introspection. "I do advise and desire you to examine your selves and to be better studied in, and acquainted with your own hearts, than, it may be, you are," enjoins Samuel Slater in *A Discourse of Closet (or Secret) Prayer* (1691).[8] The shaping premise of Wettenhall's *Enter into thy Closet* is likewise that the Christian who "would keep himself close to the waies of holiness must . . . be often alone" (4). "To that purpose," Wettenhall continues, "he should have a place convenient to retire to, which we will call a Closet" (4–5). The closet is necessary, Wettenhall maintains, because public rites of devotion "may be, and most frequently are, too general to reach our particular case and sins" (4). Dawes concurs: "every man has particular Sins to confess, particular Blessings to ask, particular Mercies to give thanks for, particular Failings both of his own and other Mens to wail." Given such individual specificities, he argues, "there neither ought to be, nor indeed can there be any provision made for these in the Devotions of the Church or Family" (vii).

The self that Dawes, Wettenhall, Slater, and the other proponents of closet devotion envisage as the object of such scrutiny is not only insistently individualized, but also ever more trenchantly interiorized. In both respects, the door of the prayer closet opens onto an incipiently modern figuration of selfhood, the work of the closet likewise hinging upon a more individuated self conceived to reside at an inward remove from outward deed and public expression. "Every man is that really which he is secretly," Brooks puts it pointedly in *The Privy Key of Heaven*. Repeating himself for emphasis, he continues:

> Never tell me, how handsomely, how neatly, how bravely, this or that man acts his part before others; but tell me, if thou canst, how he acts his part before God in his closet; for the man is that certainly, that he is secretly. There are many that sweat upon the stage, that are key-cold in their closets. (162)[9]

Strikingly, Brooks's conception of sincere devotion—how one "acts his part before God in his closet"—turns out to be nearly as theatricalized as his representation of devotional pretence. In either guise, religion is a performance. The principal gauge of its authenticity lies, according to Brooks, in the siting of the act, whether it is produced openly in public for others, or more properly on the private stage of the prayer closet.

This work of the self upon the self staged within the prayer closet is directed along increasingly introspective involutions, spiralling past what Wettenhall terms a "review of my late ways" (57) and into deeper reflection upon "my present Inward State, the temper of my mind" (59): tasks, he repeatedly insists, that "can never be performed as they should be, if we are in company" (2). One begins by "tak[ing] account of his own state and actions" and then turning inward, to "whether his heart be so stedfast in holy purposes as it has been" (2), to "what posture or temper my heart hath continued, and at present is" (271). These spiritual self-anatomies, to be performed at Wettenhall's urgings at least twice daily (12), lift out into finer and finer relief the evanescent lineaments of an inner (devotional) life. Wettenhall's prayer closet manual thus presents the self coming to awareness of itself in view of an ever-expanding repertoire of internalized affective shadings, as the devout probe whether their hearts are "soft, tender, penitent, considerative, and in awe of God; or whether dull, careless, insensible" and so on and on (271)—the affects of devotion being so mutable as to require constant tending and calibration. For it is "by our constant Performance of these Duties," Dawes reminds us, that "we shall be best able to know, whether we are indeed Christians or no, whether we only put on an outward Form of Godliness, or are inwardly full of the Power of it" (135). The point of such directed self-study, as Alan Sinfield has recognized, "was not to relax, but to savor the nuances of one's spiritual condition." "Anxious self-examination," he remarks, "was the gratification."[10]

Made available in the prayer closet is thus an experience of the self that one can "fully descend into" (to recall Parr's metaphor and its metaphysics of internal depths) only because one has withdrawn in secret. In the space of private devotion there emerges a more reclusive self to search out, scrutinize, and cultivate, something to fret over but also to dote upon. These introspective exertions accrete the ever-receding declivities of a deepening, individuating inwardness as closet effects, the recessive architecture of the closet, the place of personal retreat within the house, itself productive of what is experienced as a spatialized "deep self."

Yet, while these texts bespeak individualized interiorities, they do not advance self-awareness as a value in itself. Instead, the inwardness excavated and so rigorously probed here is done so *devotionally:* that is, only in deference to God and in the service of his divine will. Subjectivity is thus both the product and the implement of devotion. Moreover, not only the processes but also the subjectifying results of the care of the self undertaken within the closet tend to be highly scripted in format—literally so. This is evident in an early chapter of Wettenhall's handbook that addresses the directive role of Scripture in the articulation of devotion. The Psalms in particular, he instructs, equip "a man with petitions, hymns, and ejaculations of all sorts" (41).[11] Wettenhall accordingly advances a devotional regimen that would have the devout reading through the entirety of the Psalms on a regular, repeating basis. More precisely, what Wettenhall advocates is less a reading than a *praying* of the Psalms: a daily, internal reiteration of these prescripted devotions as the very terms of one's own individual experiences and desires. No proponent of extempore prayer, he believes instead that "God . . . loves to hear his own language from us" (63).

The determinative role Wettenhall accords Scripture—a virtual language machine for producing self-reflexive expression and understanding—does not render his emphasis on the personal and the individual in devotion—"our particular case," as he phrases it (4)—merely tendentious, however. The personal rather takes its contours here from a particularized, "feeling" application of Scripture to the self: a self that requires its own individual and private place of devotion, but also paradoxically a self that can comprehend and interpellate itself only in terms of the previously scripted but animate word of God.[12] This is what seventeenth-century divines called an "inner experience" of God's word and what Francis Barker (following Louis Althusser) has more recently termed, in a different Renaissance context, "the pre-constitution of the subject in its subjection."[13] At the same time, I think we need to be wary of overplaying the hegemonic within the space of religious devotion, a space with its own heterotopic possibilities: a space, we have seen, where the sacred may come to traffic with the excessive and the transgressive, even the otherwise culturally illicit.[14] Determining the meaning of the word of God that overdetermines devotional subjectivity is itself bound to be a less than wholly deterministic matter, whatever discipline an ecclesiastical leader like Wettenhall might look to impose upon the process. The disfellowshipped Baptist prophet Anne Wentworth, we may recall, finds in the Bible the authorization, indeed the imperative, that she divorce her earthly husband to remarry herself more properly to Christ. Testifying to this problem of hermeneutic containment on a much larger scale are the myriad revisionary and dissenting forms of Christianity that proliferate with an epoch-making cultural influence in the seventeenth century: "the century of revolution," as Christopher Hill aptly names it.[15] Indeed, more or less radical sectarian groups, as well as minority forms of Christianity in general, were then, as now, often among the most devoted to the Bible, which is understood—experienced—by them in the most intensely, if selectively, literalistic terms.

"DEPREHENDING" THE SELF

I desire to die, and to be dissolved in Christ.—Philippians 1:23

Until the recent revival of religion as a central concern in Renaissance studies (a matter to which I will return in a moment), the question of subjectivity and devotion has gone underlit in the efflorescence of historically and theoretically oriented scholarship on the history of selfhood, of how the self conceptualizes and represents itself. That history has been illumined for us across the public stage and atop the anatomy table, mapped in travel diaries and in encounters with New and Old World "others," excavated through the subjunctive involutions of the sonnet sequence and the Renaissance miniature, and traced along the lines of the authenticating signature of the penman's hand and in the play of shadow and light in the painter's self-portrait.[16] Yet this remarkable body of work, however elucidative, remains incomplete to the extent that much of it has tended to pass over the networks of religious acculturation that saturate so much social process in this period. The sin of omission appears all the more flagrant given that Christianity in seventeenth-century England was, as Fredric Jameson none too forcefully put it some time ago, "the cultural dominant, . . . the master-code in which issues are conceived and debated."[17]

In the first volume of *The History of Sexuality*, Foucault, too, could be seen to be working from an implicit recognition of the early modern cultural centrality of religious devotion. Despite his utopic desire to uncouple sex from the structures and strictures of subjectivity—to envision, if only momentarily at the end of the book, a postsexuality world organized around "bodies, pleasures, and knowledges" rather than subjectivities (157)—despite (or perhaps because) of this desire, Foucault's history of sexuality is concomitantly a history of selfhood, one that, as he puts it elsewhere, means to address the question of "why it is that sexuality became, in Christian cultures, the seismograph of our subjectivity" ("Sexuality and Solitude," 368). Foucault commences these imbricated histories in the space of the Roman Catholic confessional and the more inward turn the sacrament takes after the Council of Trent. " 'Tell everything,' the directors would say time and again," he reports, " 'not only consummated acts, but sensual touchings, all impure gazes, all obscene remarks . . . all consenting thoughts' " (*The History of Sexuality*, 21). I want to put forth the subjectifying apparatus of the prayer closet, and the culture of private devotion it comes to represent, as a node for another chapter in the history of the self and its passions taken up in medias res by Foucault at the Counter-Reformation confessional. Indeed, the very trajectory passing from act to thought that Foucault discerns in confession is replicated in the instruction of Wettenhall's *Enter into thy Closet*, which directs one from a "review of my late ways" into a deeper, more germane consideration of "my present Inward State, the temper of my mind." In the prayer closet, however, no mediating priest stands between God and the devotee; through Scripture and handbook that function has been both textualized and internalized. Closet devotion, in other words, is the technology by which the soul becomes a subject.

Thus far I have been considering the prayer closet in terms of the prose literature devoted to it. But the architecture of private refuge and inwardness structures the religious lyric no less than it does the manual and treatise. Here we could look, for instance, to Vaughan or Traherne or other of the meditative poets.[18] I want instead, however, to return to Donne and Herbert, divines who cannot, in fact, be numbered among the most unqualified advocates of closet devotion. I do so in the first place because their far more ambivalent, even agonistic, views onto and from within the prayer closet issue in what are among the most pressurized, most experientally nuanced accounts we have of closet devotion. Second, I want to foreground Donne and Herbert here because their closets are structured according to a markedly different set of terms from those that are underwriting a significant portion of the revival of Renaissance religious studies I referred to a moment ago, a trend that, in its devout conservatism, has emerged as a new Christian humanism.

*   *   *

Herbert, like the other writers we have been considering, advises Christians in the course of his long didactic poem "The Church-Porch," "By all means use sometimes to be alone" (line 145). At a later point in the same poem he insists, however, that corporate prayer in church remains the richest form of devotion: "Though private prayer be a brave design, / Yet public hath more promises, more love." "Pray with the most," Herbert thus concludes, "for where most pray, is heaven" (lines 397-98, 402). Donne advances much the same case in a sermon preached at St. Paul's in 1626: "Chamber-prayers, single, or with your family, Chamber-Sermons, . . . [and] Chamber-Sacraments, administered in necessity there, are blessed assistants, and supplements; they are as the almes at the gate, but the feast is within" (*Sermons*, 7:292). Private devotions—what Donne here calls "Chamber-prayers"—while commendable in themselves, are thus to be regarded as only partial and preliminary to the more sumptuous repast made available to the congregation: "he that hath a handfull of devotion at home," Donne continues, "shall have his devotion multiplyed to a Gomer here" at church.

At least in their more didactic modes, then, both Donne and Herbert appear to come down squarely favoring the congregational side of the debate over public versus private devotion—a valuation that may be attendant upon their shared occupation as priests, as pastors within a national church, charged with supervision of the corporate devotional practices of the flocks within their care. Yet the lyric poetry Donne and Herbert produce can be seen as giving expression to a rather different scheme of prioritization. As Barbara Kiefer Lewalski has noted, the religious lyric is itself intrinsically a private mode, an expressive form, she goes on to explain (though in terms that may be too anodyne for the edgy devotional affects we find in these poets), that is "concerned to discover and express the various and vacillating spiritual conditions and emotions the soul expresses in meditation, prayer, and praise" (4).

The effect of devotional privacy is deepened in Herbert's lyrics by their recurrent figurations of intimate spaces and enclosures. In "Sion," aptly nominated by Richard Strier as "one of the major 'architectural' poems in

The Temple,"[19] Herbert dramatically marks the passing of God's interest in monumental structures and edifices:

> Lord, with what glory wast thou served of old,
> When Solomon's temple stood and flourishèd!
>   Where most things were of purest gold;
>   The wood was all embellishèd
> With flowers and carvings, mystical and rare:
> All showed the builder's, craved the seer's care.
>
> Yet all this glory, all this pomp and state
> Did not affect thee much, was not thy aim;
>   Something there was, that sowed debate:
>   Wherefore thou quitt'st thy ancient claim:
> And now thy Architecture meets with sin;
> For all thy frame and fabric is within.
>
> (lines 1–12)

Strier builds his discussion of this pivotal poem around what he calls "the living temple topos." Derived from the New Testament, this topos marks the displacement of the outward form and grandeur of Solomon's temple by means of its structural replication inside the believer—as when Donne in Holy Sonnet 11 enjoins himself to reflect upon "How God the Spirit . . . / . . . doth make his temple in thy breast" ("Wilt thou love God, as he thee?" lines 3–4). My sense, however, is that what is effected in Herbert's "Sion" has less to do with the succession of one kind of temple by another—an inner temple for an outer one—than with a wholesale *replacement* of monumental architecture by inner habitations that are restructured on a more intimate scale altogether.

Consequently, and perhaps somewhat ironically for a volume titled *The Temple,* what emerges as the privileged architectural form-language of Herbert's verse is a lexicon of small, private structures—boxes, cabinets, walled gardens, urns, cells, chambers, secret rooms, and closets. In "The H. Communion," Christ thus retains "the privy key" that opens "the soul's most subtle rooms" (lines 21–22), intimate spaces that he gradually comes to occupy and even to furnish. Nicholas Ferrar's preface to the first edition of *The Temple* introduces it as the work of one who "abounded in private devotions,"[20] and it is a private chamber that serves as the site of the devotional experiences of the poem "Artillery": "As I one ev'ning sat before my cell," Herbert here begins. In "Confession" we find him structuring his own heart out of ever-more recessive hiding places, inlaying enclosure within enclosure:

> . . . within my heart I made
> Closets; and in them many a chest;
> And, like a master in my trade,
> In those chests, boxes; in each box, a till.
> (lines 2–5)

Consider also Herbert's "To All Angels and Saints," which represents Mary's virginal maternal body as a jewel case for the embryonic Christ she holds inside her: "Thou art the cabinet where the jewel lay" (line 14). This conceit of safe enclosure, Herbert confesses, nearly stirs him to a form of Marian devotion: "Chiefly to thee would I my soul unfold: / But now, alas, I dare not" (lines 15–16). The poem "Ungratefulness" works more doctrinally secure territory in presenting the mysteries of the Trinity and the Incarnation as "two rare cabinets full of treasure," the latter one being especially "packed" with "sweets" and "delights" (lines 7, 19, 24). God will unlock both chests of riches, Herbert promises, merely in exchange for ownership of man's "poor cabinet of bone": a two-for-one exchange of containers that many, he points out in dismay, are foolishly reluctant to transact with so gracious a trader (lines 28–30). Christ's macerated and opened body presents another intimately scaled space in the poem "The Thanksgiving," a space the poet wants to make "my bower" (line 14). In "Paradise" Herbert locates himself within still another kind of divine enclosure, this time representing himself as a tree nurtured and protected in God's private garden: "What open force, or hidden CHARM / Can blast my fruit, or bring me HARM, / While the inclosure is thine ARM?" (lines 4–6). To be bounded, boxed in, is for Herbert to feel more securely, more intimately possessable by God: "Inclose me still for fear I START," he nervously implores in "Paradise" (line 7). "O fill the place / And keep possession with thy grace," Herbert adds in "Good Friday," another lyric that figures the devout heart first as a box and then as a small, close room (lines 24–30).

The many small chambers, enclosures, bowers, and cabinets of Herbert's verse can be sited within the penumbra of the prayer closet and its enhanced devotional intimacies. But in his poem "Decay" we find a differently valenced meditation on God's current predilection for secret sites—both exterior structures and their interiorized mimetic doubles—as the privileged spaces for enjoying fellowship with him. Herbert here turns almost perversely nostalgic for pre-Christian times long gone by, times when, as he sees it, God was more openly sociable with his human favorites:

> Sweet were the days, when thou didst lodge with Lot,
> Struggle with Jacob, sit with Gideon,
> Advise with Abraham, when they power could not
> Encounter Moses' strong complaints and moan:
> > Thy words were then, *Let me alone.*
>
> One might have sought and found thee presently
> At some fair oak, or bush, or cave, or well.
> (lines 1–7)

Now, in contrast, God himself has taken to the closet:

> I see the world grows old, whenas the heat
> Of thy great love, once spread, as in an urn
> Doth closet up itself, and still retreat,
> Cold Sin still forcing it, till it return,
> > And calling *Justice,* all things burn.
> (lines 16–20)

In this poem, the closet emblematizes the retraction of God's favor and "Cold Sin's" rule over these latter days. God will maintain his self-sequestration, Herbert moreover concludes, until the end of the world, at which point he will reemerge in the open; this time, however, it will be not in his former guise of sociability, but rather as judgment, vengeance, and a consuming apocalyptic fury. In the meantime, the continued closeting of God's love, as it is figured in "Decay," goes without the nimbus of intimacy and comforting security that the space of enclosed refuge bears in other of Herbert's lyrics. The closet here signals instead the foreclosure of the possibility of open colloquy with God. At the same time, it also produces, paradoxically, the feeling of a kind of devotional claustrophobia — as though the closet uncomfortably brings God *too close:* "now thou dost thyself immure and close / In some one corner of a feeble heart," Herbert complains (lines 11–12).[21]

Herbert's seventeenth-century figuration of the closet as a site of immurement, housing both angry God and anxious Christian, reaches its contemporary, Middle America apocalypse in Stephen King's novel *Carrie.* In this Christian fundamentalist horror story, the prayer closet, once again neither a place of comforting intimacy nor devotional exhilaration in the enhanced presence of God, becomes simply "the worst place of all":

[Carrie and her mother] were entering the place of the altar. There was a cross on a table covered with an embroidered silk cloth. On either side of the cross there were white candles. Behind this were several paint-by-the-numbers of Jesus and His apostles. And to the right was the worst place of all, the home of terror, the cave where all hope, all resistance to God's will—and Momma's—was extinguished. The closet door leered open. Inside, below a hideous blue bulb that was always lit, was Derrault's conception of Jonathan Edwards' famous sermon, *Sinners in the Hands of an Angry God*.[22]

Here the prayer closet is a punitive site, the place to which the telekinetically gifted (and now sexually awakened) Carrie is cruelly sequestered for hours on end by her idiosyncratically fundamentalist mother: "Go to your closet. Pray in secret. Ask forgiveness for your sin. . . . There had been other times when Mother had kept her in the closet for as long as a day at a stretch—when she stole that forty-nine-cent finger ring from Shuber's Five and Ten, the time she had found that picture of Flash Bobby Pickett under Carrie's pillow—and Carrie had once fainted from the lack of food and the smell of her own waste" (56–58).

* * *

In King's novel *Carrie*, the prayer closet ironically serves as what Carol Clover, in her taxonomy of the tropes of the horror film, terms the "Terrible Place."[23] The closet is also, we shall see, something of a terrible place for Donne as well. Although less architectural than Herbert's *Temple*, Donne's devotional writings nonetheless do remark the specific emplacement of powerful—and again profoundly ambivalent—subjective experiences inside the space of the closet. In a 1622 sermon Donne thus ascertains that within the public sphere represented by the church congregation, "There is our *Nos, We*, testimonies that we are in the favour, and care of God; We, our Nation, we, our Church." "But," he continues, "I am in my Cabinet at home, when I consider, what God hath done for me, and my soule; There is the *Ego*, the particular, the individuall, I" (*Sermons*, 5:71). Here Donne not only frames subjectivity as a specifically devotional function, he also spatializes it. The *I*, the individual, the devotional monad, cites—and sites—itself in the closet; there, in "my Cabinet at home," the self faces itself and what God has done for it personally, particularly.

Concordant, then, with what we find in manuals promoting the practices of private devotion, Donne here apprehends the full flush of subjectivity as an effect of the closet. In another 1622 sermon, however, the prayer closet—now a metafigural space Donne has incorporated within himself—appears as the place in which, as he strikingly phrases it, the self "deprehend[s]" itself:

> where shall I finde the Holy Ghost? I lock my doore to my selfe, and I throw my selfe downe in the presence of my God, I devest my self of all worldly thoughts, and I bend all my powers, and faculties upon God, as I think, and suddenly I finde my selfe scattered, melted, fallen into vaine thoughts, into no thoughts; I am upon my knees, and I talke, and think nothing; I deprehend my selfe in it. (*Sermons*, 5:249–50)

Donne's prayer closet serves, not as the place for the comprehension and organization of the self, but instead as the scene of its disruption, its disarticulation: "I am upon my knees, and I talke, and think nothing." Under the heightened pressures of prayer and introspection uniquely engendered here, the self is repetitively, almost ritually, undone: "I deprehend my selfe in it," continues Donne, "and I goe about to mend it, I gather new forces, new purposes to try againe, and doe better, and I doe the same thing againe" (250). It is as though the very devotional intensities proffered by the other proponents of closet prayer become with Donne too intense, disorienting.

These devotional strainings are recounted in a passage of the sermon that commences with the image of Donne approaching his private audience with God wearing a "defaced" face and besmeared by "a menstruous conscience" (249). Nor, as we have just seen, do these viscerally disfiguring abjections lessen as he attempts to "gather new forces," to recompose himself within the self-shut closet of his private devotions: "I finde my selfe scattered, melted, fallen into vaine thoughts, into no thoughts." The psychical disintegration Donne says he experiences in the closet accords with the violence and personal violations that characterize devotional self-expression throughout the Holy Sonnets, in which the poet brands as his best those days "when I shake with fear" ("Oh, to vex me, contraries meet in one," line 14). This sermon's convulsive phenomenology of closet devotion might have issued from just such a day. Thus, rather than pass off this subjective meltdown as a blockage or absolute failure of devotion, we might see it as quite the answer to Donne's prayers—an answer, that is, to the desire for the immolation of the self voiced, among other places, in "Batter my heart," where, before inviting God to ravish him, Donne calls upon him to "bend / Your force, to break, blow, burn, and make me new" (lines 3–4). Like Paul's desire to die and be dissolved in Christ, these are all terms of self-unmaking, a process imbued in Donne's sonnet, as we have seen, with an erotic aura. The violent dispossession of the self from itself that transpires in Donne's prayer closet correlates with the subjective dissolution, the effacement of the organizational boundaries of selfhood, theorized by Bataille as the ultimate meaning of "the plethoric disorder" (104) of both mystical experience and eroticism—which, at least on the latter account, Leo Bersani (himself following Bataille) specifies in "Is the Rectum a Grave?" to passive anal sex and, as he sees it, its valuable potential for shattering male subjectivity in a *"jouissance* of exploded limits" (217, 222). For Donne, who also makes sodomy the climactic metaphor of "Batter my heart," the question then might be: is the prayer closet likewise a grave?[24] This is indeed the case in another of Donne's sermons, which (somewhat perversely) uses the occasion of Easter Sunday to meditate not so much on the Resurrection, but rather on the varieties of death:

> but I will finde out another death, *mortem raptus,* a death of rapture and of extasie, that death which S. *Paul* died more then once, The death which S. *Gregory* speaks of, *Divina contemplatio quoddam sepulchrum animae,* The contemplation of God, and heaven, is a kinde of buriall, and Sepulchre, and rest of the soule; and in this death of rapture, and extasie, in this death of the Contemplation of my interest in my Saviour, I shall finde my self, and all my sins enterred, and entombed in his wounds. (*Sermons,* 2:210–11)[25]

Here the self is envisioned as refinding itself in its private devotions, but finding itself to be dead, ensconced in the orifices of Christ's body, interred in its contemplations, annihilated into a rapture at once ecstatic and mortifying, thrilling and fearful.

THE ARCHITECTURE OF THE CLOSET: MATERIAL RELIGIOUS CULTURE

In the isolated and darkened room in which one meditates, everything is prepared for the fantastic meeting of desire, formed by the material body, and the "scene" drawn from the allegories of desolation and the Gospel mysteries.
—*Roland Barthes, on the* Exercises *of Saint Ignatius Loyola in* Sade/Fourier/Loyola

Having opened the closet as the space in which the self comes to feel itself demeaned and disintegrated, Donne returns his congregation to the more secure grounds of corporate devotion, a place where God has promised to be found dispensing blessings that are more rejuvenating than dissipating:

> I beleeve in the Holy Ghost, but doe not finde him, if I seeke him onely in private prayer. But in Ecclesia, when I goe to meet him in the Church, when I seeke him where hee hath promised to bee found . . . instantly the savour of this Myrrhe is exalted, and multiplied to me; not a dew, but a shower is powred out upon me. (Sermons, 5:250)

Others join with Donne in insisting that closet devotion is not to be pursued exclusive of attendance at church, that Christians are to be exercised in both private and public forms of piety. "Neither one, nor the other may be neglected," determines John Boughton in his catechistical handbook God and Man (1620).[26] Samuel Slater likewise admonishes in his Discourse of Closet . . . Prayer, "That while Christ doth here command and enjoyn secret duty, it is not any part of his purpose to exclude or take us from publick" (8). Yet having assumed this stance of apparent evenhandedness at the outset, Slater continues on for more than a hundred pages detailing the ways and means of "secret prayer" as both a special "Duty [and] An Advantage" (18, 22). In his prayer book Ancilla Pietatis, subtitled The Hand-Maid to Private Devotion and bestowed upon its dedicatee the Duchess of Buckingham as "a servant to attend you in your closet" (sig. A3), Daniel Featley asserts, "My intent is not to detract any thing from publike Devotion; but my desire is to adde to private" (6). "Verily," he insists, "if ever Private Devotions powring themselves forth in brinish teares, were in season, now they are" (sig. A6). Thirty years later Thomas Brooks heralds the same claim: "God by his present dispensations calls more loudly for closet prayer now than he hath done in those last twenty years that are now past over our heads" (The Privy Key of Heaven, 162).

Many English divines of varying Protestant affiliations and persuasions concurred. Hence, as the century unfolds, there amasses a considerable body of writing on private devotion—a literature of the closet—ranging from lyric poetry to book-length treatises, published sermons, how-to handbooks, and prayer miscellanies to spiritual biographies. Several of these texts we have already been considering, including Edward Wettenhall's Enter into thy Closet, Or a Method and Order For Private Devotion, a manual whose popularity earned it an impressive number of seventeenth-

Figure 14. The Christian closet. Title page from Edward Wettenhall, *Enter into thy Closet*, 1663. Courtesy of the Folger Shakespeare Library, Washington, D.C.

century editions (fig. 14). So too was the case with William Dawes's *The Duties of the Closet*, another handbook of instruction and model prayers — "soliloquies" Dawes calls them (117, 126) — offered with the express aim of bringing "Closet-Religion into Fashion" (sig. A3ᵛ). Samuel Smith's *The Christians Guide* likewise lays out guidelines in the "Rules for Closet-Devotion" (200), while Oliver Heywood supplies *Closet-Prayer, a Christian Duty*, a monograph on the same subject, but one compact enough, its preface advertises, to be as "portable as a pocket book or *vade mecum*" (xi). There is also Thomas Comber's *A Companion to the Temple and Closet* (1672), William Howell's *The Common-Prayer-Book: The Best Companion in House and Closet as well as in the Temple* (1685), and Nathanael Resbury's *Of Closet-Prayer* (1693), each handbook devoted to the promotion and practice of what Wettenhall evocatively terms "Closet-work" (216).[27]

What these pedagogically oriented treatises and manuals look to effect by means of argument, instruction, and enticement, spiritual biographies propound by way of incarnate example. Thus Richard Stock, Milton's boy-hood rector at All Hallows, uses the form of the funeral sermon to recount the model life of "John, Lord Harrington," illustrating how the deceased had organized each day so as to afford himself numerous and lengthy sequestrations in his prayer closet. Eventually published in *The Church's Lamentation for the Loss of the Godly* (1614), Stock's Puritan hagiography details an exemplary devotional regimen:

> His private exercise and course of piety was on this sort. He usually rose every morning about four or five of the clock, not willingly sleeping above six hours. As soon as ever he was thoroughly awake, he endeavored religiously to set his heart in order and to prepare it for goodness all the day after, offer-ing the first fruits of the day and of his thoughts unto God. Thus having tuned his best instrument, his heart, in the next place he read a chapter of the Holy Scripture. That done, he went to his prayers with his servants in his chamber. After this he read some divine treatise to increase his knowledge in spiritual things, and this for the greater part of an hour. . . . And all this he did besides that which was performed with all the family, with whom he joined in the order his honorable father left in the family, namely, reading of the Psalms and a chapter, together with prayer according to the order of our Church, before dinner and supper, and singing of a psalm and prayer after supper.[28]

So continues Harrington, seemingly ever at prayer or sacred study, throughout the course of his day, the habitual contours of which are mi-metically patterned into Stock's own highly repetitive recounting of it:

> But to return to his morning business: after he had bestowed the former time in the manner aforesaid, he withdrew himself to his closet, and after his own private prayer disposed himself to some serious study, if some spe-cial business interrupted not his course, for the space of three or four hours; after which time he addressed himself, if he had time before dinner, to dis-patch business, if any were required of him, and to converse with friends, to better them or be bettered by them. . . . Soon after dinner if he had the op-portunity he ordinarily withdrew himself for awhile to the meditating upon some sermons which he had lately heard, for which use he retained some five or six in his mind. (194–95)

Such ceaseless spiritual endeavor might appear to crowd out the possi-bility of maintaining any other, more this-worldly activities or concerns. Yet perhaps even more notable than Harrington's herculean devotional prowess and stamina is the degree to which his feats of personal piety are, as represented in this passage, so seamlessly textured into the matter of everyday aristocratic life, of Harrington attending to his business concerns and engaging with his friends, as well as overseeing his household, which at every turn of the day he seems likewise to be convening for prayer and spiritual instruction. One surmises that Harrington's domestic administration does not merely extend into the individual spiritual lives of his servants and his family, but actually transpires through his supervision of their devotions. Just so, John Dutton, writing in the *Athenian Mercury* at the century's end, numbers as one of the principal advantages of family prayers in the home the way in which this daily devotional ritual "conciliates respect and reverence to the head of it."[29] Religious devotion thus administers the social order of the household.

Yet separate from these overlapping spiritual ministrations and domestic administrations, we also find that Harrington reserves the closet as his own place of individual privacy within the semiprivate sphere of his household:

> After prayers with them he withdrew himself from his servants and friends, and there in a book which he kept for the account of his life he set down what he had done all that day; how he had either offended or done good, and how he was tempted and withstood them. . . . He was constantly accustomed upon Saturday at night, besides his account for the day, to call himself to strict account how he had spent the whole week, that according as he found his estate, he might better fit himself to sanctify the Sabbath following. (196–97)

The privacy of the closet, as well as the intimate nature of the processes that transpire and are recorded within it, is further underscored by the disclosure that Harrington inscribes his spiritual diary "in a peculiar character known to none," encrypting the self's secret account of itself so that it not "come to any man's view but his own and his God's" (196).

Harrington's closet appears to exist as a particular place within his house. This allocation of a specific room for personal private devotion accords with the instruction given by Brooks in *The Privy Key* and by Heywood in *Closet-Prayer,* both of which propound an insistently literal interpretation of Matthew 6:6, the founding text of closet devotion: "But thou, when thou prayest, enter into thy closet, and . . . shut thy door." "These words of our Saviour are plain, and to be taken literally, and not allegorically, for he speaketh of shutting the door of the chamber," determines Brooks (164). Similarly, Heywood advances his own claim for the materiality of the closet in view of those who understand Christ's pronouncement on closet prayer "mystically, making an allegory of it, as though it did import, *interiorem cordis recessum,* the inner recesses or emotions of the heart" (4). While granting that "it be a truth and a duty that we must pray in the closet of the heart," Heywood reiteratively emphasizes the notion of place evoked by Christ's words—of devotion in situ:

> this is not the proper meaning of the *place,* for we need not interpret the plain word in such a figurative sense . . . besides, that is not suitable to the scope of the *place,* which opposeth self-retirement to the Pharisaical modes of devotion. The word then, is to be literally taken, and, in general, imports "any secret *place,*" where a thing is laid up; . . . or . . . a close or secret chamber, a withdrawing room, retiring *place,* where a person is not seen or heard, nor yet is disturbed in his devotions by any noise or commotion; a secret conclave or apartment locked up where no company is admitted. (4; emphasis added)

By returning us, in good Protestant fashion, to the plain meaning, to the literal, Heywood takes the kind of metaphoric troping on the closet (of the heart, of the body, and so on) so pervasive in seventeenth-century devotional writing and re-places this trope within a material space, an actual closet.

We can gain a fuller sense of what Heywood is here reacting against by turning to Lewis Bayly's enormously popular devotional miscellany *The Practise of Pietie* (1620). Under the instructional heading of "How a private man must begin the Morning with Piety," Bayly appropriately cites Matthew 6:6. In this case, however, Christ's directive serves only as matter for metaphor: "as soon as ever thou awakest in the Morning, keep the doore of thy heart fast shut, that no Earthly thought may enter before God be come in first, and let him (before all others) have the first place therein."[30] While Bayly leaves unspecified whether this devotional duty would most effectively be undertaken in utter solitude, Bishop George Downame's *Godly and Learned Treatise of Prayer* (1640) maintains that no such thing is required. The spirit of Matthew 6:6 can be honored, Downame asserts, simply by praying silently within the congregation of faithful churchgoers: "then thou art to pray in the closet of thy heart without using the voice."[31]

Samuel Smith also envisions closet devotion as achievable in public: "A Soul truly devout, in such [public] places, is so collected into its self, that all the Objects which might do it an injury [i. e., the distractions of the world] cannot find it; the faithful Person is in the Closet of his own heart" (200). In this way, Smith shows Christians how to carry their closets with them to church. At the same time, the prayer closet seems to mean more to Smith than the merely rhetorical figure for devotional discipline it is in the texts of Downame and Bayly. For, unlike them, Smith remains emphatic throughout *The Christians Guide* on the need to be alone when at prayer. "Devotion requires solitude," he maintains (196). For Smith the prayer closet is thus ideally both to be established as a material *place,* a special room within the house, and, synchronistically, to be experienced as a condition of imperturbable devotional inwardness within the heart—an indwelling paraspace, so to speak. In this way, whether the Christian is at home or in public, the prayer closet remains an always proximate place of enclosed devotional refuge: either in the form of an actual, site-specific retreat, or as a kind of virtual space—a place the devout can enter from any place, an introjected structure of intensified self-possession and sharpened devotional focus, a zone in which the outer, public world falls away from the Christian in the transports of an always private devotion.

In its own terms no less compelling than Smith's virtual closet is Wettenhall's architectural realization of Matthew 6:6. And what he envisions is no ascetic's cell. "My Closet," Wettenhall proposes, "would I have no unpleasant place, as sweetly situated as any place of my house, that I might delight to be therein" (5). Accordingly, in the second chapter of his manual entitled "Of the Situations and Furniture of their Closet, who have choice," Wettenhall recommends that this chamber be provided with its own chimney "against the Winter's cold to make the place endurable, if need be, a whole night" (7). While Donne's grim "Hymn to Christ, at the Author's last going into Germany" finds that "Churches are best for Prayer, that have least light" (line 29), Wettenhall envisions a windowed prayer closet, awash with sunlight. Since high places "whence we may behold the heavens and over-look the earth . . . much raiseth the soul and elevates the affections" (5), the closet should be also be designed, Wettenhall further suggests, with what we, in our own domestication of sacred space within the bourgeois home, have come to call "cathedral ceilings." Wettenhall thus materializes the prayer closet as a private condensation of monumental sacred space within the home, "a certain secret Chappel for my self," as he renames it (9). "It's Devotion," Smith echoes, "that makes our Closets to become little Churches" (17).

The closet, Wettenhall continues, should be sited "most remote from the noise, company, and disturbance of the people, who are busied usually below" (5). Oliver Heywood similarly determines that it be "the most retired room" in house (83). The best plan, according to Wettenhall, would be to establish the prayer closet within a suite of private chambers, so that "my passage thereunto should be through two other outer rooms, at least through one, the door or doors of which I might ever have shut, when I thither retired" (6). The architectural recessiveness of the closet serves to secure it against the usual distractions and disruptions of the domestic world in motion around it. This siting also has the advantage, Wettenhall interestingly notes, of generating a private space conducive for uninhibited praying aloud—"to the end," he remarks, "that my voice, which many times I shall have occasion, for my own quickening, to use, might not be heard without." Wettenhall further specifies that the prayer closet, like Elisha's chamber, should contain "a Table, a Stool, and a Candlestick." Additionally, he recommends "an hard Couch, or a great Chair, on which I might sometimes lean my weary or aching head." He favors the couch, since "sometimes I haply might find it necessary to spend the whole night there, and might thereon take some repose" (6). In keeping with nearly every writer on private devotion, Wettenhall envisions the prayer closet as a locus of a great deal of textual activity, ranging from biblical study and rote scriptural memorization, to the recitation of prayers out of prayer books like his own, to the maintenance of a spiritual diary. Hence, along with the aforementioned table, or "praying Desk" as he later terms it (7), every closet should also be stocked with a Bible, a Book of Common Prayer, "two Paper-books" ("which when filled must be supplied by two others"), as well as pen and ink. As a final element of design, Wettenhall advises that "the wall over such Desk or Table should be hung (if I were able to do it) with some stuff of one colour . . . to the end that, when there kneeling at my Prayers, I might have in mine eye nothing to call away or divert my thoughts" (7). Wettenhall's design scheme for the prayer closet is so detailed as to specify the color green for this tabula rasa of drapery— "the best," he determines here, "for the eyes sake."

"My Closet being thus fitted," Wettenhall continues in the next chapter of his manual, "it is supposed that my recourse thereto is either more or less solemn" (8). Having structured and furnished the closet in these most materially specific ways, Wettenhall next looks to circumscribe its use as a "place principally designed for my devout retirement" (8–9). The closet, he urges, should thus no longer serve to house an array of private activities, activities that may have included, but were previously not limited to, religious ones. Evacuated of all such competing secular concerns, the closet is thus to be refurbished as the *prayer closet,* a place reserved exclusively for the business of personal devotion. "Look upon thy Closet no more as an ordinary Room," Dawes directs us, "but as the Temple of God; where he will be in a peculiar manner present" (3).[32]

Consecrate as such, the prayer closet emerges, whatever lip service its advocates may offer to the notion of not wanting to lessen the primacy of churchgoing, as the cynosure of devotional experience, the new site of privileged access to God. "Sincere saints worshipping God with others are comparatively far off," Heywood declares, "but souls in a corner or closet are admitted to come near God, and have sweet intimacy with him. . . . God will more familiarly communicate himself to the soul in secret" (23, 26). Samuel Smith concurs: "Our Lord . . . casts not his favours upon the Crowd" (197).[33] Moreover, as Nathanael Resbury reminds us, in the prayer closet we have "greater liberty in particularizing our wants before God" (13). In his enthusiasm for the closet, Brooks goes so far as to contend (perhaps heretically) that closet prayer is more efficacious, more likely to be granted, than a petition lifted up by many voices in public, in church: "Oh the prevalency of prayer behind the door! . . . [It] never returns empty; it hits the mark, it carries the day with God; it pierceth the wall of heaven" (183). Also deemed more productive in the space of the closet are those anatomizing rituals of self-examination that, as we saw in our consideration of devotional subjectivity, can sound the depths of the soul only in private. "In secret we may more freely, and more fully, and safely unbosom our souls to God," Brooks asserts (172). And in secret, Heywood confirms, God is sure to reciprocate: "God will more familiarly communicate himself to the soul in secret;" "he who is much with God in secret places," he adds, "gets into God's secret place" (26, 34).

Consequently, Wettenhall is able to conclude that one "can no wise be esteemed a serious and thorow Christian, uprightly and cordially discharging his duty towards God, who is a stranger unto privacy" (1). Yet to specify the prayer closet of Matthew 6:6 as an actual place, and not primarily an allegorical admonishment against pharisaical displays of piety, is to locate the enhanced and privileged spiritual experiences of closet devotion well beyond the material means of most Christians. Lawrence Stone and others have written about the trend toward an "architectural privacy" in the design and organization of late-seventeenth-century households, which entailed such spatial innovations as the transfer of bedrooms upstairs, away from the more public spaces below; the development of smaller, private chambers allocated for more personal pursuits; and the creation of corridors, which opened routes of circulation through the house that did not traverse these chambers and the more private activities they began to house. Such developments, Stone points out, were not confined to only the very wealthiest households; rather, they increasingly filtered down to successful yeomen and tradesmen, whose houses, Stone writes, likewise "became more varied, more subdivided and more specialized in function, and thus afforded greater privacy." [34] But even if every member of such families (not to say anything for the moment about every one of their servants) was indeed to have his or her own individual bedroom, it nonetheless would be another matter altogether for each to be provided with an *additional* private chamber or closet, exclusively dedicated, as Wettenhall's handbook enjoins, to devotional practices. [35]

It appears from Richard Stock's memorial funeral sermon that John, Lord Harrington maintained just such a room. So did Lady Anne Clifford, whose diaries record her frequent recourse to the closet for a variety of personal activities—reading, letterwriting, private conferences, even gift-giving—that were not limited (as Wettenhall would have it) strictly to devotional tasks. [36] But how many other Christians could lay claim to the same privilege, to their own, individual closets? Here then, along the differentials of wealth and class, there opens a fault line in the period's discourse on private devotion. Ironically, Jesus' injunction to pray in private appears in the course of what is perhaps the most populist sermon in the Gospels, the Sermon on the Mount (Matthew 5–7). Preaching to the multitudes, including the poor: this is the context in which Christ instructs, "When thou prayest, enter into thy closet." Accordingly, seventeenth-century proponents of closet devotion insist, "Every child of God may and must perform the duty of secret prayer" (Heywood, *Closet-Prayer*, 11). "Secretly and solitarily to hold intercourse with God is the undoubted duty of every Christian," Brooks reiterates; "the text," he further specifies, "is . . . not limited to any sort or rank of persons, whether high or low, rich or poor, bond or free, servant or master" (166, 210). In illustrating their contention, Brooks, Heywood, and Joseph Hall each call forth an impressive cast of the faithful who, as Scripture relates, performed their devotional duties in the material conditions of solitude. Among this exemplary number are Abraham, Isaac, Jacob, Moses, David, Elijah, Hannah, Daniel, Peter, and Paul—even Jonah, who, through a remarkable exercise of devotional fancy on the part of Brooks, becomes in the belly of the whale an archetype of the Christian in his closet. [37] Foremost in the performance of closet devotion is of course Christ himself, whom the Gospels regularly present, we are here reminded, in prayerful isolation atop a mountain, or tracing the desert, or secluded in some other place of retreat. Heywood quotes Mark 1:35 to this effect: "In the morning, rising up a great while before day, [Jesus] went out and departed into a solitary place, and there prayed" (19).

Wettenhall's *Enter into thy Closet* similarly opens, we have already seen, with the declaration that no one can "be esteemed a serious and thorow Christian who is a stranger unto privacy," and this imperative is repeated throughout its pages. Interestingly, such universalizing determinations are crosscut in the literature of closet devotion with an awareness that within the ranks of Christian society there exists an uneven access to the kind of architectural privacy upon which the spiritual regimens they advance so manifestly depend. Simply put, not every Christian has—or will ever have—his or her own prayer closet to retreat to. Thus the chapter in which Wettenhall details the proper furbishing of the closet as "no unpleasant place" is predicated, he specifies from the start, upon economics, upon the supposition "that my condition allows me so much choice, as that I might have it so" (5). A later chapter of the manual that addresses the question of how much time Christians are to spend in their closets is likewise carefully demarcated by the lines of class. "If I am a person of leisure, I ought daily, twice in the day, to retire to my Closet for devotion's sake," Wettenhall instructs (13). "If I be the Master or Mistress of a Family," he continues, "there is little question of it." But "if I be a servant, or one who works for my living," Wettenhall concedes, "there is indeed somewhat the more question; for that not only I may be straitned in time, but want the conveniency of privacy" (17).

I noted a moment ago that the sermon in which Christ compels Christians to their closets famously begins, "Blessed are the poor." But evidently servants, laborers, the poor were not necessarily to be so blessed as to have a closet (and all that it entails spiritually) to call their own. Nor do any of the writers we are concerned with here understand Christ's sermon as a scriptural call for an egalitarianism of devotional opportunity or even of access to God.[38] Nor, furthermore, is the literature of closet devotion especially troubled by the incommensurability between its own promotion, on one hand, of such private spiritual exercises as the sine qua non of a devotional life, and an awareness, on the other, that the material circumstances of many, indeed most Christians would never have afforded them the requisite personal privacy, not to say leisure, to nurture these essential devotional habits. Brooks's (one might think rather unhelpful) advice in *The Privy Key* to servants who feel deprived of adequate liberty for prayer is simply for them to find another master (210-11). Better still, he suggests, they could always "redeem time" for devotion from their recreations, meals, and sleep (215). Heywood's worry is that servants might deploy his claims concerning the necessity of devotional privacy as an argument for greater personal liberty, if only to spend it in prayer. To such his curt rejoinder is simply to "be content with your condition; had you more liberty, it may be your hearts would not be in so good a frame" (112–13). Wettenhall carries the discussion further, recognizing that religious devotion is no different from any social process inasmuch as "the higher matters and more curious circumstances are commended only to men of abilities, estates and leisure suitable" (sig. A6ᵛ). He thus ascertains that "private devotions of every day will be different to particular persons according as their conditions differ" (33), so that, for instance, servants need pray only as they rise from or go to bed. The class structure of spirituality is inscribed even more forthrightly by Dawes, who declares in the preface to *The Duties of the Closet*, "I design'd not this Book for the ordinary People, but for those who are in some measure Masters of their own Time, and therefore I have prescrib'd much longer Devotions than are suitable to the Conditions of Labouring People" (sig. A4).

The care of the self, Foucault has insisted, "constitute[s] not an exercise in solitude, but a true social practice."[39] So too the care of the soul. For the privacy that increasingly comes to encase the performance of religious devotion in its most intensified registers demarcates individual prayer and the protocols of spiritual self-examination all the more trenchantly as forms of social practice—and social privilege. The prayer closet thus develops a privileged devotional subjectivity that is also a subjectivity *of* privilege—one, however spiritually oriented, that manifestly bears the impress of class and economic standing. Not even all souls are fashioned equal.

PRAYING THROUGH THE BODY

And O what memorable fruits of secret prayer had David frequently? Surely he felt the sweetness of it, both in his soul and body.
— *Oliver Heywood*, Closet Prayer

As a material structure, the prayer closet houses a body as well as a soul. "Observe it," declares Heywood, "in true closet prayer there should be a confinement of the voice as well as the body" (5). Indeed, Heywood implies that the closet exists more for the sake of the body and its voice than for the soul and its interior intonations. Highlighting the corporeal here might appear to cut against the grain of the introspectively oriented closet manuals and treatises we have been considering, which spend pages detailing an inner need for undisturbed devotional privacy. Yet nearly all these same texts attend just as seriously to the comportment of the body within the closet as they do to the disposition of the soul. Dawes, for instance, would bring the body to its knees and keep it there. Kneeling, he determines, is "the Bodily Posture always to be used in Prayer, both Private and Publick"—devotion's signature posture (3). Wettenhall too asserts that "though the posture of the body seem to be a small matter, yet methinks my Prayers want their due solemnity, if not performed in a posture of worship" (77). But whereas Dawes sanctions a single position for the devout body, Wettenhall, we have seen, outfits the prayer closet with a couch, a chair, a stool, and a table, as well as a kneeler; all this is provided with the body in mind—the furniture of devotion supporting a gamut of expressive postures.

George Downame's *Godly and Learned Treatise of Prayer* allots an entire chapter to devotion's corporeal bearings, arguing that the body is no less gesturally articulate in the religious sphere than it is in the field of worldly, social affairs. God, Downame thus affirms, is both spoken to and himself speaks through "the gesture of the bodie" (118). In illustrating this claim, he catalogs a spectrum of prayerful bodily positions on display in the Bible, which include, in addition to kneeling, the motions of standing, sitting, lying in bed, prostrating oneself, "falling on the ground," walking, riding, and journeying, as well as inclining the whole body in the direction of some part or other of heaven, whether east or west (119–22). This last pose, Downame notes, was especially important in the Old Testament, but for Christians it has been rendered "a thing indifferent," by which he means something neither especially commendable nor condemnable in itself (120). For that matter, the point of Downame's postural index seems to be that all these many somatic positions are things indifferent, that the Christian body can bespeak devotion in the idiom of nearly any of its many gestural possibilities (119). Heywood, having likewise ascertained from Scripture that there are indeed "several laudable gestures in prayer," thus advises, "You may do in this as you find most advantageous in your experience: no invariable rules can be given as to these particular circumstances" (84). This is also Joseph Hall's counsel in a chapter of *The Art of Divine Meditation* titled "Of the site and gesture of the body": "In this let every man be his own master" (82). Noting that the stance or action of the body "must needs be varied according to the matter of meditation," Hall continues: "If we think of our sins, Ahab's soft pace [I Kings 16:31], the publican's dejected eyes and his hand beating his breast [Luke 19:2] are most seasonable. If of the joys of heaven, Steven's countenance fixed above [Acts 7:55] and David's hands lifted up on high [Psalms 134:2] are most fitting" (82–83).

Yet, as we can glean from the specificity of Hall's instruction, what isn't a thing indifferent, what does indeed matter, is that the demeanor of the body be enlisted in some meaningful way into the articulation of devotion, that it, too, be made to enact one's prayers and worship—that, as Hall urges it, "we use that frame of body that may both testify reverence and in some cases help to stir up further devotion" (82). "Consider, your bodies are God's, and must be presented as a sacrifice to God," Heywood likewise compels us; "he will be worshipped with the outward as well as inward man; you cannot, without dangerous sacrilege, rob him of either" (84). Downame is no less adamant on this account, insisting that "the signes of those graces which we contein in our souls must (when they may conveniently) be expressed in the body" (117). And having canvassed the range of motion of the entire body, Downame then turns with more speci-fied attention (like Hall) to "the gesture of the parts," thus expanding his kinetic system of devotionally expressive somatic possibilities, including uncovering one's head, lifting up one's eyes or casting them down, raising one's hands, knocking at one's breast, and so forth (122–23).[40]

Devotion has its voices as well as its gestures, as we find in the next chapter of Downame's exhaustive treatise, called "Of the Voyce to be used in prayer" (125). Among the attributes for which Wettenhall promotes the closet, I noted earlier in passing, is the privacy it affords for uttering those "quickening" cries of the heart, for putting breath to one's most intimate devotional longings. Similarly, Downame contends in this chapter that praying aloud "greatly serve[s] to help both the attention of the mind and the intention of the affections" (118). The claim made here is not simply that vocal intonations can be indicative of devotional feeling. Much more than this, Downame regards the voice, like both the overall carriage of the body and its discreet gestures, as an instrument that produces devotional affect, functioning, as he puts it, "to stirre up the affections of the heart" (127). Again these assertions find an echo in Heywood, who determines that worshiping God entails "both . . . the habit of our body and manner of our voice" (85). There is "both evidence and assistance in the body's humble gesture," he maintains; "it is a help to make you humble, and it is a sign that you are humble" (84).

These kinesthetic accounts of prayer posit a remarkable liaison between the corporeal and the spiritual within the space of the closet. Like a subcutaneous pulse of electricity, grace reverberates outward from the soul through the body, stimulating it into the motions and postures of devotion. The position of the body in prayer thus comes to reflect, to instantiate the demeanor of the soul. But this process transpires in the other direction as well, so that the body's movements can also stir the soul to more fervent states of devotion. "Now our bodies and members thereof, as they are the instruments so also [are they] the indices and manifesters of our souls," affirms Downame (117). In this devotional system, spiritual progress is not calibrated toward an utter repudiation of the corporeal, as though the body could only be (as it is in the most severely dualistic versions of Christianity) the prison house of the soul. Rather, to recall Heywood's formulation, the body, devotionally attuned, is actually a "help" to the soul. The body and its poses, its motions, its voicings, even its passions can thus be redeemed in the performance of prayer as the medium in which religious devotion takes on its fullest expression.

Although Downame himself does not here single out the prayer closet as necessarily the most suitable stage for the expressive performances of the devotionally activated body, a number of other writers on prayer do. "Herein"—that is, in the closet—"let the body, as well as the soul, be taken up in meet acts of worship," exhorts Wettenhall (78). Even Samuel Smith, who in his most rigidly dualistic moment espouses that "Devotion . . . disunites us from our Body" (140), recognizes later in *The Christians Guide* that "Devotion has its Actions and its Words: it impresseth its transports and motions upon the Soul; and the Body frequently may have its too" (197). For this reason, he determines that the body so engaged "should not be expos'd to the view of men who make ill Judgments thereof." This is not to imply, conversely, that the body was seen to be mute within the sphere of public worship; for this space, too, offers its own choreography of the devout body as it kneels, stands, speaks, and sings in accordance with the rhythms of the scripted church liturgy or service. Instead, as with all of the workings of closet devotion, the question is one of intensification, the closet functioning, its advocates see it, as an amplifying structure—one that might sometimes inspire the devout to "use such gestures as would not be fit in the sight of others" (Heywood, *Closet Prayer*, 22). It is worth stressing here that the texts I have been treating are not the expostulations of adherents of ecstatic Christian sects, such as the Quakers, whose galvanic bodies became the vehicles for far more spectacular flights of devotion, marked by fits of uncontrollable shaking, groans, and weeping, as well as trances.[41] On the contrary, Heywood and Smith, like Downame, Wettenhall, and Dawes, stand well within the orthodox in investing the corporeal with spiritual expressivity and significance, in, like Donne, hard-wiring the soul to the body: "All that the soul does," he thus declares in a sermon I have already cited, "it does in, and with, and by the body. . . . These two, Body, and Soule . . . concurre in all that either of them doe" (*Sermons*, 4:358).

*   *   *

In keeping with its interest in the role of the body in devotion, the literature of the prayer closet is girded with sensual imagery and erotic set pieces culled from the Song of Songs, this ensemble of epithalamic lyrics called into service here as a further enticement to the intimacies of the closet. "Love is the Source and Basis of Devotion," Samuel Smith writes in the first edition of his *Christians Guide* (1683); "it is touched with a violent desire of Union; It says with the Spouse, *Let him kiss me with the kisses of his Mouth, for his Love is sweeter than Wine*" (2). The devout, Daniel Featley's *Hand-Maid to Private Devotion* likewise intones, "alwaies shuts her selfe up in her Closet, desiring no eye to see but her Fathers in secret. Wounded she is (like the Spouse in the Canticles) with the darts of divine love and continually bleedeth" (2–3). "What place can be so proper for the Soul to meet her Beloved in, as the Closet," echoes Dawes in *The Duties of the Closet*, "where there shall be nothing to disturb or interrupt their Heavenly Conversation? . . . Here may she enjoy him, as fully as possibly she can in this Life" (138). "Here," he continues,

> she will find him, who alone is lovely, nay, and what will still more delight
> and please her, here will she find a way to the Eternal Injoyment of him,
> whom she so much loves; here will she be instructed how to behave her self
> so that her God, whom she thirsts after, may delight in her, and take her up
> from beholding his hinder parts, to that Glorious place, where she shall see
> Him Face to Face, and have a full and secure Enjoyment of Him for ever and
> ever. (140)

As Dawes frames it, the prayer closet is one's own private aperture onto heaven and its pleasures. And here the hereafter is conceived, like the closet itself, in patently sensual terms, a place where (in Dawes's bizarre, but biblically derived, corporeal conceit) one moves from beholding God's "hinder parts" to "a full . . . Enjoyment of Him" face to face.[42]

For Thomas Brooks in *The Privy Key of Heaven* the co-operations of soul and body within the closet, as well as the pleasures attendant thereupon, find an emblem in the story from Genesis of Jacob's wrestling match with an angel:

> And Jacob was left alone; and there wrestled a man with him until the breaking of the day. And when he saw that he prevailed not against him, he touched the hollow of his thigh; and the hollow of Jacob's thigh was out of joint, as he wrestled with him. And he said, Let me go, for the day breaketh. And he [Jacob] said, I will not let thee go, except thou bless me. (Genesis 32:24–26)

In his reading of this episode as a proto-closet devotional experience ("And Jacob was left alone"), Brooks sides with those biblical commentators who have identified Jacob's mysterious wrestling partner as "the Son of God in human shape." Brooks also asserts that "the nature or manner of the combat . . . was both outward and inward, both corporal and spiritual," which means, he continues, that Jacob won his blessing "as well by the strength of his body as . . . by the force of his faith." Interestingly, Brooks further specifies, evidently to enhance the sheer physicality of the encounter, that these two combatants squared off as ancient wrestlers did: Jacob and Christ, that is, wrestled each other in the nude, for "those which did wrestle of old . . . wrestle[d] naked" (178–79). The latent (or not so latent) potential for a homoerotic cathexis onto this biblical scene of two unclothed men, hand to thigh, has been thrown into relief more recently in Tony Kushner's play *Angels in America* through the character of Joe Pitt, who is handsome, married, Mormon, and gay. In the course of coming out to his wife, Joe locates the first stirrings of homosexual desire in the nervous pleasure he, as a devout boy, took in a Bible picture-book image of this very story, of a young, virile Jacob grappling with a handsome, blond angel—"a beautiful man," as Joe recalls this exciting scene of homodevotional pornography.[43] Nor is the seventeenth-century Puritan devotional treatise any more inclined than Kushner's contemporary "Gay Fantasia" to back away from the erotic energies thrown off by Jacob's markedly physical encounter with a beautiful "man." Indeed,

Brooks seems to insist upon the homoerotic by explicitly framing Jacob and Christ as (male) lovers in the course of his explanation of how a mere mortal could prevail against a divine opponent: "The angel," he analogizes, "was as freely and fully willing to be conquered by Jacob, as Jacob was willing to be conqueror. When lovers wrestle, the strongest is willing enough to take a fall of the weakest; and so it was here" (180).

The affects of the prayer closet, then, are those belonging to lovers, to the erotic: "Oh the sweet meltings, the heavenly warmings . . . with God, that Christians have found when they have been alone with God in a corner, in a closet, behind the door!" (174), we find Brooks rhapsodizing just a few pages before his exegesis of Jacob's nocturnal wrestling match. In this instance, however, he happens to be invoking the intimate relations of husband and wife, the shifting amorous analogies Brooks employs throughout *The Privy Key of Heaven* instancing for us yet again the highly labile eroticism of sacred eroticism, which can be heteroerotic or homoerotic, and both at once:

> A husband imparts his mind most freely and fully to his wife when she is alone; and so doth Christ to the believing soul. Oh the secret kisses, the secret embraces, the secret whispers, the secret cheerings, the secret sealings, the secret discoveries . . . that God gives to his people when alone. . . . Christ loves to embrace his spouse, not so much in the open street, as in a closet. (176–77)

Correspondingly, Oliver Heywood opines, "The Spouse of Christ is [herself] modest"; "here then," Heywood continues, again shifting from a connubial framework to a same-sex one, "comes in the use of and advantage of closet prayer, that a Christian may (as Jonathan and David unbosomed themselves to each other alone) open his heart to God where no eyes see" (25–26).

These amorous effusions should impress upon us not only the task of addressing the homoerotic vectors of Christian devotion, but also the need to refine prevailing critical and historical accounts that have posited the expiration of "religious enthusiasm" in the mid- or late seventeenth century (in some accounts even earlier), as well as, in its wake, what has been recently termed the "disappearance of sacred eroticism from English religious discourse."[44] Religious enthusiasm and sacred eroticism were, of course, subject to a sharpened critique throughout the seventeenth century to the Enlightenment and beyond. Thus, as I noted in the previous chapter, the incursion of erotic discourse in a devotional text is stridently pathologized in the eighteenth-century edition of the Anglican communion manual, *The Weeks Preparation;* republished as *The New Weeks Preparation,* these meditations come scrubbed of all their former defiling strains of "spiritualiz'd Concupiscence" (iv), of devotions that might "pollute the soul with luscious Images" (vi). A related animus, as Debora Kuller Shuger has noted, is operative in Alexander Pope's "Eloisa and Abelard" (1717) and its satiric exposure of the "pious fraud of am'rous charity" (177). Previous to this, Milton had essentially rewritten the corpus of seventeenth-century religious lyric devoted to the most trenchantly corporeal moments in Jesus' life with his own revisionary, chastening christological canon: "On the Morning of Christ's Nativity" (1645), "Upon the Circumcision" (1645), "The Passion" (1645), and *Paradise Regained* (1671). As we have seen, the somatically spectacular events of Christ's Nativity, Circumcision, and Passion prompted Donne, Herbert, Crashaw, and others to intense and visceral displays of devotional affect, to sighs and tears and shudders. Apart from "Upon the Circumcision," in which Christ is momentarily made naked and "bleeds to give us ease" (11), Milton's recasting of these events not only drains them of much of their potential for erotic cathexis, he also strikingly *de-*corporealizes them. In Milton's devotional corpus Christ appears hardly to have a body at all. Coincident with that absence, Milton himself hardly seems like a devotional poet. Indeed, his poem on *The Passion,* the generative site for so much of the affective and amorous devotion we have considered here, goes unfinished and, what is more, is published by Milton as such—as though it were to be the final lyric on a literally abandoned topic.[45]

Nonetheless, to report the post-Restoration "disappearance of sacred eroticism from English religious discourse" is, I think, to make the case too total, too closed. This history needs to be opened, in accordance with our opening of the prayer closet, so as to encompass the erotic energies that continue to pulse through such "late" texts as Brooks's *Privy Key of Heaven;* or Dawes's *Duties of the Closet,* which had reached at least seven editions by 1732; or Traherne's ecstatic devotional poetry, most of which was penned in the 1660s and 1670s. The narrative to which these works and the many others akin to them belong should not, then, be unfolded as the story of the utter effacement of sacred eroticism—as though this culture of somatized and sensualized Christian piety could simply be anaesthetized, repressed with only a few, idiosyncratically assigned vestiges left palpable. Rather, the history of sacred eroticism is one that is pointed toward a more particularized *emplacement,* not effacement, of its energies and expressions. Erotic devotion—religion speaking of and as sex—does not suddenly disappear sometime in the seventeenth or the eighteenth century. But it does appear to be increasingly rezoned, with its all-exciting, unsettling flexions of amplified affect, to the closet. The prayer closet: a space where the body's "transports and motions" may speak, even heighten the devotion of the soul it houses. A space where the sacred may touch the transgressive, even the profane. A place where the naked, homoerotic clutch of Jacob and his God correlates to the lovemaking of husband and wife "behind the door." The prayer closet: a structure that still resides at the core of Christianity, though often now as a site of denial and scandal.

Notes

INTRODUCTION: SACRED EROTICISMS

1 Francis Rous, *The Mysticall Marriage, or Experimentall Discoveries of the heavenly Marriage between a Soule and her Savior*, 2d ed. (London, 1631), 288–89. Further references supplied in the text.

2 Georges Bataille, *Erotism: Death and Sensuality*, trans. Mary Dalwood (San Francisco: City Lights, 1986), 21–22. Bataille offers the term "sacred eroticism" in contrast to the conventional notion of "divine love," remarking that "the love of God is a concept more familiar and less disconcerting than the idea of the love of a sacred element" (22). Similarly, my interest here turns on the permutations of eroticism that inhere in the sacred as a phenomenological structure, as well as on the libidinalities of the God/devotee dyad. See also Debora Kuller Shuger's distinctly non-Bataillean discussion of "sacred eroticism" in *The Renaissance Bible: Scholarship, Sacrifice, and Subjectivity* (Berkeley: University of California Press, 1994), 168–93. Further citations of both Bataille and Shuger supplied in the text.

On appreciating the force—even the strangeness—of a convention, see also Richard Strier's *Resistant Structures: Particularity, Radicalism, and Renaissance Texts* (Berkeley: University of California Press, 1995), 23–25. Strier treats this matter through a deft discussion of the famous clash in the 1950s between the iconoclastic William Empson and the traditionalist Rosemund Tuve over how to read Herbert's Crucifixion poem, "The Sacrifice."

3 See Leo Steinberg, *The Sexuality of Christ in Renaissance Art and in Modern Oblivion* (New York: Pantheon, 1983), recently republished in a revised and significantly expanded second edition (Chicago: University of Chicago Press, 1996); all references are according to the revised edition. See also Caroline Walker Bynum, *Holy Feast and Holy Fast: The Religious Significance of Food to Medieval Women* (Berkeley: University of California Press, 1987) and *Fragmentation and Redemption: Essays on Gender and the Human Body* (New York: Zone Books, 1992); and Peter Brown, *The Body and Society: Men, Women, and Sexual Renunciation in Early Christianity* (New York: Columbia University Press, 1988). Specific references to these works supplied in the text. Other pertinent contributions to the discussion of corporeality and spirituality include Rudolf M. Bell, *Holy Anorexia* (Chicago: University of Chicago Press,

1985), and Michael Camille, *Image on the Edge: The Margins of Medieval Art* (Cambridge: Harvard University Press, 1992).

4   Steinberg, *The Sexuality of Christ*, 18–22. Yet to look here and see sex, to suspect the erotic in Michelangelo's *all'antica* Christ, is not a reflex idiosyncratic to modern "Freudianized" viewers. Despite the strictly theological terms in which Steinberg reads this image, he himself notes the contemporary controversy surrounding the (literally) shameless nudity of the statue, as well as the fact that every sixteenth-century copy of it represents the figure as aproned. "Even now," Steinberg continues, "the original statue in Sta. Maria sopra Minerva stands disfigured by a brazen breechclout" (21). As I will be arguing at greater length in chapter 2, pre- and early modern authors were well aware of the potential of religious expressions and representations to signify erotically as well as — or sometimes even instead of — devotionally. Some found this troubling; others enabling, even exhilarating.

5   See particularly chapters 5 ("Transgression"), 8 ("From religious sacrifice to eroticism"), and 11 ("Christianity") of *Erotism*.

6   At the beginning of the lengthy "Retrospect" Steinberg appends to the expanded edition of his book, he remarks that "Christianity's greatest taboo [is] Christ's sexuality," and he cites a variety of scholars echoing this claim (219). Yet far more taboo, I would maintain, is any consideration of Christ's "sexuality" that would take us outside the terms of a presumptive heterosexuality. Steinberg claims that in responding both to the critics and to the admirers of *The Sexuality of Christ* he has attended "to every alternative view produced by the criticism of the past decade" (221). But the alternative that the sexuality of Christ might also be the site of erotic interests and energies that are other than strictly heteroerotic is nowhere addressed in Steinberg's nearly two-hundred-page rejoinder, apart from a singular reference in one of his footnotes to Malcolm Boyd's article, similarly titled "The Sexuality of Jesus" (*Witness 74* [July–August 1991]: 14–16), which, as Steinberg notes (but considers no further), "argued that Jesus was gay" (326). Perhaps the other (non-)moment in which homoeroticism is (not) addressed in Steinberg's discussion is his assuaging response to the "X-rating" of his book in its review by Michael Levey, which, as Steinberg reprises it here, "warned readers of the *Washington Post* that certain parts of . . . *The Sexuality of Christ* would only appeal to perverts of a particular persuasion." What this particular persuasion is and what these "perverts" would find appealing here is left unspecified by both Levey and Steinberg, though the latter assures us that "there is no cause for alarm" (298).

7   In addition to Bynum's work, a number of other treatments of female religiosity have appeared in recent years, including Karma Lochrie, *Margery Kempe and the Translations of the Flesh* (Philadelphia: University of Pennsylvania Press, 1991); Kathy Lavezzo, "Sobs and Sighs between Women," in *Premodern Sexualities,* ed. Louise Fradenburg and Carla Freccero (New York:

Routledge, 1996), 175-98; Kathryn Bond Stockton, *God between Their Lips: Desire between Women in Irigaray, Bronte, and Eliot* (Stanford: Stanford University Press, 1994); and Phyllis Mack, *Visionary Women: Ecstatic Prophecy in Seventeenth-Century England* (Berkeley: University of California Press, 1992).

8 See Michel Foucault, "Sexuality and Solitude," in *On Signs,* ed. Marshall Blonsky (Baltimore: Johns Hopkins University Press, 1985), 367. See also *The Care of the Self,* the third volume in Foucault's *The History of Sexuality,* trans. Robert Hurley (New York: Random House, 1988), 37-68.

9 Thomas Brooks, *The Privy Key of Heaven, or Twenty Arguments for Closet-Prayer* (1665), in *The Complete Works of Thomas Brooks,* ed. Alexander B. Grosart, 3 vols. (Edinburgh: James Nichol, 1866), 2:162. Further references supplied in the text.

1 CHRIST'S GANYMEDE

1 The 1995 *Adam Gay Video Guide,* for instance, heralds *More of a Man* (dir. Jerry Douglas; 1990) for being "as much a revelation as it is a revolution in gay video making" (90). *Adult Video News* similarly praises the videotape for elevating "the adult feature into the realm of cinematic art without sacrificing the sexual intensity," and it acclaims the video's screenplay as "what may be the best . . . in the 20 year history of gay adult features" (November 1990, 72). The video, its director, and its star (the late Joey Stephano) were, moreover, honored with a number of adult industry awards.

Not only has *More of a Man* been feted within its own industry, the video has also recently become the subject of several critical studies. My treatment of it, especially its opening scene, draws upon Mandy Merck's provocative discussion in "*More of a Man*: Gay Porn Cruises Gay Politics," one of the essays in her book *Perversions: Deviant Readings* (New York: Routledge, 1993), 217-35. Mark Simpson provides another interesting consideration of *More of a Man* in "A World of Penises: Gay Videoporn," in *Male Impersonators: Men Performing Masculinity* (New York: Routledge, 1994), 131-49. I consider the fairly ambitious cultural work of this videotape and the interplay within it of the codes of (gay) masculinity and (gay) eroticism at greater length in "Homodevotion," in *Cruising the Performative: Interventions into the Representation of Ethnicity, Nationality, and Sexuality,* ed. Sue-Ellen Case, Philip Brett, and Susan Leigh Foster (Bloomington: Indiana University Press, 1995), 71-89.

2 See Merck, *Perversions,* 224.

3 Eve Kosofsky Sedgwick, *Epistemology of the Closet* (Berkeley: University of California Press, 1990), 140. Further references supplied in the text.

4 Here I am adapting and somewhat retooling Merck's formulation: "In the eerie blue light of the float's plastic-lined interior (which itself suggests the

inside of a giant condom) sex and religion finally come together. . . . [T]he couple consummate their romance and rejoin the march, leaving behind a used condom juxtaposed in a final freeze-frame with the abandoned rosary" (*Perversions*, 234). Unlike Merck, however, I do not see the rosary and the type of devotion it represents as so much "abandoned" as erotically recuperated and revalenced, in keeping with the video's array of homodevotional pleasures.

5　The sort of amatory gestures I cite here from representative lyrics by Donne, Herbert, and Crashaw are not confined to the verse of male Christian poets. Aemilia Lanyer, for instance, figures Christ as the lover "In whom is all that Ladies can desire" in a dedicatory poem "To the Ladie *Katherine* Countesse of Suffolke" (line 85), in *The Poems of Aemilia Lanyer*, ed. Susanne Woods (New York: Oxford University Press, 1993). In *Salve Deus Rex Judaeorum* (1611), the long poem on Christ's Passion that follows, Lanyer goes on to blazon "His alablaster breast, his bloody side" (line 1162) in terms of the same white-and-red color scheme amorously employed by Herbert and Crashaw. I examine female devotional desire at greater length in chapter 2.

6　Samuel Rutherford, *Christ Dying and Drawing Sinners to Himself* (London, 1647), 285. Further references supplied in the text.

7　Both as cited in Steinberg, *The Sexuality of Christ*, 17 (emphasis added).

8　*The Mysterie of Christs Nativitie* (London, 1614), sig. D2^{v}.

9　*Sermons* 4:358. Donne (still drawing upon Tertullian) continues: "These two, Body, and Soule, cannot be separated for ever, which, whilst they are together, concurre in all that either of them doe."

　　For an extended consideration of the materializations of the body in Donne's writings, see John Carey's tour de force, *John Donne: Life, Mind and Art*, rev. ed. (London: Faber and Faber, 1990), esp. chap. 5 ("Bodies"), chap. 6 ("Change"), and chap. 7 ("Death"). Elaine Scarry offers another eloquent discussion of Donne's corporeal poetics in "Donne: 'But yet the body is his booke,'" in *Literature and the Body: Essays on Populations and Persons*, ed. Elaine Scarry (Baltimore: Johns Hopkins University Press, 1988), 70–105. Yet as illuminating as Scarry's account of Donne's incorporation of the material body into his textual corpus is, this discussion is limited insofar as it remains surprisingly unconcerned with matters having to do with Donne's poetics and the *gendered* body. This is also the case with Carey's study.

10　See also Louis L. Martz's classic study *The Poetry of Meditation: A Study in English Religious Literature of the Seventeenth Century*, rev. ed. (New Haven: Yale University Press, 1962), which seeks to establish contiguities between seventeenth-century Protestant English devotional poetry and medieval and Counter-Reformation meditational methodologies. Particularly germane is Martz's discussion of the influence on metaphysical verse of Saint Ignatius Loyola's *Exercises* and their demand for a devotional "application of the senses"—that is, an intense corporealized imaging, stripe by stripe, nail by nail, of the events of Christ's Passion, or other biblical scenes (43–56, 71–82, and passim). The erotics of this influential devotional practice have been argued by Roland Barthes in *Sade/Fourier/Loyola*, trans. Richard Miller (Baltimore: Johns Hopkins University Press, 1997): " 'The *Exercises*,' says a Jesuit commentator, 'is an area at once formidable and desirable. . . . ' Indeed, anyone reading the *Exercises* cannot help but be struck by the mass of desire which agitates it. The immediate force of this desire is to be read in the very materiality of the objects whose representations Ignatius calls for: places in their precise, complete dimensions, characters in their costumes, their attitudes, their actions, their actual words. The most abstract things (which Ignatius calls 'invisibles') must find some material movement where they can picture themselves and form a *tableau vivant*. . . . [T]he basis, the force of materiality, the immediate total of desire, is of course the human body; a body incessantly mobilized into image by the play of imitation which establishes a literal analogy between the corporeality of the exercitant and that of Christ, whose existence, almost physiological, is to be rediscovered through personal anamnesis" (62).

11 Samuel Johnson, "Life of Cowley," in *Johnson's Lives of the Poets: A Selection*, ed. J. P. Hardy (Oxford: Clarendon Press, 1971), 12–13. The metaphysicals have continued to accrue charges of impropriety well past the time of Johnson, with Donne and Crashaw particularly being singled out. For example, C. S. Lewis, no great lover of Donne, terms Elegy 19 ("To His Mistress Going to Bed") "a pornographic poem," in "Donne and Love Poetry in the Seventeenth Century," in *Seventeenth-Century Studies Presented to Sir Herbert Grierson* (Oxford: Clarendon Press, 1938), 75–76. Indeed, this elegy was one of the poems censored from the posthumous publication of Donne's collected verse in 1633. See also Wilbur Sanders, *John Donne's Poetry* (Cambridge: Cambridge University Press, 1971), on Holy Sonnet 14 ("Batter my heart"): "In a queer way—queer when you think about the alleged subject [that is, Donne's desire to be raped into redemption]—the sonnet has a kind of knockabout vitality, as if the whole affair had been staged and could be enjoyed on that level" (130).

Perhaps even more than is the case with Donne, reading Crashaw has been critically constituted as something of a dirty pleasure. Here is T. S. Eliot: "Crashaw's images, even when entirely preposterous . . . give a kind of intellectual pleasure—it is a deliberate conscious perversity of language." See *For Lancelot Andrewes* (London: Faber and Faber, 1928), 96. In *Seven Types of Ambiguity* (New York: New Directions, 1947), William Empson similarly finds—and enjoys—"something weird and lurid" in Crashaw's verse (222). Commenting on the protean liquids of Crashaw's infamous poem "The Weeper," Robert Martin Adams likewise remarks, "The transformation of salt tears to milk is queer; raising the butterfat content to make cream is odder yet"; see his "Taste and Bad Taste in Metaphysical Poetry: Richard Crashaw and Dylan Thomas," *Hudson Review* 8 (1955): 66.

12 John Davies, *The Holy Roode or Christs Crosse,* in *The Complete Works of John Davies of Hereford,* 2 vols., ed. Alexander B. Grosart (New York: AMS Press, 1967), 1:10. Further references are according to page number and will be supplied in the text.

13 Mary Douglas, *Purity and Danger* (London: Routledge and Kegan Paul, 1969).

14 John Hayward, *The Sactuarie of a troubled soule* (London, 1604), pt. 2, 213.

15 "Meditation 1.10," *The Poems of Edward Taylor,* ed. Donald E. Stanford (New Haven: Yale University Press, 1960), 20-22. All citations of Taylor's poetry are according to this edition.

16 The senator from North Carolina denounced the photograph as a "sickening, abhorrent, and shocking act by an arrogant blasphemer." Letter from Helms to his constituents, 17 July 1989, cited in Steven C. Dubin, *Arresting Images: Impolitic Art and Uncivil Actions* (New York: Routledge, 1992), 97.

17 Barbara Kiefer Lewalski briefly treats Donne's "The Cross" in relation to Lipsius's *De Cruce* in *Protestant Poetics and the Seventeenth-Century Religious Lyric* (Princeton: Princeton University Press, 1979), 201-2. Further references supplied in the text.

18 This desire for a beautiful Christ remains culturally viable today. For instance, while casting for a 1996 revival of his hit 1970 musical *Jesus Christ Superstar,* composer Andrew Lloyd Webber insisted that the show's "Jesus has got to have sex appeal and real star quality" (*Newsweek,* 29 January 1996, 19). Thanks to Allys Dierker for calling my attention to this sound bite.

On Christ as a specifically homoerotic icon of male beauty, consider the following letter to the editor in a 1955 issue of *Physique Pictorial,* a (pre-hard core pornography) male "physical culture" magazine: "I would like to see [George] Quaintance portray a scene of Christ on the cross," writes one reader, identified only as "D. W., Michigan." "Though some pieces of evidence would indicate he was crucified nude, this would be offensive to good taste so he should be depicted in a loin cloth, but the two thieves could be shown nailed naked to their crosses. Such a painting could depict in the persons of the thieves the physical torture and humiliation of crucifixion, while emphasizing in the figure of Christ the transcendent spiritual values of this central event." See "Letters," *Physique Pictorial* 5 (winter 1955).

19 As cited in the accompanying program for the New Museum's retrospective of "Andres Serrano: Works 1983-1993." For Serrano's claim that "My religious imagery owes a lot to Renaissance art," see Lucy R. Lippard, "Andres Serrano: The Spirit and the Letter," *Art in America* 78 (April 1990): 240.

20 Vaughan develops a similar conceit of the body as closet in his poem "The Feast," where the soldier's penetrating spear is envisioned as "the key / Opening the way" to "my bed of rest!" (lines 63-65).

21 Curiously, what Crashaw imagines as being raped here is the water that passes over (and fails to cleanse) Pilate's guilty hands. Revisiting and rewriting the

story of Niobe, Crashaw's epigram enacts a second metamorphosis on the unfortunate nymph. Having already once been changed from maiden girl to "well-fam'd Fountaine," the Roman proctor's washing his hands of responsibility for Christ's death is an "Adult'rous touch" that alters Niobe yet again from flowing water to "Nothing but Teares."

22 See George Walton Williams, *Image and Symbol in the Sacred Poetry of Richard Crashaw* (Columbia: University of South Carolina Press, 1963), 119–23. Leah Marcus notes a similar thematic in Crashaw's verse in *Childhood and Cultural Despair: A Theme and Variations in Seventeenth-Century Literature* (Pittsburgh: University of Pittsburgh Press, 1978), 148.

23 Compare Aemilia Lanyer's lyric "To the Ladie *Lucie,* Countesse of Bedford," which likewise depicts Christ's residence within the closet of the heart:

> Me thinkes I see faire Virtue readie stand,
> T'unlocke the closet of your lovely breast,
> Holding the key of Knowledge in her hand,
> Key of that Cabinne where your self doth rest,
> To let him in, by whom her youth was blest
>> The true-love of your soule, your hearts delight,
>> Fairer than all the world in your cleare sight.
>
> . . . .
>
> Loe here he coms all stucke with pale deaths arrows:
>> In whose most pretious wounds your soule may reade
>> Salvation, while he (dying Lord) doth bleed.

(lines 1–7, 12–14)

Anne Clifford, another of Lanyer's female patrons, is similarly urged to "lodge him in the closet of your heart" ("To the Ladie *Anne,* Countesse of Dorcet," line 143).

24 Even George Walton Williams, Crashaw's usually rather reserved editor, seems unable to restrain himself here. Apparently taking his cues from his poet, Williams himself turns punningly indecorous in his commentary on this passage: " 'soft bowells . . . discharge,' however, by the process of elimination, has quite a different meaning," he notes; "it may be thought not in the best taste to introduce scatology into eschatology—the stanza has no Latin original" (*The Complete Poetry of Richard Crashaw,* 191).

25 Adams, "Taste and Bad Taste," 67.

26 Suggesting that we see sentimentality not so much as a specific "thematic or a particular subject matter but as a structure of relation, typically one involving the author-or-audience-relations of spectacle," Sedgwick calls attention in *Epistemology of the Closet* to a seemingly never-abating proliferation of deeply sentimentalized depictions of the exposed body of Jesus on the cross—in his pain and his passion—and links them to what she terms a "vast national wash of masculine self-pity" as expressed, for instance, in such genre writing di-

rected to men as the *New York Times* "About Men" column, country music, and the sports pages (142–45). "If the sentimental, as we have been taught, coincides topically with the feminine, with the place of women," Sedgwick asks, "then why should the foregrounded *male* physique be in an indicative relation to it?" (142). Noting how feminist criticism has successfully reversed the negative valuation of the category of "the sentimental," Sedgwick calls for further work in the "somewhat similar" rehabilitation of sentimentality as an important gay male project as well (144–45). This endeavor, I want to suggest, can be pushed back beyond the nineteenth-century novel (its usual starting point) to the enticing vagaries of Renaissance devotional materials and especially to Crashaw, who has regularly been derided for what are seen to be the effeminizing sentimental excesses of his devotional poetry.

27 On early modern conceptions of the body's solubility, see Gail Kern Paster's important, richly materialist account of humoral physiology and psychology, *The Body Embarrassed: Drama and the Disciplines of Shame in Early Modern England* (Ithaca: Cornell University Press, 1993). "Every subject," Paster writes, "grew up with a common understanding of his or her body as a semipermeable, irrigated container in which humors moved sluggishly." "This body," she continues, was "characterized by corporeal fluidity, openness, and porous boundaries" (8). In these terms, Crashaw's epigrammatic figurations show Christ incarnated as the hyperbolized body, as the ecstatic superflux of the corporealities described by Paster.

28 See Williams, *Image and Symbol*, 84–104. See also Austin Warren, *Richard Crashaw: A Study in Baroque Sensibility* (Baton Rouge: Louisiana State University Press, 1939): "All things flow. Crashaw's imagery runs in streams; the streams run together; image turns into image. His metaphors are sometimes so rapidly juxtaposed as to mix—they occur, that is, in a succession so swift as to prevent the reader from focusing separately upon each. The effect is often that of phantasmagoria" (192). Crashaw the poet, moreover, has become mingled with his own liquescent poetics: "a religious pourer forth of his divine Raptures and Meditations" is how he is nominated in William Winstanley's *Lives of the Most Famous English Poets* (1687), facsimile edition, with an introduction by William Riley Parker (Gainesville, Fla.: Scholars Facsimiles and Reprints, 1963), 101–2.

29 Linda Williams's *Hard Core: Power, Pleasure, and the "Frenzy of the Visible"* (Berkeley: University of California Press, 1989) offers a powerful account of (principally heterosexual) pornography's will-to-knowledge of the body; see esp. 48–57. According to Williams, pornography can be read as a discourse of the body, one motored by a "principle of maximum visibility"—a fetishizing drive to probe and to bring into heightened visibility the body's surfaces, orifices, and interior mechanisms.

30 Compare Mikhail Bakhtin on the grotesque body: "All these convexities and

orifices have a common characteristic; it is within them that the confines between bodies and between body and the world are overcome: there is an exchange and an interorientation" (Bakhtin, *Rabelais and His World*, trans. Hélèna Iswolsky [Bloomington: Indiana University Press, 1984], 317).

31 Michael C. Schoenfeldt, *Prayer and Power: George Herbert and Renaissance Courtship* (Chicago: University of Chicago Press, 1991), 249–50. Further references supplied in the text. Schoenfeldt cites the English translations of these Latin poems provided in *The Latin Poetry of George Herbert: A Bilingual Edition*, ed. Mark McCloskey and Paul R. Murphy (Athens: Ohio University Press, 1965).

32 In contrast, Schoenfeldt (following Robert Graves) discerns the feminine surfacing in the poem in terms of an allegorized female figure of Despair: "Graves perhaps overstates the case, but he is close to the truth when he suggests that 'the Divine Figure in the "The Bag" is fused with the figure of the temptress and at the end of the poem subordinate to her, when it has distinct feminine characteristics'" (249). (The citation here is to Graves's *Poetic Unreason and Other Studies* [London: Cecil Palmer, 1925], 62.) I am not sure whether or not "The Bag" presents a *personification* of despair, but, even if it does, it is a further stretch for Graves to envision such a personification as female, as "the temptress." What necessitates the gendering of "Despair" as female? Spenser's *The Faerie Queene*, for instance, allegorizes Despair as a male personification.

33 On the sexual meaning of "come" in the Renaissance, see Eric Partridge, *Shakespeare's Bawdy* (London: Routledge, Kegan and Paul, 1968), 81.

34 Empson accords Crashaw's epigram the distinction of instantiating his seventh and final type of ambiguity: "This is to show the unearthly relation to earth of the Christ, and with a sort of horror to excite adoration. . . . The second couplet is 'primitive' enough; a wide variety of sexual perversions can be included in the notion of sucking a long bloody teat which is also a deep wound. The sacrificial idea is aligned with incest, the infantile pleasures, and cannibalism; we contemplate the god with a sort of savage chuckle; he is made to flower, a monstrous hermaphrodite deity, in the glare of a short-circuiting of the human order" (*Seven Types of Ambiguity*, 221). Though his interpretations continue to vex most Crashavians, Empson remains the poet's best critic, appropriately matching in such readings Crashaw's extravagances with his own.

As a kind of modern cinematic analogue to the unsettling familial relations conceived in Crashaw's epigram, I would offer one of the most perverse moments in the 1973 film *The Exorcist* (directed by William Friedkin). This film is no less—perhaps all the more—seriously suffused with faith, ritual, and Christian religiosity for all its spectacularized blasphemies and violence. Indeed, three Roman Catholic priests were employed as consultants on the film, and two of them were given acting parts in it as well. The particular scene I have in mind occurs well into Regan's grotesque possession. Having barricaded her horrified mother in her bedroom and calling her a "bitch," the demonized child uses superhuman strength to mount her mother and force her head into her crotch. "Lick me! Eat me!" Regan orders. In addition to its sheer sexual vulgarity, this highly emblematic moment—like the final couplet of Crashaw's epigram—perversely upends proper parent/child roles. For here the child looks to give suck to the mother, rather than the mother nursing the child. Describing the scene in just such terms, William Paul's *Laughing Screaming: Modern Hollywood Horror and Comedy* (New York: Columbia University Press, 1994) rates it "the grossest inversion the film can muster" (304). Apparently Crashaw too envisioned this kind of familial inversion ("The Mother then must suck the Son") as profoundly unsettling, perhaps even horrifying: that is, as shocking but also, in keeping with metaphysical poetics, as devotionally provocative.

35 See Thomas Laqueur's *Making Sex: Body and Gender from the Greeks to Freud* (Cambridge: Harvard University Press, 1990), particularly chapter 4, for an extended historical discussion of the elasticity of gender in early modern biological conceptions: "The body," Laqueur shows at length here, "was far less fixed and far less constrained by categories of biological difference than it came to be after the eighteenth century" (106). See also Anthony Fletcher's *Gender, Sex, and Subordination in England 1500-1800* (New Haven: Yale University Press, 1995), esp. 3-98. Apart from the matter of same-sex—particularly female same-sex—eroticism, which is given a rather cursory treatment here, Fletcher's book usefully sums up a substantial amount of recent historical scholarship on the cultural ideologies and practices of gender and sex in early modern England.

36 Compare Jonathan Goldberg's reading of "Artillery," and other of Herbert's "Sacred Poems and Private Ejaculations" (as they are termed on the title page of *The Temple*), in *Voice Terminal Echo: Postmodernism and Renaissance Texts* (New York: Methuen, 1986), 110-11: "A scene of scattered seed, shooting stars, and the ejaculative traces of a forestalled and productive path: how to enter the poem, how to be on the page, where the words stay, yet nonetheless come."

37 The androgynizing formulations I cite are taken from (in order) Janel Mueller, "Women among the Metaphysicals: A Case, Mostly, of Being Donne For," *Modern Philology* 87 (1989): 153; E. Pearlman, "George Herbert's God," *English Literary Renaissance* 13 (1983): 107; Bynum, *Holy Feast and Holy Fast*, 261; Schoenfeldt, *Prayer and Power*, 250; and Marcus, *Childhood and Cultural Despair*, 148. An important exception to the practice of rerouting the homoerotic vectors of devotion to Christ along heterosexual circuits is Walter Hughes's " 'Meat Out of the Eater': Panic and Desire in American Puritan Poetry," in *Engendering Men: The Question of Male Feminist Criticism*, ed.

Joseph A. Boone and Michael Cadden (New York: Routledge, 1990), 102-21.

38 Eve Kosofsky Sedgwick, "Gosh, Boy George, You Must Be Awfully Secure in Your Masculinity!" in *Constructing Masculinity,* ed. Maurice Berger, Brian Wallis, and Simon Watson (New York: Routledge, 1995), 16. Sedgwick contextualizes her insight in terms of the work of Sandra Bem on psychological androgyny: Bem "had people rated on two scales, one measuring stereotypically female-ascribed traits and one measuring stereotypically male-ascribed ones; and found that many lucky people score high on both, many other people score low on both, and most importantly that a high score on either of them does not predict a low score on the other."

39 Steinberg himself cites Levey's appraisal as an epigraph to one of the new chapters he adds to his revised and substantially expanded edition of *The Sexuality of Christ,* 298.

40 Among the critics who have been applying Bynum's work on medieval female piety to Renaissance lyric poetry are Schoenfeldt, *Prayer and Power;* Shuger, *The Renaissance Bible;* Thomas F. Healy, "Crashaw and the Sense of History," in *New Perspectives on the Life and Art of Richard Crashaw,* ed. John R. Roberts (Columbia, Missouri: University of Missouri Press, 1990), 49-65; Eugene R. Cunnar, "Crashaw's 'Sancta Maria Dolorum': Controversy and Coherence," also in Roberts, *New Perspectives,* 99-126; and Anthony Low, *The Reinvention of Love: Poetry, Politics, and Culture from Sidney to Milton* (Cambridge: Cambridge University Press, 1993).

41 Caroline Walker Bynum, "The Body of Christ in the Later Middle Ages: A Reply to Leo Steinberg," in *Fragmentation and Redemption,* 79-118. This essay first appeared in *Renaissance Quarterly* 39 (1986): 399-439.

42 See the revised edition of *The Sexuality of Christ,* 364-89, for Steinberg's own, highly polemical response to Bynum's critique, in which, among many other demurrals, he remarks the dubiety of Bynum's adducing the mystical writings of medieval nuns and saints as a master gloss on the range of meanings of the *Renaissance* painters he considers.

43 Bynum herself makes this point in *Fragmentation and Redemption,* 85. See also Arnold I. Davidson, "Sex and the Emergence of Sexuality," *Critical Inquiry* 14 (1987): 16-48, esp. 26. Steinberg, however, remains unmoved by this criticism, whether given in the form of Bynum's refusal of sexual meanings or Davidson's Foucauldian constructionism (see *The Sexuality of Christ,* 326-29).

44 Richard C. Trexler, "Gendering Jesus Crucified," in *Iconography at the Crossroads,* ed. Brendan Cassidy (Princeton: Department of Art and Archeology, Princeton University, 1993), 108. Further references supplied in the text.

45 Wendy Doniger, *Women, Androgynes, and Other Mythical Beasts* (Chicago: University of Chicago Press, 1980), 87-93.

46 See, for instance, Parama Roy, "As the Master Saw Her," in *Cruising the Performative,* 112-29, for a more complex account of the erotics of Hindu

devotion, one that recognizes the devotional mobilizations of homoerotic as well as heteroerotic forms of desire.

47   For example, see Bynum's chapter on "Women Mystics and Eucharistic Devotion" in *Fragmentation and Redemption*, 123, 131–34. Interestingly, this essay originally appeared in 1984, several years before the publication of *Holy Feast and Holy Fast*, a book, I have been arguing, that prefers and valorizes thematics of food and feeding over those having to do with sex. Bynum's earlier essay allows not only more erotic scope to female devotional expression, but also more latitude for the heterodox and the transgressive: "We misunderstand the power of the erotic, nuptial mysticism of Low Country figures like Hadewijch and Beatrice of Nazareth if we project onto their image of lover seeking Lover stereotyped notions of brides as passive and submissive. Their search for Christ took them through a frenzy they called insanity (*orewoet* in Flemish, *aestus* or *insania amoris* in Latin)" (134).

48   *The Letters of St. Catherine of Siena*, trans. and ed. Suzanne Noffke (Binghamton, N.Y.: Medieval and Renaissance Texts and Studies, 1988), 128. Bynum notes elsewhere that in a vision the Viennese Beguine Agnes Blannbekin received Christ's foreskin in her mouth and found it as sweet as honey (*Fragmentation and Redemption*, 186).

49   Interestingly, Catherine's male biographer Raymond of Capua reports a vision of his own, in which Catherine's female face metamorphosed into a bearded, male one. Such regenderings, Bynum suggests, functions as miraculous endorsements of "the woman's visionary ability authenticated either by seeing her as male or by seeing a male Christ acting through her" (*Fragmentation and Redemption*, 39). The homoerotic possibilities of such mystic transsexualism are, however, left unexplored here.

50   Consider also Bynum's emphatic de-eroticization of breast imagery in devotional iconography: "There is reason to think that medieval viewers saw bared breasts (at least in painting and sculpture) not primarily as sexual but as the food with which they were iconographically associated" (*Fragmentation and Redemption*, 86). As evidence, she points to numerous late medieval pictorial representations that situate the lactating Virgin Mary in a grape arbor or associate her nourishing breast with other modes of food production and distribution. Furthermore, Bynum contends that Bernard of Clairvaux's textual gloss on Song of Songs 1:1–2 ("For your breasts are better than wine, smelling sweet of the best ointments")

> makes clear not only the medieval tendency to associate breasts with food (*rather than sex*) but also the medieval tendency to assimilate Church as Christ's spouse with Church as Christ's body. Bernard said explicitly that Christ's bride is the Church who nurses us, and that the bride-Church nurses from Christ who is also therefore a mother, and that this motherly body is all of us. (93; emphasis added)

Yet is Bernard, as Bynum paraphrases him, really directing us to understand that breasts are so exclusively to be associated with food instead of sex? Rather, there appears to be as much talk of the conjugal in Bernard's exegesis of this text as there is of maternal nursing. Moreover, given Bynum's emphasis on the polysemous nature of the body and its meanings, why force an interpretive choice between *either* the nutritive body *or* the sexual one? Certainly such a division does not obtain in seventeenth-century devotional literature, which explores the breast imagery of the Canticles in ways, as I will be discussing in chapter 2, that remain patently erotic, as well as, in some cases, maternal.

Also relevant here is Foucault's discussion of the recurrent conjoining of sex and food in Greek philosophical texts concerned with the appetitive:

> This association between the ethics of sex and the ethics of the table was a constant factor in ancient culture. . . . Food, wines, and the relations with women and boys constituted analogous ethical material; they brought forces into play that were natural, but that always tended to be excessive; and they all raised the same question: how could one, how must one, "make use" (*chrēsthai*) of this dynamics of pleasures, desires, and acts? A question of right use. As Aristotle expresses it, "all men enjoy in some way or another both savoury foods and wines and sexual intercourse, but not all men do so as they ought." (*The History of Sexuality,* vol. 2, *The Use of Pleasure,* trans. Robert Hurley [New York: Vintage, 1986], 50–52)

Eating and having sex have also been conceptually coupled by Christian philosophers. "There are," Augustine writes, "two works of the flesh upon which the preservation of mankind depends. . . . The first . . . has to do with taking nourishment. . . . But men subsist by this support only as far as they themselves are concerned; for they do not take measures for a succession by eating and drinking, but by marrying. . . . Since, then, the human race subsists in such a wise that two supports . . . are indispensable, the wise and faithful man descends to both from a sense of duty; he does not fall into them through lust" (Sermon 1, 23–24, as cited in Steinberg, *The Sexuality of Christ,* 133).

Approaching Bynum's work from a different but related vantage, Kathleen Biddick provides a searching critique of the essentialism that underwrites both Bynum's medieval historiography and her feminism in "Genders, Bodies, Borders: Technologies of the Visible," *Speculum* 68 (1993): 389–418.

51 See also Bynum's *Fragmentation and Redemption,* 92: "If we as modern people find Steinberg's argument more titillating and Steinberg's illustrations more fascinating than those I will consider now, this may suggest merely that there is a modern tendency to find sex more interesting than feeding, suffering or salvation. It may also suggest that, pace Huizinga, twentieth-century readers and viewers are far more literal-minded in interpreting symbols than were

the artists, exegetes and devotional writers of the fifteenth and sixteenth centuries."

52 According to Bataille, the very eroticism of the erotic likewise subsists in its taboo components: "The simple taboo created eroticism in the first place . . . pleasure was bound up with transgression" (*Erotism*, 127).

53 J. C. Levenson, "Donne's *Holy Sonnets*, XIV" (1954), repr. in part in *John Donne's Poetry*, 2d ed., ed. Arthur L. Clements (New York: Norton, 1992), 327.

54 John E. Parish, "No. 14 of Donne's *Holy Sonnets*" (1963), also excerpted in Clements, *John Donne's Poetry*, 332. See too George Knox, "Donne's *Holy Sonnets*, XIV" (1956), likewise reprinted in Clements: "The sexual ravishment involves no bisexuality on the part of the poet nor does it require our imagining literally the relation between man and God in heterosexual terms. The traditions of Christian mysticism allow such symbolism of ravishment as a kind of 'as if' " (329).

55 "Oh my black soul! now thou art summoned / By sickness, death's herald, and champion; / Thou art like a pilgrim, which abroad hath done / Treason, and durst not turn to whence *he* is fled, / Or like a thief, which till death's doom be read, / Wisheth *himself* delivered from prison; / But damned and haled to execution / Wisheth that still *he* might be imprisoned" (lines 1–8; emphasis added).

56 William Kerrigan, "The Fearful Accommodations of John Donne," *English Literary Renaissance* 4 (1974): 340. Further references supplied in the text.

57 Stanley Fish, "Masculine Force: Donne and Verbal Power," in *Soliciting Interpretation: Literary Theory and Seventeenth-Century English Poetry*, ed. Elizabeth D. Harvey and Katharine Eisaman Maus (Chicago: University of Chicago Press, 1990), 242, 241.

58 Wilbur Sanders, *John Donne's Poetry*, 129. See also Anthony Low, *The Reinvention of Love: Poetry, Politics and Culture from Sidney to Milton*, 79: "The only poem in which Donne assumes the female part unequivocally to the end is 'Batter my heart.'" Arthur F. Marotti's *John Donne, Coterie Poet* (Madison: University of Wisconsin Press, 1986) provides a notable exception to the spate of heterosexualing readings of this sonnet: "The sexualization of the speaker's relationship to God at the end of the sonnet is shocking partly because it has the shape of a passive homosexual fantasy." The full implications of this insight for an analysis of gender and desire in Donne's poetics are left unexplored by Marotti, however, in the elaboration of his larger "Love is not Love" argument that what appears to be amorous courtship in Renaissance poetry is actually an encoded solicitation of aristocratic patronage in a homosocial courtly sphere: "Being loved in the spiritual homoerotic context of 'Batter my heart' corresponded to being favored in the political order" (259–

60). See also David Loewenstein's chapter on "Politics and Religion" in *The Cambridge Companion to English Poetry: Donne to Marvell*, ed. Thomas N. Corns (Cambridge: Cambridge University Press, 1993): "In the sonnet 'Batter my heart,' Donne's Calvinistic God . . . becomes, in the poem's three successive quatrains, a metal worker, a warrior-king, and a male lover" (11).

59   Ann Baynes Coiro, "New-found-land: Teaching Metaphysical Poetry from the Other Side," in *Approaches to Teaching the Metaphysical Poets*, ed. Sidney Gottlieb (New York: Modern Language Association of America, 1990), 86. Further references supplied in the text. Compare Katharine Eisaman Maus, *Inwardness and Theater in the English Renaissance* (Chicago: University of Chicago Press, 1995), 193: "When Donne in *Holy Sonnets* 14 asks to be raped by God, takes on a position that seems 'feminine' or passive, the point is that his position is already feminine, insofar as God is always already inside him."

60   Achsah Guibbory, "John Donne," in *The Cambridge Companion to English Poetry: Donne to Marvell*, 141–42.

61   On the cultural, as well as political or civic, feminization of the penetrated or "passive" partner, see David M. Halperin, *One Hundred Years of Homosexuality and Other Essays on Greek Love* (New York: Routledge, 1990), 32–36, 47, and passim. For a discussion of penetration and virility within the economies of gender in contemporary gay pornography, see Rambuss, "Homodevotion," in *Cruising the Performative,* esp. 82–84.

It would be an oversimplification, however, to claim that it was always the case in early modern culture that sodomy categorically regendered the sodomized male as female. For a striking counterexample, see Donne's anti-Jesuitical polemic, *Ignatius His Conclave,* and its account of the lechery of an Italian cardinal who gave "full reine to his licentiousnesse," piling outrageous transgression upon transgression:

> his stomacke was not towards young beardlesse boyes, nor such greene fruit; for hee did not thinke, that hee went farre inough from the right Sex, *except hee had a manly,* a reverend, and a bearded Venus. Neither staied he there; but his witty lust proceeded further; . . . striving to equall the licentiousnesse of Sodomits, which would have had the Angels . . . he tooke a Cleargy-man, one of the portion and lot of the Lord: and so made the maker of God, a Priest subject to his lust; . . . that his Venus might bee the more monstrous, hee would have her in a Mitre. And yet his prodigious lust was not at the height; as much as hee could he added; and having found a Man, a Cleargy-man, a Bishop, he did not sollicite him with entreaties, & rewards, but ravished him by force. (*Ignatius His Conclave,* ed. T. S. Healy [Oxford: Oxford University Press, 1969], 41, 43; emphasis added)

In certain respects, Donne's invective against the Catholic cardinal who sodomizes a priest—a grown or bearded man, that is, not a youth—can be seen to mark not so much the opposite but the obverse, the demonic doubling, of the ravishment Donne himself desires in "Batter my heart." In the episode I have cited above (as is also the case, I would suggest, in Holy Sonnet 14), the transgressivity of the cardinal's buggery is heightened by the marked virility of the buggered, his "bearded Venus." The implication here is that the act would be less spectacularly abominable if it had been perpetrated against "young beardlesse boyes," a class of males more readily seen as androgynous or effeminized.

62   The figure of Ganymede—the boy-bride/servant—may also be looming behind these lines from one of John Saltmarsh's devotional lyrics, with their conflation of the lover/page role: "Who would not be thy spouse? O let me be / But a poore page to wait on thee." In John Saltmarsh, "Poems Upon Some Holy raptures of David," in *Poemata Sacra Latine et Anglice Scripta* (Cambridge, 1636), 15.

63   Thomas Blount, *Glossographia: Or a Dictionary Interpreting the Hard Words of Whatsoever Language, Now Used in our Refined English Tongue* (London, 1670), 596.

64   Leonard Barkan, *Transuming Passion: Ganymede and the Erotics of Humanism* (Stanford: Stanford University Press, 1991), 26. Mignault, Barkan suggests, "may be operating out of such a peaceful orthodoxy that none of the (somewhat risible) implications that occur to us would occur to him. That we cannot claim to know, nor does any amount of History of Ideas qualify us to limit what a person in a certain age is capable of thinking. But we do not have the warrant to assume that only we are clever enough—or sufficiently unblinded by belief—to be aware of the difficulties in the equation between pederasty and sacred rapture" (26).

65   Alexander Ross, *Mystagogus Poeticus, or the Muses Interpreted* (1647), ed. John R. Glenn (New York: Garland, 1987), 335.

66   On the figure of Ganymede in Renaissance schemes of representation, in addition to Barkan's eloquent *Transuming Passion*, see James M. Saslow, *Ganymede in the Renaissance: Homosexuality in Art and Society* (New Haven: Yale University Press, 1986). While Saslow's encyclopedic study treats both the erotic and the religious significances of Ganymede, he tends to keep these sets of meanings more binarized than Traherne's poem "Love," or even some of the images and texts Saslow himself discusses, show them to be. Saslow's discussion appears to be premised on the notion that a spiritualized employment of the Ganymede trope would necessarily preclude any concurrent activation of its erotic valences—an ahistorical polarization of the religious and the erotic that I want here to challenge.

67   The starting point here would have to be Michel Foucault's vastly influential study of *The History of Sexuality*, especially vol. 1, *An Introduction*, trans.

Robert Hurley (New York: Vintage 1990). See also the crucial work of Alan Bray in *Homosexuality in Renaissance England* (London: Gay Men's Press, 1982) and "Homosexuality and the Signs of Male Friendship in Elizabethan England," *History Workshop Journal* 29 (1990): 1–19. Bray's essay is reprinted in *Queering the Renaissance*, ed. Jonathan Goldberg (Durham: Duke University Press, 1994). This anthology presents essays that engage and extend the groundbreaking work of Foucault and Bray in highly productive ways. Other historically oriented, book-length studies of pre- and early modern sexuality that have been especially useful to me here are Halperin, *One Hundred Years of Homosexuality;* Goldberg, *Sodometries: Renaissance Texts, Modern Sexualities* (Stanford: Stanford University Press, 1992); Valerie Traub, *Desire and Anxiety: Circulations of Sexuality in Shakespearean Drama* (London: Routledge, 1992); Eve Kosofsky Sedgwick, *Between Men: English Literature and Male Homosocial Desire* (New York: Columbia University Press, 1985); and Alan Sinfield, *The Wilde Century: Effeminacy, Oscar Wilde, and the Queer Moment* (New York: Columbia University Press, 1994). George Chauncey's important revisionary work on American homosexual cultures in the early decades of the twentieth century suggests that the full consolidation of distinct subjectivities based on sexual identity (rather than—or along with—gender identity) occurs even later than the series of late-nineteenth-century turning points posited by Foucault. See his *Gay New York: Gender, Urban Culture, and the Making of the Gay Male World, 1890–1940* (New York: Harper Collins, 1994).

Most recently, Mark D. Jordan's *The Invention of Sodomy in Christian Theology* (Chicago: University of Chicago Press, 1997) provides an acute exposé of the crucial, if not always coherent, processes in medieval moral theology by which various homoerotic acts and desires became abstracted into the vilified categories of first sodomy and then the sodomite. "The credit—or rather, the blame—for inventing the word *sodomia*, 'Sodomy,' must go," Jordan writes, "to the eleventh-century theologian Peter Damian. He coined it quite deliberately on analogy to *blasphemia*, 'blasphemy,' which is to say, on analogy to the most explicit sin of denying God. Indeed, and from its origin, Sodomy is as much a theological category as trinity, incarnation, sacrament, or papal infallibility" (29). Jordan's scholarship stands as complementary to Foucault's in many respects, but it is also marked by some notable conceptual and historical departures. For instance, although he agrees that "Being a Sodomite is . . . not an identity in ways that might occur to a modern reader" (57), Jordan recovers the conceptual terms by which a specifically medical analysis of same-sex copulation is undertaken in Avicenna's *Canon of Medicine,* thus demonstrating that "there is no need [contra Foucault] to wait for the nineteenth-century 'homosexual' in order to have some same-sex behavior reduced to a medical identity" (123). Avicenna's diagnosis, Jordan recounts, suggests that sodomitic behavior could be due to naturally occurring physiology, thus raising the possibility that the proper response to this condition, if any is needed, would be medical rather than moral or legal (see also 156, 163–64).

68 John Rainolds, *Th'Overthrow of Stage-Players* (London, 1599), 10, 32, quoted in Bray, *Homosexuality in Renaissance England*, 17.

69 Thomas Shepard, *The Sincere Convert* (1641), in *The Works of Thomas Shepard*, 3 vols. (Boston: Doctrinal Tract and Book Society, 1853; repr. New York: AMS Press, 1967), 1:28. See Warner, "New England Sodom," 348–49, in *Queering the Renaissance*, for a discussion of this text.

70 Cited in Jonathan Ned Katz, *Gay/Lesbian Almanac* (New York: Harper and Row, 1983), 95–96.

71 This recognition has also motored a substantial amount of some of the most compelling scholarship on Shakespeare and Renaissance drama in recent years. See, among many such exemplary instances, the following book-length studies: Jeffrey Masten, *Textual Intercourse: Collaboration, Authorship, and Sexualities in Renaissance Drama* (Cambridge: Cambridge University Press, 1997); Stephen Orgel, *Impersonations: The Performance of Gender in Shakespeare's England* (Cambridge: Cambridge University Press, 1996); Valerie Traub, *Desire and Anxiety*; Jonathan Goldberg, *Sodometries*, esp. chaps. 4–5; and Marjorie Garber, *Vested Interests: Cross-Dressing and Cultural Anxiety* (New York: Routledge, 1992), chap. 3.

72 Michael Warner, "Tongues Untied: Memoirs of a Pentecostal Boyhood," *Village Voice Literary Supplement* (February 1993), 14; repr. in *The Material Queer: A LesBiGay Cultural Studies Reader*, ed. Donald Morton (Boulder, Colo.: Westview Press, 1996), 39–45.

73 Schoenfeldt offers a more extended reading of this poem in *Prayer and Power*, noting how in the next stanza entering into the church "is likened to the entry into another's body": "Now I in you without a body move, / Rising and falling with your wings: / We both together sweetly live and love" (lines 5–7). "'Comfort, I'le die,' declares the speaker," Schoenfeldt continues, "anticipating a death which is both spiritual and sexual" (241).

74 Compare Bataille: "The one who sacrifices is free, . . . free to throw himself suddenly *outside of himself*" ("Sacrificial Mutilation and the Severed Ear of Vincent Van Gogh," in *Visions of Excess: Selected Writings*, ed. Allan Stoekl [Minneapolis: University of Minnesota Press, 1985], 70).

75 Leo Bersani, "Is the Rectum a Grave?" in *AIDS: Cultural Analysis, Cultural Activism*, ed. Douglas Crimp (Cambridge: MIT Press, 1988), 217–18. Further references supplied in the text. Bersani polemically advances this revaluation of sex against what he terms "the redemptive reinvention of sex" that has been undertaken by both feminist and gay and lesbian theorists of sexuality, a project with a "frequently hidden agreement about sexuality as being, in its essence, less disturbing, less socially abrasive, less violent, more respectful of 'personhood' than it has been in a male-dominated, phallocen-

tric culture" (215). In this respect, Bersani perversely aligns himself with the position of antipornography crusaders Andrea Dworkin and Catherine Mac-Kinnon. Dworkin and MacKinnon regard all pornography as inherently violent, whether or not it involves rape or explicit sadomasochism, because they see pornography as eroticizing operations of patriarchal power and inequality that inhere in essentially all "real world" sexual and social interactions between men and women. Bersani parts company with them, however, in the positive value he ascribes to sex understood in terms of a phantasmatic of power and dominance. Whereas the connection between sex and power makes pornography (and apparently most forms of sex for that matter) hateful to Dworkin and MacKinnon, Bersani would have us value it for just these reasons:

> [Dworkin and MacKinnon] have given us the reasons why pornography must be multiplied and not abandoned, and, more profoundly, the reasons for defending, for cherishing the very sex they find so hateful. Their indictment of sex—their refusal to prettify it, to romanticize it, to maintain that fucking has anything to do with community or love—has had the immensely desirable effect of publicizing, of lucidly laying out for us, the inestimable value of sex as—at least in certain of its ineradicable aspects—anticommunal, antiegalitarian, antinurturing, antiloving. (215)

Sex, then, isn't a good thing because one happily acquires a sense of an integrated self from it; rather, the experience of sex—which Bersani correlates with passive anal sex—is a good thing because its shattering power prevents us from unabatingly maintaining our subjectivities. The penetrated rectum thus serves as the "grave" in which "the masculine ideal . . . of proud subjectivity is buried" (222). Given this notion of the sexual, however, Bersani's discussion seems to presuppose that everyone having sex is in this "passive," penetrated position—that everyone is in fact a bottom. Yet of course every bottom requires a top. What thus goes unelaborated in Bersani's account of the phantasmatic power of sex—an account clearly written from the vantage of the bottom—is the structure of experience of the partner who performs the role of the top.

76 Milton's anti-licensing tract *Aeropagitica* instances this conception of the perverse. Discussing the heresy of Arminianism (a theology that asserted free choice and agency over Calvinistic predestination), Milton notes how "the acute and distinct Arminius was perverted merely by the perusing of a nameless discourse written at Delft, which at first he took in hand to confute." (249). See also Jonathan Dollimore, *Sexual Dissidence: Augustine to Wilde, Freud to Foucault* (Oxford: Clarendon Press, 1991), 119–47, for a fascinating discussion of what Dollimore terms "the theology rather than the sexology of perversion" (27).

Donne himself was a religious convert, having turned away from Catholicism—a literal perversion from the faith of his family, whose ancestors included the sister of Thomas More. Furthermore, one of Donne's uncles, Jasper Heywood, headed the Jesuit mission in England during the poet's youth.

77 See Bray, *Homosexuality in Renaissance England,* 19-30, where he argues that homosexuality "was not part of the chain of being, or the harmony of the created world or its universal dance. . . . It was none of these things because it was not conceived of as part of the created order at all; it was part of its dissolution. And as such it was not a sexuality in its own right, but existed as a potential for confusion and disorder in one undivided sexuality" (25).

78 On the indictment of Christian/Jewish marriage as a sodomitical violation of the cultural order, see Theo van der Meer, "The Persecutions of Sodomites in Eighteenth-Century Amsterdam: Changing Perceptions of Sodomy," in *The Pursuit of Sodomy: Male Homosexuality in Renaissance and Enlightenment Europe,* ed. Kent Gerard and Gert Hekma (New York: Harrington Park Press, 1989), 265. On the importance of structures of alliance—"a system of marriage, of fixation and development of kinship ties, of transmission of names and possessions"—in the regulation of sexuality, see Foucault, *The History of Sexuality,* vol. 1, *An Introduction,* 106-14.

No one, it seems to me, has taken up the homophobically performative diffusions and confusions of the (still) slippery category of sodomy more masterfully than Jonathan Goldberg does in *Sodometries;* see esp. 1-26. See also Janet E. Halley, "*Bowers v. Hardwick* in the Renaissance," in *Queering the Renaissance,* 15-39. Halley masterfully anatomizes the 1986 Supreme Court decision against consensual "sodomy" and the warrant for such a ruling the Court sought to locate in early modern proscriptions against sodomy—proscriptions ahistorically misunderstood by the court to retain a strictly homosexual meaning.

79 Cited in Steinberg, *The Sexuality of Christ,* 46.

80 See Dubin's *Arresting Images,* 90-93, for a summary of the religious controversy surrounding the theatrical release of Scorsese's film version of *The Last Temptation of Christ.*

81 Richard Baines, "A note Containing the opinion on Christopher Marly Concerning his damnable Judgment of Religion, and scorn of Gods word," in *Marlowe: The Critical Heritage, 1588-1896,* ed. Millar Maclure (London: Routledge, 1979), 37. Interestingly, Marlowe, according to Baines, ascribed a transitivity of erotic object choice (both male and female) to Christ that is analogous to what we have seen expressed in sexualized devotional lyrics of Donne and Traherne. For, in addition to Christ's sodomizing of John, we are told that "the woman of Samaria & her sister were whores & that Christ knew them dishonestly."

Baines's scandalous accusations were reiterated by Thomas Kyd. Kyd, however, shifts (and, to a certain extent, veils) his expression of Marlowe's notions about Christ and male/male love by replacing Baines's gospel framework with a Virgilian referent: Kyd thus writes to Sir John Puckering that Marlowe "wold report St John to be our saviour Christes Alexis. I cover it with reverence and trembling that is that Christ did love him with an extraordinary love" ("Kyd's Unsigned Note to [Sir John] Puckering," in *The Life of Marlowe and The Tragedy of Dido Queen of Carthage*, ed. C. F. Tucker Brooke [London: Methuen, 1930], 107).

82 On this point see Bray, *Homosexuality in Renaissance England*, 19–30, and Goldberg, *Sodometries*, 19–20.

83 Tony Kushner, *Angels in America: A Gay Fantasia on National Themes, Part 1, Millennium Approaches* (New York: Theatre Communications Group, 1992), act 2, scene 5, and act 3, scenes 1 and 6; and *Part 2, Perestroika* (New York: Theatre Communications Group, 1994), act 2, scene 2.

84 Jonathan Weinberg provides a more extended treatment of homoeroticism in Hartley's work in *Speaking for Vice: Homosexuality in the Art of Charles Demuth, Marsden Hartley, and the First American Avant-Garde* (New Haven: Yale University Press, 1993). See 29–31 and 180–81 for Weinberg's discussion of this particular painting.

85 See Juan Davila and Paul Foss, *The Mutilated Pietà* (Surry Hills, Australia: Artspace Publications, 1985).

86 On Donne's dress rehearsal for his death/marriage to Christ see Izaak Walton's "Life of Donne" (1640): "A monument being resolved upon, Dr. Donne sent for a carver to make for him in wood the figure of an urn, giving him directions for the compass and height of it; and to bring with it a board, of the just height of his body. 'These being got, then without delay a choice painter was got to be in readiness to draw [Donne's] picture, which was taken as followeth.—Several charcoal fires being first made in his large study, he brought with him into that place his winding-sheet in his hand, and having put off all his clothes, had this sheet put on him, and so tied with knots at his head and feet, and his hands so placed as dead bodies are usually fitted, to be shrowded and put into their coffin, or grave. Upon this urn he thus stood, with his eyes shut, and with so much of the sheet turned aside as might shew his lean, pale, and death-like face, which was purposely turned towards the East, from whence he expected the second coming of his and our Saviour Jesus.' In this posture he was drawn at his just height; and when the picture was fully finished, he caused it to be set by his bed-side, where it continued and became his hourly object till his death" (Izaak Walton, *The Complete Angler and The Lives of Donne, Wotton, Hooker, Herbert and Sanderson,* ed. Alfred W. Pollard [London: Macmillan, 1906], 234).

87 Sigmund Freud, "Psycho-Analytic Notes on an Autobiographical Account of a Case of Paranoia (Dementia Paranoides)" (1911), in *The Standard Edition of the Complete Psychological Works of Sigmund Freud,* 24 vols., ed. James Strachey (London: Hogarth Press, 1953–74), 12:32. Further citations supplied in the text.

2 DEVOTION AND DESIRE

1 "The Rapture," lines 105, 114. Cited according to *The Poems of Thomas Carew,* ed. Rhodes Dunlap (Oxford: Clarendon Press, 1957). For this poem's nomination as "the sexiest of the century," see William Kerrigan and Gordon Braden, *The Idea of the Renaissance* (Baltimore: Johns Hopkins University Press, 1989), 180.

2 It is worth noting that Crashaw does not simply appropriate the terms and figures of Carew's seductive lyric for his devotional purpose. In Carew's poem, it is a male lover who looks forward to "Deflowring the fresh virgins of the Spring" and "rifl[ing] all the sweets, that dwell / In my delicious Paradise" (lines 58–60). Crashaw, in echoing Carew's lyric, regenders these cavalierisms, reassigning the active role from the male lover (Christ in this case) to the devout female addressee of his ode.

3 See, in particular, Barbara Lewalski's *Protestant Poetics and Seventeenth-Century Religious Lyric:* "Crashaw writes out of a very different aesthetics emanating from Trent and the continental Counter Reformation, which stresses sensory stimulation and church ritual (rather than scripture) as means to devotion and to mystical transcendence" (12). Lewalski's account presents Crashaw as always already a disciple of Rome, when in reality his conversion occurred relatively late in his career, and probably had more to do with the fact that, by the 1640s, the Laudian Anglicanism with which Crashaw was identified was no longer a viable option in England.

4 In this study, I am less interested in parsing the differences between Catholicism and Protestantism, or even between the strands of Protestantism itself, than I am in working from their points of confluence and their shared devotional lexicons. My sense is that English devotional expression in this period is a more pliable cultural formation than it would appear from the overly streamlined Reformation contours accorded it in Lewalski's influential *Protestant Poetics and Seventeenth-Century Religious Lyric.* In her drive to filter a distinctly "Protestant poetics," Lewalski, as I noted previously, not only effectively exiles Crashaw—and the kinds of religious, national, and stylistic hybridity he so powerfully represents—from the authentic line of English religious lyric; she also downplays significant and productive cross-filiations that transpire between continental Catholic devotional materials and the other,

"more mainstream" English Protestant authors (Donne, Herbert, Vaughan, and Taylor) who serve as the focus of her study.

Conversely, Helen C. White's *English Devotional Literature (Prose): 1600–1640* (Madison: University of Wisconsin Press, 1931) makes the case that English authors were rather enviously impressed by the wealth of continental Catholic devotional materials (65). This richness was measured not only by volume and variety, but also in terms of the spiritual luster of Catholic texts—an allure English writers themselves felt had not yet widely been achieved by the Reformation's own, albeit more doctrinally sound, devotional endeavors. White further points out that the task of translating (and theologically amending where necessary) Catholic devotional works into English was not only permitted but was sometimes even encouraged. Indeed, many English Protestant divines were more than willing, when it came to matters of devotion, to supplement Scripture and sermon with what had been drawn from outside the purview of the Reformed. Thus we find Richard Brathwait's devotional miscellany *The Spiritual Spicerie* (London, 1638) stocked with the savor of prayers, meditations, and "Motives to Piety" culled from Augustine, Bernard, Bonaventure, and Aquinas, among others. Alexander Grosse opens his *Sweet and Soule-Perswading Inducements Leading Unto Christ* (London, 1632) with a tone-setting epigraph taken from Saint Bernard's sermons on the *Canticles,* a body of devotional commentary that remained influential throughout the period. Similarly, William Crashaw (father of the poet, though himself a staunch Puritan) bestows his English verse translation of *The Complaint or Dialogue Betwixt the Soule and the Bodie of a damned man* (London, 1616), a text that was also thought to have been composed by Bernard, on "an age that needs al helps to holinesse, and inticements to devotion" (sig. A3ᵛ). What's more, White points out that it was common practice for English Protestants traveling abroad to carry or to post home copies of Catholic prayer books and spiritual treatises not available in England (142–43). On the relation between Romanist and English devotional writings, see also Martz, *The Poetry of Meditation,* esp. 6–13.

5 John Saltmarsh, "A Meditation upon the Song of Songs," in his *Poemata sacra,* 13.

6 Sarah Davy, *Heaven Realized, or the holy pleasure of daily intimate communion with God* (London, 1670), sig. A3. Further references supplied in the text. Although the title page informs us that this memoir/devotional handbook is "a part of the precious relics written with [Davy's] own hand," it is worth bearing in mind that this text was compiled, edited, and published after Davy's death by her minister "A. P." (Anthony Palmer?). The male editorship of *Heaven Realized* complicates any unmediated ascription of the designation of "women's writing" to this text, as well as others like it penned by women but published (posthumously or not) under male editorial supervision.

7 Alexander Grosse, *Sweet and Soule-Persuading Inducements Leading Unto Christ* (London, 1632), sig. A2. Further references supplied in the text.

8 "G. B.," *A Weeks Preparation Towards a Worthy Receiving of the Lords Supper* (London, 1679), 38, 79–80. Further references supplied in the text.

9 John Saltmarsh, *Holy Discoveries and Flames* (London, 1640), 18.

10 In his edition of Taylor's poetry, Stanford glosses the term *Spermodote* as "giver of seeds." On Taylor's devotional erotics and homoerotics, see Walter Hughes, " 'Meat Out of the Eater,' " in *Engendering Men*, ed. Boone and Cadden, 102–21. Hughes scrutinizes the tensions in Taylor's poetry, as well as in the religious writings of Michael Wigglesworth, attendant upon their usage of erotic desire as a means for expressing passionate devotion to Christ. Hughes terms such expression "an anomaly in their lives"—"lives," he continues, "that could not *legitimately* include passionate, erotic attachments to other men." The result for these poets, as Hughes draws out, appears to be a jumble of affects, including fascinated excitement, anxiety, repulsion, and "what we would today call . . . 'homosexual panic' " (107). Yet, in contrast to what Hughes ascertains in these American Puritan authors, I find it striking how little panic is registered over similar expressions of male/male devotional eroticism in the poetry of Donne, Herbert, Crashaw, Traherne, and other English authors.

11 For an important and more expansive account of sacred eroticism and Herbert's verse, see Schoenfeldt, *Prayer and Power*, 230–73.

12 Francis Quarles, *Sions Sonets* (1625), in *The Complete Works in Prose and Verse*, 3 vols., ed. Alexander B. Grosart (Edinburgh: University of Edinburgh Press, 1880), 2:120–32. Here I cite the "Bridegroome's Sonet" XII, st. 5. Further references supplied in the text. Compare Quarles's analogy of an opened book to an uncovered female body and the porno-devotional conclusion of Donne's infamous elegy "To his Mistress Going to Bed": "For laymen, are all women thus arrayed; / Themselves are mystic books, which only we / Whom their imputed grace will dignify / Must see revealed" (lines 40–43).

13 "Mris. Elizabeth Moores Evidences for Heaven," in Edmund Calamy, *The Godly Mans Ark* (London, 1657), 239–45.

14 An Collins, *Divine Songs and Meditacions* (London, 1653), 2, 9, 30. Further references supplied in the text. A substantial selection from the *Divine Songs* is available as Augustan Reprint Society Publication no. 94, edited by Stanley N. Stewart (Los Angeles: Clark Library, 1961).

15 See the commentary on this poem offered in *Her Own Life: Autobiographical Writings by Seventeenth-Century Englishwomen*, ed. Elspeth Graham et al. (London: Routledge, 1989), 70.

16 *Eliza's Babes: or The Virgins-Offering. Being Divine Poems and Meditations. Written by a Lady* (London, 1652), 22.

17 Isaac Watts, Preface to Elizabeth Singer (Rowe), *Devout Exercises of the Heart*, 6th ed. (London, 1754), 9. Further references supplied in the text.

18 Anne Wentworth, *A Vindication* (London, 1677), 2. Further references supplied in the text.

19 On Wentworth's rhetorical strategy of reversal see the introduction to her writings provided in *Her Own Life*: "Thus the fraught issues of duty and loyalty to one's husband, the immodesty and vainglory of a woman writing for publication, are turned on their heads, and protecting the self becomes an act of selflessness" (182).

20 Anne Wentworth, *A true Account of Anne Wentworths Being cruelly, unjustly, and unchristianly dealt with by some of those people called Anabaptists* (London, 1676), 8.

21 See Graham et al., *Her Own Life*, 195.

22 John Donne, *Devotions upon Emergent Occasions* (Ann Arbor: University of Michigan Press, 1959), 124.

23 Anthony Horneck, *The Passion of our blessed Lord and Saviour Jesus Christ, or, Cryes of the Son of God* (London, 1700?), 2. In this context, compare the following passage on Pentecostalist ecstasy from Michael Warner's "Tongues Untied," in which Warner places side by side ecstatic religious experience and erotic abandonment, his correlation culminating in the same sensual image we find in Horneck: "The bliss of Pentecostalism is, among other things, a radical downward revaluing of the world that despises Pentecostalists. Like all religions, Pentecostalism has a world-canceling moment; but its world-canceling gestures can also be a kind of social affirmation, in this case of a frequently despised minority. I suspect that the world-canceling rhetorics of queer sexuality work in a similar way. If you lick my nipple, the world suddenly seems comparatively insignificant. Ressentiment doubles your pleasure" (15).

24 *Diary of Anne Bathurst* (1692), cited in Phyllis Mack, *Visionary Women*, 117.

25 Pierre Bourdieu, *The Logic of Practice*, trans. Richard Nice (Stanford: Stanford University Press, 1990), 68; Sarah Beckwith cites Bourdieu's claim in her compelling study *Christ's Body: Identity, Culture, and Society in Late Medieval Writings* (London: Routledge, 1993), 45.

26 See, for instance, in addition to Lewalski's *Protestant Poetics*, Ira Clark, *Christ Revealed: The History of the Neotypological Lyric in the English Renaissance* (Gainesville: University Press of Florida, 1982).

27 William Sherlock, *A Practical Discourse Concerning Death* (London, 1689), 12. Further references supplied in the text. See also John Sommerville's discussion of Sherlock's treatise in *Popular Religion in Restoration England* (Gainesville: University Press of Florida, 1977), 54.

28 The heightened affectivity of early modern friendship has been much discussed recently. See in particular Alan Bray, "Homosexuality and the Signs of

Male Friendship in Elizabethan England," and, on the interrelations between friendship and religious piety, Forrest Tyler Stevens, "Erasmus's 'Tigress': The Language of Friendship, Pleasure, and the Renaissance Letter." Both of these essays appear in *Queering the Renaissance*. Two other selections in this volume—Dorothy Stephens's "Into Other Arms: Amoret's Evasion" and Valerie Traub's "The (In)Significance of 'Lesbian' Desire in Early Modern England"—treat the affective and erotic contours of female friendships.

29 See "The Church Militant" for one of the few instances in which Herbert employs bridal metaphors. Significantly, Christ's spouse in this case is the corporate Church, not the individual Christian soul. Herbert's nationalist poem "The British Church" also alludes to the Church as Christ's spouse, distinguishing the English church from the Roman one in terms of bride-versus-whore imagery.

The lack of marital metaphors in Herbert's devotional verse is also noted by Anthony Low in his chapter on the poet in *The Reinvention of Love*, 87–107. Low rightly calls attention to the other sets of familiar relations by which Herbert instead frames sacred love, including those of father/child and master/servant. I am skeptical, however, that what follows from such metaphors is the utter de-eroticization of divine love Low attributes to Herbert: "He was clearly uncomfortable with the use of sexual imagery in certain religious contexts in a way that Donne was not. . . . His poems evoke the seductive, the sensual, and the scatological only in order to exemplify sin or temptation" (101). What Low doesn't address here is the ways in which these other social relations favored by Herbert have been culturally imbued with their own erotics. (On the amorous metaphors used to express, for instance, the intimacy between the master and secretary—Herbert several times figures himself as God's secretary—see Richard Rambuss, *Spenser's Secret Career* [Cambridge: Cambridge University Press, 1993], 40–43.) In general, Low's exploration of erotic love is impeded by its structuring declination to conceive of eroticism existing outside the sphere of husband and wife. Apparently for Low there is only one kind of eroticism (heterosexual sexuality) and one place for it (marriage). Thus in his reading of Donne Low remarks that, although "Donne's experience with human love enabled him to write some of the best and most innovative love lyrics in the language," "that experience did not carry over successfully into the divine poems." This is so, Low argues, because Donne "could not surrender himself to a specific, personal, masculine Christian God." Here, without someone to play wife to God's impersonation of the divine husband, there can be no "successful" figuration of sacred eroticism; hence Low writes of "The repeated failure of love in Donne's divine poems" (85).

30 On the affective bonds that make masters and servants beholden to each

other, see Alan Bray's important essay, "Homosexuality and the Signs of Early Modern Friendship," in *Queering the Renaissance*.

31 See Michael Parks, "King David Was Gay? Rabbis Cry Blasphemy," in *The Los Angeles Times,* as reprinted in *The New Orleans Times-Picayune,* Thursday, 11 Feb. 1993, sec. A, p. 24. The claim was made in the course of a speech by Yael Dayan, a member of the Labor Party. Among the numerous denunciations elicited by her assertions, those of Rabbi Yosef Arzan are particularly cogent. After threatening, "We will blow up this leftist coalition," Rabbi Arzan goes on to declare that "they [the leftists in the governing coalition] are simply *raping* all of the people we Israelis hold to be holy" (emphasis added)—as though the verbal imputation of homosexuality to a figure of whom one wants (needs) to believe otherwise is itself to enact a homosexual rape upon him.

32 On the development of companionate marriage, see the classic account of Lawrence Stone, *The Family, Sex, and Marriage in England, 1500-1800* (New York: Harper, 1977), particularly 100-101, 217-18. Further references supplied in the text.

33 Jeffrey Masten, "My Two Dads: Collaboration and the Reproduction of Beaumont and Fletcher," in *Queering the Renaissance, 281.*

34 See Jeffrey Masten on the web of early modern meanings for the term *conversation:* "dwelling among; interchange between; commerce, society, intimacy; sexual intercourse or intimacy; conversion" (Masten, "Playwrighting: Authorship and Collaboration," in *A New History of Early English Drama,* ed. John D. Cox and David Scott Kastan [New York: Columbia University Press, 1997], 360).

35 John Winthrop, "Modell of Christian Charity" and "Address of John Winthrop to the Company of the Massachusetts Bay," in *The Winthrop Papers,* 5 vols., ed. Stewart Mitchell (Boston: Massachusetts Historical Society, 1929-47), 2:283, 2:176, as cited in Michael Warner, "New England Sodom," in *Queering the Renaissance, 339.*

36 For the suggestion that Davy's initial encounter with this female friend "reads like falling in love," see Graham et al., *Her Own Life,* 166-67; rather unhelpfully, however, this discussion applies an ahistorical notion of homosexuality to the evocation of female homoeroticism in Davy's conversion narrative.

37 On Quaker women and the renegotiations of gender, female roles, and social order that afforded for such public activities, see Phyllis Mack's continually illuminating *Visionary Women.*

38 Katharine Evans and Sarah Cheevers, *A True Account of the Great Tryals and Cruel Sufferings undergone by those two faithful Servants of God* (London, 1663), 27. Further references supplied in the text.

39 For similar points, though adduced in rather different terms, see Shuger, *The Renaissance Bible,* 176-80; and Bynum, *Holy Feast and Holy Fast,* 248.

40 Duke of Newcastle, preface, *New Week's Preparation . . . The Whole being Purified from those Extatic and Carnal Expressions* (London, 1737), ii. Further references supplied in the text. Sommerville discusses this revised edition in *Popular Religion*, 39–40.

41 Watts—who may put too fine a point on it—even specifies that "Mrs Rowe had been sought early on by several Lovers, so she spent several Years of younger Life in the connubial State with a Gentleman" (*Devout Exercises*, 12).

42 See, for instance, Bynum, *Holy Feast and Holy Fast*, 300–301.

43 *The Complete Works of Saint John of the Cross*, ed. E. Allison Peers, 2 vols. (Westminster, Md.: Newman Bookshop, 1945), 1:361. Further references supplied in the text. I am grateful to Debora Shuger for calling my attention to this passage.

44 *Abusive Furniture Catalog*, Bouchard Wood Products, Ltd. (San Francisco, 1976), 14.

45 Donna J. Haraway, "A Cyborg Manifesto: Science, Technology, and Socialist-Feminism in the Late Twentieth Century," in *Simians, Cyborgs, and Women: The Reinvention of Nature* (New York: Routledge, 1991), 149.

46 Ibid. Though Haraway interestingly later locates herself in this discussion as "an Irish Catholic girl" (173), the terms of her fidelity and apostasy are applied at the outset to the project of constructing "an ironic political myth faithful to feminism, socialism, and materialism" (149). At the center of Haraway's techno-feminist myth—"my blasphemy," she terms it—is the image of the cyborg, a posthuman, postgender hybrid of organism and machine.

47 Compare the narrative Debora Shuger offers in the chapter called "Saints and Lovers" in *The Renaissance Bible:* "The representation of sexual desire in the Middle Ages borrows heavily from the affective spirituality of Augustine and the twelfth-century Cistercians. That is, medieval secular eroticism (courtly love) is itself modeled on the analysis of spiritual longing, so that the latter is theoretically anterior to the former, rather than the reverse" (176). Shuger also posits a historical distinction between the erotic and the sexual: "The identification of the erotic with sexuality . . . emerged sometime after 1650." "Before 1650," she continues, "erotic desire was represented as a process originating in the desirable object (especially the eyes), whose simulachrum enters the erotic subject through his own eyes, traveling thence to the imagination or fancy and finally dwelling in the heart" (178). In Shuger's model, the sexual, on the other hand, is reduced to being, historically speaking, merely a matter of genital stimulation: "After the Restoration, the identification of eroticism with genital sexuality becomes standard" (180). As much as I admire the rigor of Shuger's historicism, her aim here to cordon off the erotic from the sexual (along with the implicit privileging of the former) seems overly schematic. It also evokes for me the endeavors of some in contemporary pornography de-

bates to separate out—which is to say again to privilege—representations of eroticism over "hard-core" depictions of sex.

3 THE PRAYER CLOSET

1 William Dawes, *The Duties of the Closet. Being an Earnest Exhortation to Private Devotion*, 5th ed. (London, 1709), 142–43, ii. As far as I can ascertain, Dawes's manual appears to have been first published in 1693. Further citations supplied in the text.

2 S[amuel] Smith, *The Christians Guide to Devotion*, 2d ed., (London, 1685), 196. Further citations supplied in the text.

3 Edward Wettenhall, *Enter into thy Closet, or a Method and Order for Private Prayer and Devotion*, 5th ed., rev. (London, 1684), 23. The earliest edition of Wettenhall's manual I have found is from 1663. Further citations supplied in the text.

4 Daniel Featley, *Ancilla Pietatis: The Hand-Maid to Private Devotion* (London, 1633), 6. Further citations supplied in the text.

5 Elnathan Parr, *Abba Father* (London, 1636), 4.

6 Joseph Hall, *The Art of Divine Meditation* (London, 1633), repr. in Frank Livingstone Huntley, *Bishop Joseph Hall and Protestant Meditation in Seventeenth-Century England* (Binghamton, N.Y.: Center for Medieval and Early Renaissance Studies, 1981), 80 (emphasis added). Further citations are according to Huntley's edition and are supplied in the text.

7 Oliver Heywood, *Closet Prayer* (London, 1668), repr. in *The Whole Works of the Rev. Oliver Heywood, B.A.*, 5 vols. (London: John Vint, 1825), 3:13. Further citations are to this modern edition and are supplied in the text.

8 Samuel Slater, *A Discourse of Closet (or Secret) Prayer from Matthew 6:6* (London, 1691), 78. Further citations supplied in the text.

9 On the notion of a recessive, interiorized selfhood constituted within the conditions of privacy, see Patricia Fumerton, *Cultural Aesthetics: Renaissance Literature and the Practice of Social Ornament* (Chicago: University of Chicago Press, 1991).

Whereas the purview of Fumerton's study is chiefly secular, Anne Ferry considers a range of devotional materials, including homilies, prayer books, and lyric poems in *The "Inward" Language: Sonnets of Wyatt, Sidney, Shakespeare, Donne* (Chicago: University of Chicago Press, 1983), her important investigation of the expressive terms of selfhood in the sixteenth and early seventeenth century. See in particular 45–55 for Ferry's treatment of "the closet of the heart" topos: "Sixteenth-century descriptions of examining one's internal state were most commonly based on metaphorical comparisons to entering a room in a house: a chamber, closet, or cabinet" (46). Ferry briefly contextualizes these metaphorical patterns in terms of both physiology ("The *O.E.D.* cites a quotation in which a heart is also said to have chambers") and household architecture. Yet she remains skeptical that the use of private chambers and closets for religious devotion can be taken as evidence "for a growing individualism among sixteenth-century Englishmen," or for the emergence of "a conception of a private self leading an inner life" (52). Ferry points out that the word *private* in the sixteenth century typically referred not to the condition of being alone, but rather to the domestic sphere as distinct from the public world. Hence she argues that "collections of what were called private prayers consisted of devotions suitable for recitation by families and their servants at home in the chapels or closets of 'private houses' rather than in church. They did not otherwise differ from public prayers in greater intimacy of style, or closer application to individuals, or more detailed scrutiny of the heart" (53).

My contention here, however, is that what Ferry's salutary historical contextualizations do not admit of the late-fifteenth- and sixteenth-century materials her study treats can indeed be posited of closet devotion as a seventeenth-century cultural formation. Brooks, Heywood, Wettenhall, Dawes, and its other advocates zealously advocate the practice of private devotion precisely on the grounds of its essential differences from public worship—differences they calibrate in terms of specific activities that can properly be performed only when one is alone in the closet—as well as the enhanced efficacy and intensity of private prayer. As I will discuss later, some of this amplified intensity devolves from the greater role allotted to the body and its gestures in solitary devotional expression.

Furthermore, we find that the degree of privacy insisted upon in closet devotion has become far more circumscribed by the mid–seventeenth century. Here private means not the domestic sphere but *individual* solitude, as in Wettenhall's exhortation that a Christian must be "often presenting himself *alone* before God" (1; emphasis in the original). Accordingly, the prayer closet increasingly comes to be materially cordoned off from the rest of the domestic space. See also Daniel Featley's prefatory claim that his model prayers, "though they are fitted to thy *private closet,* yet with a little *alteration* they may serve for more *publicke use* in the *Familie,* or elsewhere" (no page number). In Featley's distinction between private and public, the domestic sphere is aligned with the latter—the public domain—and not with the former as Ferry supposes is always the case. Or consider Thomas Brooks's presentation of the biblical story of Jacob's private, nighttime wrestling match with the angel as an emblem of private prayer. Brooks's exegesis pointedly distinguishes between the space of individual privacy and that of family: "Jacob did never so enjoy the presence of God as when he had left the company of men. Oh! the sweet communion that Jacob had with God when he was retired from his family, and was all alone with his God by the ford Jabbok!" (179). Once again, the space of devotional privacy is framed in contrast to the more public sphere of the family and the household. Here private does indeed mean individual solitude.

10 Alan Sinfield, "Protestantism: Questions of Subjectivity and Control," in *Faultlines: Cultural Materialism and the Politics of Dissident Reading* (Berkeley: University of California Press, 1992), 159. I am indebted to Sinfield's probing discussion of the "technology of the soul" (164), a technology I look here to *spatialize* in and around the structure of the prayer closet.

11 See also Dawes: "The Book of Psalms is the best Book of Devotions in the World" (12).

12 Making a similar case for the directive role of the Bible in framing the self's narrative of itself, Sacvan Bercovitch describes this process of illumination as involving "intricate correlations between personal and scriptural events, culminating in the fusion of self and subject." See Bercovitch's seminal study *The Puritan Origins of the American Self* (New Haven: Yale University Press, 1975), 29.

Moreover, Helen White points out that prayer books that endeavored to instruct users on how to compose their own prayers are much rarer than those that supply, usually as a supplement to the *Book of Common Prayer,* prescripted prayers for a wide range of personal occasions and circumstances. One handbook that does offer such how-to-do-it-yourself instruction, White notes, is John Clarke's *Holy Incense for the Censers of the Saints* (London, 1634). Yet, as we can ascertain from the prolix subtitle of Clarke's book, the Bible plays a formative role in determining even extempore prayers and, with them, the structure of individual devotional subjectivity. Clarke thus calls his manual "A Method of Prayer, with matter and formes in selected Sentences of Sacred Scripture. Also a Praxis upon the Holy Oyle shewing the Use of Scripture-Phrases. And Choyse Places taken out of the singing Psalmes, digested into a Method of Prayer and Praises" (see White, *English Devotional Literature,* 176–78).

13 Barker, *The Tremulous Private Body* (London: Methuen, 1984), 60.

14 I take the notion of heterotopic space from Foucault's brief essay "Of Other Spaces" (*Diacritics* 16 [1986]: 22–27): "There are also, probably in every culture, in every civilization, real places—places that do exist and that are formed in the very founding of society—which are something like countersites, a kind of effectively enacted utopia in which the real sites, all the other real sites that can be found within the culture, are simultaneously represented, contested, and inverted" (24).

15 Christopher Hill, *The Century of Revolution, 1603-1714* (New York: Norton, 1982). See also Hill's *The World Turned Upside Down: Radical Ideas during the English Revolution* (London: Maurice Temple Smith, 1972), and, more

recently, *The English Bible and the Seventeenth-Century Revolution* (London: Penguin, 1994).

16 Some of the important studies of early modern subjectivities I have in mind here are Catherine Belsey, *The Subject of Tragedy: Identity and Difference in Renaissance Drama* (London: Methuen, 1985); Francis Barker, *The Tremulous Private Body: Essays on Subjection* (London: Methuen, 1984); Stephen Greenblatt, *Marvelous Possessions: The Wonder of the New World* (Chicago: University of Chicago Press, 1991); Joel Fineman, *Shakespeare's Perjured Eye: The Invention of Poetic Subjectivity in the Sonnets* (Berkeley: University of California Press, 1986); Patricia Fumerton, *Cultural Aesthetics;* Jonathan Goldberg, *Writing Matter: From the Hands of the English Renaissance* (Stanford: Stanford University Press, 1990); and Harry Berger Jr., "Fictions of the Pose: Facing the Gaze in Early Modern Portraiture," *Representations* 46 (1994): 87–120. See also Katharine Eisaman Maus, *Inwardness and Theater in the English Renaissance.* Adducing numerous sixteenth- and early-seventeenth-century examples of "the separability of a privileged, 'true' interior and a socially visible, falsifiable exterior" (4), Maus contests the claim advanced in a number of these studies that personal inwardness is a post-Renaissance cultural production. She stops short, however, of making the early modern "inwardness topos" (15) she treats here fully commensurate with the structures and practices of modern subjectivity (29).

Among the exceptions to the prevailing tendency in Renaissance scholarship to underplay the shaping role of religious contexts in subject formation, and in cultural production in general, are Alan Sinfield, *Faultlines;* Michael Schoenfeldt, *Prayer and Power;* Stephen Greenblatt, *Renaissance Self-Fashioning: From More to Shakespeare* (Chicago: University of Chicago Press, 1980), esp. chap. 2, "The Word of God in the Age of Mechanical Reproduction"; and Debora Kuller Shuger, *Habits of Thought in the English Renaissance: Religion, Politics, and the Dominant Culture* (Berkeley: University of California Press, 1990), esp. 93–105.

17 Fredric Jameson, "Religion and Ideology: A Political Reading of *Paradise Lost,*" in *Literature, Politics, and Theory: Papers from the Essex Conference, 1976–1984,* ed. Francis Barker et al. (London: Methuen, 1986), 37.

18 Vaughan's poem "Righteousness," for instance, sites God's presence and favor —his "hidden treasures"—in various bower-like retreats and private places, while extolling the Christian "who loves / Heav'n's secret solitude" (lines 1–12). Similarly, in "Jacob's Pillow and Pillar," Vaughan locates "true worship" in "private and selected hearts," spatialized in terms that conflate the prayer closet and the Hebrew Ark of the Covenant as "that awful Cell, / That secret Ark, where the mild Dove doth dwell" (lines 11–12, 27–28). "Vanity of Spirit" presents the poet himself in private devotional retreat, turning inward "To search my self" (line 15), while in the poem "Dressing" he beseeches God to

unlock the "desolate rooms" of his heart with "thy secret key" (lines 4–5). Consider also Traherne's "Thoughts I," which shows him enjoying "springs / Of inward pleasure" that issue from the several sites of devotion, including the closet: "Like bees they fly from flower to flower, / Appear in every closet, temple, bower; / And suck the sweet from thence, / No eye can see: / As tasters to the Deity" (lines 51–52, 73–78). Even Crashaw, whose poetic corpus is perhaps better known for its swelling church hymns and liturgical offices, recurrently sites devotion within private spaces, ranging from organic retreats like nests, hives, and bowers to the manmade architecture of wardrobes, cabinets, and closets.

19 Richard Strier, *Love Known: Theology and Experience in George Herbert's Poetry* (Chicago: University of Chicago Press, 1983), 179.

20 Ferrar goes on to add, however, that Herbert also "went every morning and evening with his familie to the Church; and by his example, exhortations, and encouragements drew the great part of his parishioners to accompanie him dayly in the publick celebration of Divine Service" ("The Printers to the Reader").

21 Compare Schoenfeldt on "Decay" in *Prayer and Power,* 174. This important revisionary account of Herbert subtly explicates the poet's devotional ambivalences—Herbert's desire to withdraw from as well as to draw near his God.

22 Stephen King, *Carrie* (New York: Signet, 1975), 54.

23 See Carol J. Clover, *Men, Women, and Chain Saws: Gender in the Modern Horror Film* (Princeton: Princeton University Press, 1992), 30–31. Thus in King's novel, Carrie is "whirled into the closet headfirst and she struck the far wall and fell on the floor in a semidaze. The door slammed and the key turned. She was alone with Momma's angry God. The blue light glared on a picture of a huge and bearded Yahweh who was casting screaming multitudes of humans down through cloudy depths into an abyss of fire. Below them, black horrid figures struggled through the flames of perdition while the Black Man sat on a huge flame-colored throne with a trident in one hand. His body was that of a man, but he had a spiked tail and the head of a jackal" (57). Here the corporealizations of Christianity are troped in Carrie's prayer closet as a literal chamber of horrors. Such embodied terrors—as vivid in premodern devotional literature as they are in King's novel (see, for instance, the enormously popular ballad, "The Complaint or Dialogue Betwixt the Soule and the Bodie of a damned man")—stand as the more sinister cousin to the body-as-ecstasy trope I have been principally concerned with in this study.

24 I owe this formulation to Robert Stalker.

The disruption of the self—a sometimes ecstatic, sometimes terrible dispossession of the self's conception of being centered and self-knowing, of being continuous with itself—all this points to the other turn of closet devotion as a technology of the self, one whose processes press correlatively (and, in cases like Donne, hyperbolically) toward both self-involvement and self-denial. In *The Puritan Origins of the American Self,* Sacvan Bercovitch proposes that "the militancy they [the Puritans] hoped would abase the self released all the energies of the self, both constructive and destructive" (18–19). The closet writings of Donne and Herbert suggest, however, that these subjectifying excitations are less idiosyncratic of a distinctly Puritan dilemma of selfhood than Bercovitch's account implies.

25 I am indebted to Brendan Corcoran and his work on Donne for bringing this passage to my attention.

26 J[ohn] B[oughton], *God and Man, Or, A Treatise Catechisticall, wherein the saving knowledge of God and Man is plainely, and briefly declared* (London, 1620), 107.

27 The literature of closet devotion also flourished throughout the eighteenth century. Some of the pertinent titles are Robert Murrey, *Closet Devotions* (London, 1713); *The Book of Psalms Made Fit for the Closet* (anon.) (London, 1719); *The Christian's Closet-Piece* (anon.) (London, 1719); Timothy Byfield, *A Closet Piece: The Experimental Knowledge . . . of God* (London, 1721); Benjamin Bennet, *The Christian Oratory; of the Devotions of the Closet display'd* (London, 1725); Thomas Ken, *The Retired Christian . . . Meditations for the closet* (London, 1737); *The Devout Christian's Best Companion in the Closet; or a Manual of private devotions, collected from the Best Authors* (anon.) (London, 1738); and *An Humble Attempt to assist the Devotions of the Closet, in the most important work of self-examination* (anon.) (London, 1757).

Manuals and treatises on closet devotion continue to appear throughout the nineteenth century as well. Among many such titles, see, for example, James Bennett, *The Religion of the Closet* (Portsea, 1804); Horatius Bonar, *The Door of the Closet Shut* (1838?); J. Boulby, *The Closet Companion* (London, 1840); and Robert Meek, *Christian Duties in the Closet* (London, 1851). Other such texts designate specific audiences by their titles: see John Armstrong, *The Pastor in his Closet* (Oxford, 1847); Helen Allingham, *A Closet Companion for Daughters of Zion* (London, 1850); and Alexander Fletcher, *Closet Exercises for the Young* (London, 1859). Interestingly, a number of the eighteenth-century texts of closet devotion, as well as many of those published in the nineteenth century, conceive of closet devotion as contiguous with the family's devotions. For example: George Redford, *The Family and Closet Expositor* (London, 1830); Mrs. S. Cocks, *Original Hymns for the Family and the Closet* (London, 1831); and Richard Cope, *Pietas Private. Daily Prayer for the Closet and the Family* (London, 1857). This elision of closet devotion and family prayer contrasts with emphasis on individual solitude and architectural privacy we find in the earlier seventeenth-century handbooks and treaties. (See note 9 in this section.)

28 Richard Stock, *The Church's Lamentation for the Loss of the Godly* (London,

1614), 63–88. Everett H. Emerson's *English Puritanism from John Hooper to John Milton* (Durham: Duke University Press, 1968) offers a modern edition of the sermon, which I cite here. This passage appears on pages 194–95; further citations supplied in the text.

29 John Dutton, cited in Stone, *The Family, Sex, and Marriage*, 168–69.

30 Lewis Bayly, *The Practise of Pietie, Directing a Christian how to walke that he may please God*, 12th ed. (London, 1620), 236. White reports in *English Devotional Literature (Prose)* that this devotional guide ran to at least thirty-six editions between 1612 and 1636 (163).

31 George Downame, *A Godly and Learned Treatise of Prayer* (Cambridge, 1640), 155. Further citations supplied in the text.

32 For an illuminating materialist consideration of the secular activities sheltered in the closet or private study and their theoretical implications for notions of self and spatiality, see Mark Wigley, "Untitled: The Housing of Gender," in *Sexuality and Space*, ed. Beatriz Colomina (New York: Princeton Architectural Press, 1992), esp. 347–49. Wigley writes persuasively on how new conditions of architectural privacy in the home "mark a new subjectivity rather than simply modify a preexisting one" (345).

33 Ramie Targoff's important essay, "The Performance of Prayer: Sincerity and Theatricality in Early Modern England," *Representations* 60 (1997): 49–69, calls to the fore a different group of Renaissance texts on prayer, emphasizing the other side of this debate—that is, the performative dynamics of congregational worship and the interest of English reformers "in subsuming rituals of private confession and prayer within the public service of the church" (55). While a number of the works from which Targoff adduces the promotion of public over private devotion appear much earlier than the seventeenth-century texts upon which my argument turns, I do not think this implies a straightforward narrative of historical "development" that takes us over time toward the inevitable privileging of the private self and its activities. Rather, I see Targoff's account and mine, with their varying emphases, as complementary, illustrating just how central and controversial the debate over the location and supervision of devotion was throughout this time.

One of the texts Targoff considers in some detail is Tyndale's *Exposition of Matthew* (1533). In his aim to promote the practice of public prayer over private, Tyndale recasts the prooftext of closet devotion, Matthew 6:6, in metaphorical terms as a warning about pharisaical performances of devotion. Interestingly, however, Tyndale does allow for a literal interpretation of Christ's call to the closet in the case of those who are particularly gifted with what he terms "the spirit of praying," those (as Targoff puts it) "whose fervent manner of prayer extends beyond the normative standards of the public realm" (55–56). The prayer closet thus becomes in Tyndale's account the place where "thou mayest be free to use thy words as thou lustest, and whatsoever gestures and behaviours do move thee to devotion, is necessary and good" (*Doctrinal treatises and introductions to different portions of the Holy Scriptures,* ed. Henry Walter [Cambridge: Cambridge University Press, 1848], 257). Hence, even this promoter of public prayer recognizes the greater devotional intensity of the closet. Moreover, whereas Tyndale circumscribes this experience only to a spiritually gifted few, the writers with whom I am concerned want to make this enhanced devotional experience available to every Christian—or at least, as we shall see, to those whose social and economic circumstances will afford them the privilege of maintaining a prayer closet.

34 Stone, *The Family, Sex, and Marriage,* 169–70. See also a number of the essays gathered in Roger Chartier, ed., *A History of Private Life,* vol. 3, *Passions of the Renaissance,* trans. Arthur Goldhammer (Cambridge: Belknap Press of Harvard University Press, 1989); Mark Girouard, *Life in the English Country House: A Social and Architectural History* (New Haven: Yale University Press, 1978) and *Robert Smythson and the Elizabethan Country House* (New Haven: Yale University Press, 1983); Alice T. Friedman, *House and Household in Elizabethan England: Wollaton Hall and the Willoughby Family* (Chicago: University of Chicago Press, 1989); and, most recently, Lena Cowen Orlin, *Private Matters and Public Culture in Post-Reformation England* (Ithaca: Cornell University Press, 1994), 35–40, 185–89.

35 The floor plans for a number of the aristocratic households examined in Girouard's *Life in the English Country House* reveal closets sited off individual bedchambers. See, for instance, Coleshill House, Berkshire, c. 1650–62 (123); Ragley Hall, Warwickshire, c. 1679 (135); Nether Lypiatt Manor, Gloucestershire, c. 1700–1705 (151); and Chatsworth, Derbyshire, 1687–88 (155). It remains unclear, however, whether these rooms served as the strictly devotional retreats called for by Wettenhall and Dawes or whether they were "all-purpose" closets.

36 *The Diary of Anne Clifford, 1616-1619: A Critical Edition,* ed. Katherine O. Acheson (New York: Garland, 1995), particularly the various entries for January 1617, April 1617, May 1617, December 1618, and November 1619. See also the diary of Lady Margaret Hoby, in which nearly every entry shows her beginning the day with a period of private prayer (*Diary of Lady Margaret Hoby, 1599-1605,* ed. Dorothy M. Meads [Boston: Houghton Mifflin, 1930]).

37 See Brooks, *The Privy Key,* 9–19, 167, 181; Heywood, *Closet-Prayer,* 12–20; and Hall, *The Art of Divine Meditation,* 80.

38 This is not to say, however, that social egalitarianism found no expression among seventeenth-century English Christians. For biblically based versions of "communism," see Christopher Hill's essay "The Bible and Radical Politics," *The English Bible,* 196–250.

39 Foucault, *The Care of the Self,* 51. On the early modern closet (principally in its secular form) as a socially and politically crucial "transactive space,"

see Alan Stewart, "The Early Modern Closet Discovered," *Representations* 50 (1995): 76–100.

40 Compare the protocols of closet prayer detailed in these manuals and prayer books to the requisite material conditions for undertaking Loyola's *Exercises,* which, as enumerated by Roland Barthes, entail "retreat in a place shut away, solitary, and above all unaccustomed, lighting conditions (adapted to the subject of the meditation), dispositions of the room where the exercitant is to stay, positions (kneeling, prostrate, standing, sitting, gazing upward), facial expression, which must be restrained, and above all, of course, the organization of time, completely governed by the code, from waking to sleeping, including the day's most ordinary occupations (dressing, eating, lying down, sleeping)" (*Sade/Fourier/Loyola,* 48–49).

41 On the role of the body in Quaker religious expression see Mack's *Visionary Women,* 150–57: "Quakers were at once ascetics, rejecting both carnal reason and carnal sensuality, and celebrators of bodily sensation as a vehicle for experiencing and expressing the soul's new capacity to discern truth" (151).

42 Stephen Moore offers an imaginative exposé of the corporealization of the God of the Hebrew Bible in *God's Gym: Divine Male Bodies of the Bible* (New York: Routledge, 1996), 75–105.

43 Kushner, *Angels in America, Part 1,* act 2, scene 2.

44 Shuger, *The Renaissance Bible,* 179. Shuger attributes this loss to what she sees as an indicatively modern identification of the erotic with the sexual, as well as with what she disapprovingly terms (here following Bynum, I assume) "the modern definition of the body as the sexual body" (181).

45 Appended to the poem in its incomplete state is this note: "This subject the author finding to be above the years he had when he wrote it, and nothing satisfied with what was begun, left it unfinished."

WORKS CITED

Abusive Furniture Catalog. Bouchard Wood Products, Ltd. San Francisco, 1976.

Adams, Robert Martin. "Taste and Bad Taste in Metaphysical Poetry: Richard Crashaw and Dylan Thomas." *Hudson Review* 8 (1955): 61-77.

Allingham, Helen. *A Closet Companion for Daughters of Zion*. London, 1850.

Andres Serrano: Works 1983-1993. Curated by Patrick T. Murphy. Essays by Robert Hobbs, Wendy Steiner, and Marcia Tucker. Philadelphia: Institute of Contemporary Art, University of Pennsylvania, 1994.

Andres Serrano: Works 1983-1993. Exhibition pamphlet. New York: The New Museum of Contemporary Art, 1994.

Armstrong, John. *The Pastor in his Closet*. Oxford, 1847.

Baines, Richard. "A note Containing the opinion on Christopher Marly Concerning his damnable Judgment of Religion, and scorn of Gods word." *Marlowe: The Critical Heritage, 1588-1896*. Ed. Millar Maclure. London: Routledge, 1979. 36-38.

Bakhtin, Mikhail. *Rabelais and His World*. Trans. Hélèna Iswolsky. Bloomington: Indiana University Press, 1984.

Barkan, Leonard. *Transuming Passion: Ganymede and the Erotics of Humanism*. Stanford: Stanford University Press, 1991.

Barker, Francis. *The Tremulous Private Body: Essays on Subjection*. London: Methuen, 1984.

Barthes, Roland. *Sade/Fourier/Loyola*. Trans. Richard Miller. Baltimore: Johns Hopkins University Press, 1997.

Bataille, Georges. *Erotism: Death and Sensuality*. Trans. Mary Dalwood. San Francisco: City Lights, 1986.

———. *Visions of Excess: Selected Writings*. 1927-1939. Ed. Allan Stoekl. Trans. Alan Stoekl, with Carl R. Lovitt and Donald M. Leslie Jr. Minneapolis: University of Minnesota Press, 1985.

Bayly, Lewis. *The Practice of Pietie, Directing a Christian how to walke that he may please God*. 12th ed. London, 1620.

Bell, Rudolf M. *Holy Anorexia*. Chicago: University of Chicago Press, 1985.

Bennet, Benjamin. *The Christian Oratory; or the Devotions of the Closet display'd*. London, 1725.

Bennett, James. *The Religion of the Closet*. Portsea, 1804.

Bercovitch, Sacvan. *The Puritan Origins of the American Self*. New Haven: Yale University Press, 1975.

Berger, Jr., Harry. "Fictions of the Pose: Facing the Gaze in Early Modern Portraiture." *Representations* 46 (1994): 87–120.

Bersani, Leo. "Is the Rectum a Grave?" In *AIDS: Cultural Analysis, Cultural Activism*. Ed. Douglas Crimp. Cambridge: MIT Press, 1988. 197–222.

Biddick, Kathleen. "Genders, Bodies, Borders: Technologies of the Visible." *Speculum* 68 (1993): 389–418.

Blount, Thomas. *Glossographia: Or a Dictionary Interpreting the Hard Words of Whatsoever Language, Now Used in our Refined English Tongue*. London, 1670.

The Book of the Psalms Made Fit for the Closet. London, 1713.

Bonar, Horatius. *The Door of the Closet Shut*. 1838.

Boughton, John. *God and Man, Or, A Treatise Catechisticall, wherein the saving knowledge of God and Man is plainely, and briefly declared*. London, 1620.

Boulby, J. *The Closet Companion*. London, 1840.

Bourdieu, Pierre. *The Logic of Practice*. Trans. Richard Nice. Stanford: Stanford University Press, 1990.

Boyd, Malcolm. "The Sexuality of Jesus." *Witness* 74 (1991): 14–16.

Brathwait, Richard. *The Spiritual Spicerie*. London, 1638.

Bray, Alan. *Homosexuality in Renaissance England*. London: Gay Men's Press, 1982.

———. "Homosexuality and the Signs of Male Friendship in Elizabethan England." In *Queering the Renaissance*. Ed. Jonathan Goldberg. Durham: Duke University Press, 1994. 40–61.

Brooks, Thomas, *The Complete Works of Thomas Brooks*. 3 vols. Ed. Alexander B. Grosart. Edinburgh: James Nichol, 1866–1867.

Brown, Peter. *The Body and Society: Men, Women, and Sexual Renunciation in Early Christianity*. New York: Columbia University Press, 1988.

Byfield, Timothy. *A Closet Piece: The Experimental Knowledge . . . of God*. London, 1721.

Bynum, Caroline Walker. *Fragmentation and Redemption: Essays on Gender and the Human Body*. New York: Zone Books, 1992.

———. *Holy Feast and Holy Fast: The Religious Significance of Food to Medieval Women*. Berkeley: University of California Press, 1987.

Calamy, Edmund. *The Godly Mans Ark*. London, 1657.

Camille, Michael. *Image on the Edge: The Margins of Medieval Art*. Cambridge: Harvard University Press, 1992.

Carew, Thomas. *The Poems of Thomas Carew*. Ed. Rhodes Dunlap. Oxford: Clarendon Press, 1957.

Carey, John. *John Donne: Life, Mind, and Art*. Rev. edition. London: Faber and Faber, 1990.

Catherine of Siena. *The Letters of St. Catherine of Siena*. Trans. and ed. Suzanne

Noffke. Binghamton, N.Y.: Medieval and Renaissance Texts and Studies, 1988.

Chartier, Roger, ed. *A History of Private Life*. Vol. 3, *Passions of the Renaissance*. Trans. Arthur Goldhammer. Cambridge: Belknap Press of Harvard University Press, 1989.

Chauncey, George. *Gay New York: Gender, Urban Culture, and the Making of the Gay Male World, 1890–1940*. New York: Harper Collins, 1994.

The Christian's Closet-Piece. London, 1719.

Clark, Ira. *Christ Revealed: The History of Neotypological Lyric in the English Renaissance*. Gainesville: University Press of Florida, 1982.

Clarke, John. *Holy Incense for the Censers of the Saints*. London, 1634.

Clifford, Anne. *The Diary of Anne Clifford, 1616–1619: A Critical Edition*. Ed. Katherine O. Acheson. New York: Garland, 1995.

Clover, Carol J. *Men, Women, and Chain Saws: Gender in the Modern Horror Film*. Princeton: Princeton University Press, 1992.

Cocks, Mrs. S. *Original Hymns for the Family and the Closet*. London, 1831.

Coiro, Ann Baynes. "New-found-land: Teaching Metaphysical Poetry from the Other Side." In *Approaches to Teaching the Metaphysical Poets*. Ed. Sidney Gottlieb. New York: Modern Language Association of America, 1990. 81–88.

Collins, An. *Divine Songs and Meditacions*. London, 1653.

Cope, Richard. *Pietas Private. Daily Prayer for the Closet and the Family*. London, 1857.

Crashaw, Richard. *The Complete Poetry of Richard Crashaw*. The Stuart Editions. Ed. George Walton Williams. New York: New York University Press, 1972.

Crashaw, William. *The Complaint or Dialogue Betwixt the Soule and the Bodie of a damned man*. London, 1616.

Cunnar, Eugene R. "Crashaw's 'Sancta Maria Dolorum': Controversy and Coherence." In *New Perspectives on the Life and Art of Richard Crashaw*. Ed. John R. Roberts. Columbia: University of Missouri Press, 1990. 99–126.

Davidson, Arnold I. "Sex and the Emergence of Sexuality." *Critical Inquiry* 14 (1987): 16–48.

Davies, John. *The Holy Roode or Christs Crosse*. In *The Complete Works of John Davies of Hereford*. 2 vols. Ed. Alexander B. Grosart. New York: AMS Press, 1967.

Davila, Juan, and Paul Foss. *The Mutilated Pietà*. Surry Hills, Australia: Artspace Publications, 1985.

Davy, Sarah. *Heaven Realized, or the holy pleasure of daily intimate communion with God*. London, 1670.

Dawes, William. *The Duties of the Closet. Being an Earnest Exhortation to Private Devotion*. 5th ed. London, 1709.

The Devout Christian's Best Companion in the Closet; or a Manual of private devotions, collected from the Best Authors. London, 1738.

Works Cited

Dollimore, Jonathan. *Sexual Dissidence: Augustine to Wilde, Freud to Foucault.* Oxford: Clarendon Press, 1991.

Doniger, Wendy. *Women, Androgynes, and Other Mythical Beasts.* Chicago: University of Chicago Press, 1980.

Donne, John. *Devotions upon Emergent Occasions.* Ann Arbor: University of Michigan Press, 1959.

———. *Ignatius His Conclave.* Ed. T. S. Healy. Oxford: Oxford University Press, 1969.

———. *John Donne.* The Oxford Authors. Ed. John Carey. Oxford: Oxford University Press, 1990.

———. *The Sermons of John Donne.* Ed. George R. Potter and Evelyn M. Simpson. 10 vols. Berkeley: University of California Press, 1953–1962.

Douglas, Mary. *Purity and Danger.* London: Routledge and Kegan Paul, 1969.

Downame, George. *A Godly and Learned Treatise of Prayer.* Cambridge, 1640.

Dubin, Steven C. *Arresting Images: Impolitic Art and Uncivil Actions.* New York: Routledge, 1992.

Eliot, T. S. *For Lancelot Andrewes: Essays on Style and Order.* London: Faber and Faber, 1928.

Eliza's Babes: or The Virgins-Offering. Being Divine Poems, and Meditations. Written by a Lady. London, 1652.

Emerson, Everett H. *English Puritanism from John Hooper to John Milton.* Durham: Duke University Press, 1968.

Empson, William. *Seven Types of Ambiguity.* New York: New Directions, 1947.

Evans, Katharine, and Sarah Cheevers. *A True Account of the Great Tryals and Cruel Sufferings undergone by those two faithful Servants of God.* London, 1663.

Featley, Daniel. *Ancilla Pietatis: The Hand-Maid to Private Devotion.* London, 1633.

Ferry, Anne. *The "Inward" Language: Sonnets of Wyatt, Sidney, Shakespeare, Donne.* Chicago: University of Chicago Press, 1983.

Fineman, Joel. *Shakespeare's Perjured Eye: The Invention of Poetic Subjectivity in the Sonnets.* Berkeley: University of California Press, 1986.

Fish, Stanley. "Masculine Force: Donne and Verbal Power." In *Soliciting Interpretation: Literary Theory and Seventeenth-Century English Poetry.* Ed. Elizabeth D. Harvey and Katharine Eisaman Maus. Chicago: University of Chicago Press, 1990. 223–52.

Fletcher, Alexander. *Closet Exercises for the Young.* London, 1859.

Fletcher, Anthony. *Gender, Sex, and Subordination in England 1500–1800.* New Haven: Yale University Press, 1995.

Foucault, Michel. *The History of Sexuality.* Vol. 3, *The Care of the Self.* Trans. Robert Hurley. New York: Vintage, 1988.

———. *The History of Sexuality.* Vol. 1, *An Introduction.* Trans. Robert Hurley. New York: Vintage, 1990.

Works Cited

———. *The History of Sexuality.* Vol. 2, *The Use of Pleasure.* Trans. Robert Hurley. New York: Vintage, 1986.

———. "Of Other Spaces." *Diacritics* 16 (1986): 22–27.

———. "Sexuality and Solitude." In *On Signs.* Ed. Marshall Blonsky. Baltimore: Johns Hopkins University Press, 1985. 365–72.

Freud, Sigmund. *The Standard Edition of the Complete Psychological Works of Sigmund Freud.* Trans. and ed. James Strachey. 24 vols. London: Hogarth Press, 1953–1974.

Friedman, Alice T. *House and Household in Elizabethan England: Wollaton Hall and the Willoughby Family.* Chicago: University of Chicago Press, 1989.

Fumerton, Patricia. *Cultural Aesthetics: Renaissance Literature and the Practice of Social Ornament.* Chicago: University of Chicago Press, 1991.

Garber, Marjorie. *Vested Interests: Cross-Dressing and Cultural Anxiety.* New York: Routledge, 1992.

"G. B." *A Weeks Preparation Towards a Worthy Receiving of the Lords Supper.* London, 1679.

———. *New Week's Preparation . . . The Whole being Purified from those Extatic and Carnal Expressions.* Preface by the Duke of Newcastle. London, 1737.

Girouard, Mark. *Life in the English Country House: A Social and Architectural History.* New Haven: Yale University Press, 1978.

———. *Robert Smythson and the Elizabethan Country House.* New Haven: Yale University Press, 1983.

Goldberg, Jonathan, ed. *Queering the Renaissance.* Durham: Duke University Press, 1994.

———. *Sodometries: Renaissance Texts, Modern Sexualities.* Stanford: Stanford University Press, 1992.

———. *Voice Terminal Echo: Postmodernism and Renaissance Texts.* New York: Methuen, 1986.

———. *Writing Matter: From the Hands of the English Renaissance.* Stanford: Stanford University Press, 1990.

Graham, Elspeth, et al., eds. *Her Own Life: Autobiographical Writings by Seventeenth-Century Englishwomen.* London: Routledge, 1989.

Graves, Robert. *Poetic Unreason and Other Studies.* London: Cecil Palmer, 1925.

Greenblatt, Stephen. *Marvelous Possessions: The Wonder of the New World.* Chicago: University of Chicago Press, 1991.

———. *Renaissance Self-Fashioning: From More to Shakespeare.* Chicago: University of Chicago Press, 1980.

Grosse, Alexander. *Sweet and Soule-Perswading Inducements Leading Unto Christ.* London, 1632.

Guibbory, Achsah. "John Donne." In *The Cambridge Companion to English Poetry: Donne to Marvell.* Ed. Thomas N. Corns. Cambridge: Cambridge University Press, 1993. 123–47.

Works Cited

Haley, Janet. "*Bowers v. Hardwick* in the Renaissance." In *Queering the Renaissance*. Ed. Jonathan Goldberg. Durham: Duke University Press, 1994. 15–39.

Hall, Joseph. *The Art of Divine Meditation* (1633). In *Bishop Joseph Hall and Protestant Meditation in Seventeenth-Century England*, by Frank Livingstone Huntley. Binghamton, N.Y.: Center for Medieval and Early Renaissance Studies, 1981.

Halperin, David M. *One Hundred Years of Homosexuality and Other Essays on Greek Love*. New York: Routledge, 1990.

Haraway, Donna J. *Simians, Cyborgs, and Women: The Reinvention of Nature*. New York: Routledge, 1991.

Hayward, John. *The Sanctuary of a troubled soule*. London, 1604.

Healy, Thomas F. "Crashaw and the Sense of History." In *New Perspectives on the Life and Art of Richard Crashaw*. Ed. John R. Roberts. Columbia: University of Missouri Press, 1990. 49–65.

Herbert, George. *George Herbert and Henry Vaughan*. The Oxford Authors. Ed. Louis L. Martz. Oxford: Oxford University Press, 1986.

———. *The Latin Poetry of George Herbert: A Bilingual Edition*. Trans. Mark McCloskey and Paul R. Murphy. Athens: Ohio University Press, 1965.

Heywood, Oliver. *The Whole Works of the Rev. Oliver Heywood, B.A.* 5 vols. London: John Vint, 1825.

Hill, Christopher. *The Century of Revolution, 1603-1714*. New York: Norton, 1982.

———. *The English Bible and the Seventeenth-Century Revolution*. London: Penguin, 1994.

———. *The World Turned Upside Down: Radical Ideas during the English Revolution*. London: Maurice Temple Smith, 1972.

Hoby, Lady Margaret. *Diary of Lady Margaret Hoby, 1599-1605*. Ed. Dorothy M. Leads. Boston: Houghton Mifflin, 1930.

Horneck, Anthony. *The Passion of our blessed Lord and Saviour Jesus Christ, or, Cryes of the Son of God*. London, 1701.

Howell, William. *The Common-Prayer-Book: The Best Companion in House and Closet as well as in the Temple*. London, 1685.

Hughes, Walter. " 'Meat Out of the Eater': Panic and Desire in American Puritan Poetry." In *Engendering Men: The Question of Male Feminist Criticism*. Ed. Joseph A. Boone and Michael Cadden. New York: Routledge, 1990. 102–21.

An Humble Attempt to assist the Devotions of the Closet, in the most important work of self-examination. London, 1757.

Jameson, Fredric. "Religion and Ideology: A Political Reading of *Paradise Lost*." In *Literature, Politics and Theory: Papers from the Essex Conference, 1976-1984*. Ed. Francis Barker et al. London: Methuen, 1986. 35–56.

John of the Cross. *The Complete Works of Saint John of the Cross*. 2 vols. Ed. E. Allison Peers. Westminster, Md.: Newman Bookshop, 1945.

Johnson, Samuel. *Johnson's Lives of the Poets: A Selection.* Ed. J. P. Hardy. Oxford: Clarendon Press, 1971.

Jordan, Mark D. *The Invention of Sodomy in Christian Theology.* Chicago: University of Chicago Press, 1997.

Katz, Jonathan Ned. *Gay/Lesbian Almanac.* New York: Harper and Row, 1983.

Ken, Thomas. *The Retired Christian . . . Meditations for the Closet.* London, 1737.

Kerrigan, William. "The Fearful Accommodations of John Donne." *English Literary Renaissance* 4 (1974): 337–63.

Kerrigan, William, and Gordon Braden. *The Idea of the Renaissance.* Baltimore: Johns Hopkins University Press, 1989.

King, Stephen. *Carrie.* Signet: New York, 1975.

Knox, George. "Donne's *Holy Sonnets, XIV.*" Repr. in part in *John Donne's Poetry.* Ed. Arthur L. Clements. 2d ed. New York: Norton, 1992. 328–29.

Kushner, Tony. *Angels in America: A Gay Fantasia on National Themes.* Part 1, *Millenium Approaches.* New York: Theatre Communications Group, 1992.

———. *Angels in America: A Gay Fantasia on National Themes.* Part 2, *Perestroika.* New York: Theatre Communications Group, 1994.

Kyd, Thomas. "Kyd's Unsigned Note to [Sir John] Puckering." *The Life of Marlowe and the Tragedy of Dido Queen of Carthage.* Ed. C. F. Tucker Brooke. London: Methuen, 1930. 107–8.

Laqueur, Thomas. *Making Sex: Body and Gender from the Greeks to Freud.* Cambridge: Harvard University Press, 1990.

Lanyer, Aemilia. *The Poems of Aemilia Lanyer.* Ed. Susanne Woods. New York: Oxford University Press, 1993.

Lavezzo, Kathy. "Sobs and Sighs between Women." *Premodern Sexualities.* Ed. Louise Fradenburg and Carla Freccero. New York: Routledge, 1996. 175–98.

Lefebvre, Henri. *The Production of Space.* Trans. Donald Nicholson-Smith. Oxford: Blackwell, 1991.

Levenson, J. C. "Donne's *Holy Sonnets, XIV.*" Repr. in part in *John Donne's Poetry.* Ed. Arthur L. Clements. 2d ed. New York: Norton, 1992. 326–28.

Levey, Michael. "Behold the Man." Review of Leo Steinberg's *The Sexuality of Christ* in *The Washington Post Book World,* 1 April 1984.

Lewalski, Barbara Kiefer. *Protestant Poetics and the Seventeenth-Century Religious Lyric.* Princeton: Princeton University Press, 1979.

Lewis, C. S. "Donne and Love Poetry in the Seventeenth Century." In *Seventeenth-Century Studies Presented to Sir Herbert Grierson.* Oxford: Clarendon Press, 1938.

Lippard, Lucy R. "Andres Serrano: The Spirit and the Letter." *Art in America* 78 (April 1990): 238–45.

Lochrie, Karma. *Margery Kempe and the Translations of the Flesh.* Philadelphia: University of Pennsylvania Press, 1991.

Works Cited

Loewenstein, David. "Politics and Religion." In *The Cambridge Companion to English Poetry: Donne to Marvell*. Ed. Thomas N. Corns. Cambridge: Cambridge University Press, 1993. 3–30.

Low, Anthony. *The Reinvention of Love: Poetry, Politics, and Culture from Sidney to Milton*. Cambridge: Cambridge University Press, 1993.

Mack, Phyllis. *Visionary Women: Ecstatic Prophecy in Seventeenth-Century England*. Berkeley: University of California Press, 1992.

Marcus, Leah. *Childhood and Despair: A Theme and Variations in Seventeenth-Century Literature*. Pittsburgh: University of Pittsburgh Press, 1978.

Marotti, Arthur F. *John Donne, Coterie Poet*. Madison: University of Wisconsin Press, 1986.

Martz, Louis L. *The Poetry of Meditation: A Study in English Religious Literature of the Seventeenth Century*. Rev. ed. New Haven: Yale University Press, 1962.

Masten, Jeffrey. "My Two Dads: Collaboration and the Reproduction of Beaumont and Fletcher." In *Queering the Renaissance*. Ed. Jonathan Goldberg. Durham: Duke University Press, 1994. 280–309.

———. "Playwrighting: Authorship and Collaboration." In *A New History of Early English Drama*. Ed. John D. Cox and David Scott Kastan. New York: Columbia University Press, 1997. 357–82.

———. *Textual Intercourse: Collaboration, Authorship, and Sexualities in Renaissance Drama*. Cambridge: Cambridge University Press, 1997.

Maus, Katharine Eisaman. *Inwardness and Theater in the English Renaissance*. Chicago: University of Chicago Press, 1995.

Meek, Robert. *Christian Duties in the Closet*. London, 1851.

Merck, Mandy. *Perversions: Deviant Readings*. New York: Routledge, 1993.

Milton, John. *John Milton*. The Oxford Authors. Ed. Stephen Orgel and Jonathan Goldberg. Oxford: Oxford University Press, 1990.

Moore, Stephen. *God's Gym: Divine Male Bodies of the Bible*. New York: Routledge, 1996.

Mueller, Janel. "Women among the Metaphysicals: A Case, Mostly, of Being Donne For." *Modern Philology* 87 (1989): 142–58.

Murrey, Robert. *Closet Devotions*. London, 1713.

The Mysterie of Christs Nativitie. London, 1614.

Orgel, Stephen. *Impersonations: The Performance of Gender in Shakespeare's England*. Cambridge: Cambridge University Press, 1996.

Orlin, Lena Cowen. *Private Matters and Public Culture in Post-Reformation England*. Ithaca: Cornell University Press, 1994.

Parish, John E. "No. 14 of Donne's *Holy Sonnets*." Repr. in part in *John Donne's Poetry*. Ed. Arthur L. Clements. 2d ed. New York: Norton, 1992. 329–33.

Parr, Elnathan. *Abba Father*. London, 1636.

Partridge, Eric. *Shakespeare's Bawdy*. London: Routledge, Kegan and Paul, 1968.

Works Cited

Paster, Gail Kern. *The Body Embarrassed: Drama and the Disciplines of Shame in Early Modern England*. Ithaca: Cornell University Press, 1993.

Paul, William. *Laughing Screaming: Modern Hollywood Horror and Comedy*. New York: Columbia University Press, 1994.

Penney, Norman, ed. *Extracts from State Papers Relating to Friends, 1654-1672*. London: Headley Bros., 1913.

Quarles, Francis. *Francis Quarles: The Complete Works in Prose and Verse*. 3 vols. Ed. Alexander B. Grosart. Edinburgh: University of Edinburgh Press, 1880.

Rainolds, John. *Th'Overthrow of Stage-Players*. London, 1599.

Rambuss, Richard. "Homodevotion." In *Cruising the Performative: Interventions into the Representation of Ethnicity, Nationality, and Sexuality*. Ed. Sue-Ellen Case, Philip Brett, and Susan Leigh Foster. Bloomington: Indiana University Press, 1995. 71-92.

———. *Spenser's Secret Career*. Cambridge: Cambridge University Press, 1993.

Redford, George. *The Family and Closet Expositor*. London, 1830.

Resbury, Nathanael. *Of Closet-Prayer*. London, 1693.

Ross, Alexander. *Mystagogus Poeticus, or the Muses Interpreted*. Ed. John R. Glenn. New York: Garland, 1987.

Rous, Francis. *The Mysticall Marriage, or Experimentall Discoveries of the heavenly Marriage between a Soule and her Savior*. 2d ed. London, 1631.

Rowe, Elizabeth (Singer). *Devout Exercises of the Heart*. 6th ed. Preface by Isaac Watts. London, 1754.

Roy, Parama. "As the Master Saw Her." In *Cruising the Performative: Interventions into the Representation of Ethnicity, Nationality, and Sexuality*. Ed. Sue-Ellen Case, Philip Brett, and Susan Leigh Foster. Bloomington: Indiana University Press, 1995. 112-29.

Rutherford, Samuel. *Christ Dying and Drawing Sinners to Himself*. London, 1647.

Saltmarsh, John. *Holy Discoveries and Flames*. London, 1640.

———. *Poemata Sacra Latine et Anglice Scripta*. Cambridge, 1636.

Sanders, Wilbur. *John Donne's Poetry*. Cambridge: Cambridge University Press, 1971.

Saslow, James M. *Ganymede in the Renaissance: Homosexuality in Art and Society*. New Haven: Yale University Press, 1986.

Scarry, Elaine. "Donne: 'But yet the body is his booke.'" In *Literature and the Body: Essays on Populations and Persons*. Ed. Elaine Scarry. Baltimore: Johns Hopkins University Press, 1988. 70-105.

Schoenfeldt, Michael C. *Prayer and Power: George Herbert and Renaissance Courtship*. Chicago: University of Chicago Press, 1991.

Sedgwick, Eve Kosofsky. *Between Men: English Literature and Male Homosocial Desire*. New York: Columbia University Press, 1985.

———. *Epistemology of the Closet*. Berkeley: University of California Press, 1990.

———. "Gosh, Boy George, You Must Be Awfully Secure in Your Masculinity!" In *Constructing Masculinity*. Ed. Maurice Berger, Brian Wallis, and Simon Watson. New York: Routledge, 1995. 11–20.

Shepard, Thomas. *The Works of Thomas Shepard*. 3 vols. Boston: Doctrinal Tract and Book Society, 1853; repr. New York: AMS Press, 1967.

Sherlock, William. *A Practical Discourse Concerning Death*. London, 1689.

Shuger, Debora Kuller. *Habits of Thought in the English Renaissance: Religion, Politics, and the Dominant Culture*. Berkeley: University of California Press, 1990.

———. *The Renaissance Bible: Scholarship, Sacrifice, and Subjectivity*. Berkeley: University of California Press, 1994.

Simpson, Mark. *Male Impersonators: Men Performing Masculinity*. New York: Routledge, 1994.

Sinfield, Alan. *Faultlines: Cultural Materialism and the Politics of Dissident Reading*. Berkeley: University of California Press, 1992.

———. *The Wilde Century: Effeminacy, Oscar Wilde, and the Queer Moment*. New York: Columbia University Press, 1994.

Slater, Samuel. *A Discourse of Closet (or Secret) Prayer from Matthew 6:6*. London, 1691.

Smith, S[amuel]. *The Christians Guide to Devotion*. London, 1683.

———. *The Christians Guide to Devotion*. 2d ed. London, 1685.

Sommerville, John. *Popular Religion in Restoration England*. Gainesville: University Press of Florida, 1977.

Steinberg, Leo. *The Sexuality of Christ in Renaissance Art and in Modern Oblivion*. Rev. ed. Chicago: University of Chicago Press, 1996.

Stephens, Dorothy. "Into Other Arms: Amoret's Evasion." In *Queering the Renaissance*. Ed. Jonathan Goldberg. Durham: Duke University Press, 1994. 190–217.

Stevens, Forrest Tyler. "Erasmus's 'Tigress': The Language of Friendship, Pleasure, and the Renaissance Letter." In *Queering the Renaissance*. Ed. Jonathan Goldberg. Durham: Duke University Press, 1994. 124–40.

Stewart, Alan. "The Early Modern Closet Discovered." *Representations* 50 (1995): 76–100.

Stewart, Stanley N., ed. *An. Collins: Divine Songs and Meditacions*. The Augustan Reprint Society, No. 94. Los Angeles: Clark Memorial Library, 1961.

Stock, Richard. *The Church's Lamentation for the Loss of the Godly*. London, 1614.

Stockton, Kathryn Bond. *God between Their Lips: Desire between Women in Irigaray, Bronte, and Eliot*. Stanford: Stanford University Press, 1994.

Stone, Lawrence. *The Family, Sex, and Marriage in England, 1500–1800*. New York: Harper, 1977.

Strier, Richard. *Love Known: Theology and Experience in George Herbert's Poetry*. Chicago: University of Chicago Press, 1983.

Works Cited

———. *Resistant Structures: Particularity, Radicalism, and Renaissance Texts*. Berkeley: University of California Press, 1995.

Targoff, Ramie. "The Performance of Prayer: Sincerity and Theatricality in Early Modern England." *Representations* 60 (1997): 49–69.

Taylor, Edward. *The Poems of Edward Taylor*. Ed. Donald E. Stanford. New Haven: Yale University Press, 1960.

Traherne, Thomas. *Thomas Traherne: Selected Poems and Prose*. Ed. Alan Bradford. London: Penguin, 1991.

Traub, Valerie. *Desire and Anxiety: Circulations of Sexuality in Shakespearean Drama*. London: Routledge, 1992.

———. "The (In)Significance of 'Lesbian' Desire in Early Modern England." In *Queering the Renaissance*. Ed. Jonathan Goldberg. Durham: Duke University Press, 1994. 62–83.

Trexler, Richard C. "Gendering Jesus Crucified." In *Iconography at the Crossroads*. Ed. Brendan Cassidy. Princeton: Department of Art and Archaeology, Princeton University, 1993. 107–19.

Tyndale, William. *Doctrinal treatises and introductions to different portions of the Holy Scriptures* (1533). Ed. Henry Walter. Cambridge: Cambridge University Press, 1848.

Van der Meer, Theo. "The Persecutions of Sodomites in Eighteenth-Century Amsterdam: Changing Perceptions of Sodomy." In *The Pursuit of Sodomy: Male Homosexuality in Renaissance and Enlightenment Europe*. Ed. Kent Gerard and Gert Hekma. New York: Harrington Park Press, 1989. 263–310.

Vaughan, Henry. *George Herbert and Henry Vaughan*. The Oxford Authors. Ed. Louis L. Martz. Oxford: Oxford University Press, 1986.

Walton, Izaak. "The Life of Dr. Donne" (1640). In *The Complete Angler and The Lives of Donne, Wotton, Hooker, Herbert, and Sanderson*. Ed. Alfred W. Pollard. London: Macmillan, 1906.

Warner, Michael. "New England Sodom." In *Queering the Renaissance*. Ed. Jonathan Goldberg. Durham: Duke University Press, 1994. 330–58.

———. "Tongues Untied: Memoirs of a Pentecostal Boyhood." *Village Voice Literary Supplement*, February 1993, 13–15.

Warren, Austin. *Richard Crashaw: A Study in Baroque Sensibility*. Baton Rouge: Louisiana State University Press, 1939.

Weinberg, Jonathan. *Speaking for Vice: Homosexuality in the Art of Charles Demuth, Marsden Hartley, and the First American Avant-Garde*. New Haven: Yale University Press, 1993.

Wentworth, Anne. *A true Account of Anne Wentworths Being cruelly, unjustly, and unchristianly dealt with by some of those people called Anabaptists*. London, 1676.

———. *A Vindication*. London, 1677.

Works Cited

Wettenhall, Edward. *Enter into thy Closet, or a Method and Order for Private Prayer and Devotion.* Rev. 5th ed. London, 1684.

White, Helen C. *English Devotional Literature (Prose): 1600–1640.* Madison: University of Wisconsin Press, 1931.

Wigley, Mark. "Untitled: The Housing of Gender." In *Sexuality and Space.* Ed. Beatriz Colomina. New York: Princeton Architectural Press, 1992. 327–89.

Williams, George Walton. *Image and Symbol in the Sacred Poetry of Richard Crashaw.* Columbia: University of South Carolina Press, 1963.

Williams, Linda. *Hard Core: Power, Pleasure, and the "Frenzy of the Visible."* Berkeley: University of California Press, 1989.

Winstanley, William. *Lives of the Most Famous English Poets* (1687). Facsimile edition prepared by William Riley Parker. Gainesville, Fla.: Scholars Facsimiles and Reprints, 1963.

Winthrop, John. *The Winthrop Papers.* 5 vols. Ed. Stewart Mitchell. Boston: Massachusetts Historical Society, 1929–1947.

INDEX

Index

Index

Index

Index

Index

Richard Rambuss is Associate Professor in the Department of English at Emory
University. He is the author of *Spenser's Secret Career*.

*   *   *

Library of Congress Cataloging-in-Publication Data
Rambuss, Richard.
Closet devotions / Richard Rambuss.
p.   cm.
Includes bibliographical references and index.
ISBN 0-8223-2180-7 (alk. paper). — ISBN 0-8223-2197-1 (pbk. : alk. paper)
1. Devotional literature, English—History and criticism.   2. English literature—Early
modern, 1500-1700—History and criticism.   3. Homosexuality and literature—
Great Britain—History—17th century.   4. Christianity and literature—Great
Britain—History—17th century.   5. Body, Human—Religious aspects—
Christianity—History of doctrines—17th century.   6. Homosexuality—Religious
aspects—Christianity—History of doctrines—17th century.   7. Erotic literature,
English—History and criticism.   8. Body, Human, in literature.   9. Desire in
literature.   10. Sex in literature.   I. Title.
PR438.D48R36   1998
820.9'3823'09032—dc21   98-19598   CIP